2003

Evaluation for Continuing Education

Alan B. Knox

Evaluation for Continuing Education

A Comprehensive
Guide to Success

JOSSEY-BASS
A Wiley Company
www.josseybass.com

Published by

JOSSEY-BASS
A Wiley Company
989 Market Street
San Francisco, CA 94103-1741

www.josseybass.com

Copyright © 2002 by John Wiley & Sons, Inc.

Library of Congress Cataloging-in-Publication Data

Knox, Alan Boyd, 1931-
    Evaluation for continuing education: a comprehensive guide to success/Alan B. Knox.
      p.   cm. — (The Jossey-Bass higher and adult education series)
Includes bibliographical references (p. 311) and index.
    ISBN 0-7879-6143-4 (alk. paper)
    1. Continuing Education—Evaluation.   2. Adult education—Evaluation.
    I. Title.   II. Series.
LC5225.A75 K66   2002
374'.12—dc21   2002001867

FIRST EDITION
HB Printing   10 9 8 7 6 5 4 3 2 1

Contents

Part III: Guidelines for Improving Evaluation Practice

Preface

Everyone associated with educational programs for adults makes evaluative judgments about program worth and effectiveness. (You have undoubtedly done so yourself.) However, they may not do so explicitly. Experienced program coordinators recognize the value of these judgments in guiding their decision making. Writers about adult and continuing education program development and evaluation tout the importance of evaluation. Unfortunately, evaluation is underused in practice. One reason is the lack of useful guidelines and examples to ensure that program evaluation is worth the effort. The goal in using this book is a successful evaluation.

Various resources can enhance your success with evaluation. One type of resource is reflected in publications on evaluation pertinent to educational programs for adults, such as those listed in the references for this book. Another type is the evaluation expert, who can help plan and conduct a specific evaluation. The ideas in this book enable you to select and work with an evaluation specialist. A third, underappreciated resource is your own growing expertise as a program instructor, coordinator, or administrator.

Expanding and deepening evaluation expertise can occur as you gain experience with evaluation procedures and results, which you use when planning and conducting subsequent evaluations. This has been my experience. In evaluating hundreds of continuing education conferences and institutes at Syracuse University and the

University of Nebraska during the 1950s and early 1960s, I confronted diverse issues, contexts, and expectations that influenced the focus and procedures of individual evaluation. During the late 1960s and the 1970s at Teachers College Columbia University and the University of Illinois, some large-scale evaluation projects focused on adult basic education, with special emphasis on attracting and retaining participants and on helping their instructors improve the teaching-learning transaction. Subsequent evaluation activities at the University of Wisconsin have emphasized extension, continuing professional education, organization development, and international comparative perspectives.

Such a biographical perspective on your attention to evaluation is especially important to help you reflect on lessons learned that can be applied in subsequent evaluations. Each evaluation is distinctive regarding program history and goals, stakeholder expectations, evaluation focus and resources, and desirable timing and procedures. A successful evaluation is responsive to distinctive program features. With each evaluation, you are likely to more readily recognize program features that you hope to better understand through evaluation.

However, some features of evaluation are generic. There are broad parallels between evaluation, the teaching and learning transaction, and a search for values and wisdom in life generally. For millennia, philosophers have clarified values including procedures for judging values and their relation to daily life. Such clarification includes criteria for assessing what is and what ought to be. Some people progress beyond an active search for meaning, and they reflect on hierarchies of values related to life choices. A comparative perspective enables us to deal with uncertainty and pluralism by reflecting on our own values while respecting the perspectives of other people.

Effective teaching and learning transactions include such an active search for meaning and clarification of values, focused on the inquiry purpose and process of each educational activity. The essence of the word and concept *evaluation* is valuing. Evaluation procedures aim to make the valuing process explicit to enable stake-holders to make valid judgments and relate them to educational decisions. Meta-evaluation entails assessing the evaluation process and conclusions to enhance both the evaluation and the educational activity generally.

My selection and discussion of evaluation reports reflects my own experience with various evaluation projects. The chapters are organized to help you select those program aspects on which such a focus would be timely for you now. Questions are found at the beginning of Chapters Four through Eleven to encourage you to reflect at the outset of each chapter on your likely use of ideas presented therein, and at the end on promising applications in your own context. Typically, contextual factors greatly influence evaluation.

Purpose

The intent of this book is to give you such useful and practical guidelines and sufficient rationale to indicate the *why* of evaluation as well as the *how*. As you use the guidelines, you enhance your understanding of evaluation concepts and procedures. This enhancement entails using manageable methods to enable you to include evaluation activities selectively as an integral part of program planning, implementation, and justification. Evaluation that is part of program development should be focused and relevant to multiple stakeholders.

The key to a successful evaluation that improves an educational program for adults is a basic rationale for why and how. It contributes to stakeholder cooperation, which is essential for conducting most evaluations and using the conclusions. This book seeks to enhance your rationale as you plan and conduct a specific evaluation, since evaluations vary in focus and scale.

This book has several features to enhance your ability to select and develop a useful rationale. It does so by suggesting and illustrating some fundamental evaluation concepts and procedures, by distinguishing a program aspect on which a specific evaluation project focuses, and by summarizing examples of evaluation reports that reflect various types of provider and scale on which evaluations are conducted. Varied examples enable you to reflect on implications for your own evaluation and inductively fashion guidelines and procedures that fit your own situation. This is not an ordinary handbook because it emphasizes contextual influence and your active role in your evolving evaluation expertise.

A central function of evaluation is to help program stakeholders explain how the educational program works and what might strengthen it. Evaluation conclusions can thus contribute to sound choices and decisions. This doesn't occur in general; it is context-specific. This book is therefore designed to encourage insight that fits your specific evaluation concerns. Because most people who conduct evaluations related to an educational program for adults have limited access to pertinent writings and reports on evaluation, this book contains wide-ranging examples.

Audience

Adult and continuing education program coordinators are in a strategic position to provide leadership for program evaluation. In every type of organization and group that makes educational opportunities available to adults, the program coordinator or administrator interacts with people in various roles who have a stake in program quality and benefits. These stakeholders are adult learners whom coordinators seek to attract and retain as participants, and teachers whom coordinators select and supervise. Some stakeholders are not directly engaged in a teaching-learning transaction but make a valuable contribution as an administrator, policy maker, funder, or external evaluator. Although any stakeholder could benefit from practical evaluation concepts and procedures, in practice it is the adult and continuing education program coordinator or administrator who has the background, role, and interests that encourage and enable strengthening program evaluation.

Overview

The book is in three parts. In the first part, three chapters introduce basic concepts and relationships to help you focus on the aspects of evaluation to emphasize so that the evaluation process is both manageable and well worth the effort in a specific instance.

The core of the book comprises eight chapters in Part Two, "Applications to Various Program Aspects," each of which focuses on an aspect of the program and provider agency that an evaluation effort might address: needs, context, goals, staff, participants, program, materials, and outcomes. Each chapter combines practical guidelines, examples from types of provider agency in which the aspect is especially important, and ways to engage the stakeholder in the evaluation process (especially in using findings for planning, improvement, and accountability).

Each chapter includes all basic guidelines, but the organization of the chapter reflects distinctive features and the interconnectedness of decisions. The guidelines can increase the benefits and success of an evaluation effort. You might read only one or two of the eight chapters, those pertaining to an intended evaluation project of your own. Chapter Four, on needs assessment, opens Part Two and is the longest because the second part, on data collection and analysis, applies to evaluation generally.

Part Three reviews the main procedures and rationale regarding program evaluation and explores implications for strengthening continuing education program evaluation in a specific setting.

Assumptions

I assume that you the reader are already familiar with basic evaluation concepts and procedures and want to use this guidebook to strengthen future evaluation. I realize that readers' evaluation expertise ranges from novice to expert. As a program coordinator rather than an evaluation specialist, you might appreciate having separate chapters that focus on evaluation applied to specific aspects such as needs assessment, materials development, or impact studies. As a practitioner, you might recognize that the context of your type of provider agency should be considered. Thus inclusion of summaries of evaluation reports from various types of educational programs for adults is useful in several ways. One is that a familiar example promotes relevance and application. A second is that reflection on a contrasting example can promote comparative analysis and encourage innovation.

I also assume that you may approach a book of this sort with some experience and interest in strengthening your evaluations. Thus you may appreciate the inductive process in the book, in which an example yields guidelines and you actively extract insights that fit your situation and evolving evaluation practice. Reference to pertinent writings about evaluation also allows you to pursue promising concepts and procedures in depth.

The use of examples from all types of educational programs for adults reflects both similarities and differences across various types of providers. The term *continuing education* embraces extension, training, literacy, community development, staff development, and continuing professional education. Greater familiarity with practice across provider types can promote sharing and collaboration.

The Author

Alan B. Knox has been professor of continuing education at the University of Wisconsin in Madison since 1981. He received his bachelor's degree, two master's degrees, and his doctorate (1958) from Syracuse University, from which he received the Distinguished Alumnus Award in 1980. His scholarly activities focus on leadership of continuing education and comparative adult education, and on helping adults learn.

Knox has published more than one hundred articles, chapters, and books on many aspects of continuing education of adults. Among his published books are *Developing, Administering, and Evaluating Adult Education* (1980); *Leadership Strategies for Meeting New Challenges* (1983); *Helping Adults Learn* (1985); *Strengthening Adult and Continuing Education* (1993); and *Evaluating Adult and Continuing Education* (1998). Between 1979 and 1984, he served as editor-in-chief of the quarterly sourcebooks on continuing education published by Jossey-Bass. He received two Okes Awards, in 1977 for outstanding research for *Adult Development and Learning* (1977) and in 1980 for coauthoring *Last Gamble on Education*, from the American Association for Adult and Continuing Education (where he served as president in 1984–85).

Knox has held teaching, research, and administrative positions at various locations, among them Syracuse University, the University of Nebraska, Teachers College Columbia University, and the

University of Illinois at Urbana-Champaign (where he served as associate vice-chancellor for academic affairs and director of continuing education and public service between 1973 and 1977). He also chaired the Commission of Professors of Adult Education in 1975–77. He has conducted hundreds of evaluations during the past forty years.

Evaluation for
Continuing Education

Part I

Basic Evaluation Concepts and Rationale

1

Overview

Before I offer useful suggestions about strengthening your evaluation, consider some of the questions about evaluation that you now care about. Why do you want to enhance your evaluation expertise? How might this book help?

An evaluation project usually depends on contributions from several people with a stake in the effectiveness of the educational program. Such stakeholders include learners, instructors, coordinators, policy makers, and funders. As noted in the Preface, each stakeholder makes evaluative judgments, however informal. Each does so from his or her current level of expertise regarding evaluation. The stakeholder typically engages in evaluation in relation to decisions about what to accomplish and how to do so. Clarifying the expertise and expectations of your main stakeholders can help you decide on the focus of a specific evaluation.

This book is organized to help you select chapters that pertain to your current evaluation concerns and to postpone reading other chapters until their focus is timely for you. The three chapters in Part One present a framework of generic concepts and varied examples; they present basic decisions that are usually made when planning and conducting an evaluation. These decisions pertain to evaluation purpose, stakeholder involvement, planning procedures, coordination role, data sources and collection, analysis and conclusion, and encouraging use of findings. In Part Two, Chapters Four through Eleven each contain concepts and examples to guide planning and conducting an evaluation of a program aspect on which you want to focus. Selection of an evaluation focus typically reflects your reason for evaluating, be it responsiveness, planning, improvement, accountability, and the like.

The purpose of this book is to present important program evaluation concepts and illustrate their use to strengthen a variety of adult education programs. Such concepts enable you to make evaluation more explicit and useful. The usefulness of this book depends on your considering its contents in relation to your evaluation purposes and expertise. As you reflect on this relationship, consider how you and other stakeholders will use desirable timing, resources, and conclusions.

As you read the first three chapters (and select others that address program aspects central to your evaluation plans), consider these questions:

- What experience and familiarity with evaluation concepts and procedures do you already have?

- What is the focus of any evaluation project(s) you are likely to undertake in the near future?

- Who has or should have a stake in the process and conclusions of the evaluation project?

Practical evaluation is useful because the evaluator combines sound procedures with a rationale for addressing issues valued by specific program stakeholders. A successful evaluation reflects both valuable concepts and responsiveness to local contingencies; explicit understanding of stakeholder values helps you address them. But how do you know if you have sufficient background to conduct a successful evaluation?

Fortunately, you have ideas available from dozens of books on evaluation and hundreds of evaluation reports. These ideas are in

the form of examples, guidelines, models, cautions, and recommendations that can guide and strengthen your ongoing evaluation
activity. This chapter gives you an overview of the examples and
guidelines in the subsequent chapters that constitute a rationale for
evaluation to improve all types of adult education programs. On the
basis of your current evaluation experience and expertise, this
overview can help guide your selection of chapters in Part Two that
fit your evaluation focus.

Thinking of your adult and continuing education provider and
program as a system helps connect useful ideas from other people's
experience to your own experience at a specific time and place.
Evaluation can address any aspect of your program. Systemically,
your agency program attracts participants, instructors, money, facilities, equipment, materials, and staff. These ingredients (inputs)
interact to enable the adult and continuing education program to
function (process) and produce the benefits (outcomes) for participants, other people associated with them, society in general, and
your provider agency. Evaluative feedback can assess the degree of
satisfactoriness of any aspect taken separately, but it usually analyzes
relationships among selected aspects of interest to program stakeholders.

You can better understand program functioning and estimate
likely results of a proposed evaluation by conducting a small preliminary assessment. The results can be used to guide decisions
about the main evaluation. An evaluability assessment analyzes
potential goals, procedures, and resources to guide planning of an
evaluation; it is illustrated in Chapter Six in the section on planning and assessing goal setting.

As an adult and continuing education program is planned and
implemented, various stakeholders make decisions. An example is
the adult learner who decides whether to participate in a program.
Another is the program instructor contemplating whether to teach
in a program and how to arrange learning activities. A third example is the program coordinator deciding if a program should be

offered, along with the many subsequent decisions about attracting participants, selecting instructors, and obtaining funding. A fourth example is the policy maker in the parent organization or funding agency who has to decide whether to devote resources to a program.

Evaluation conclusions contribute to such decisions. They do so on the basis of evidence of worth, or a relationship that can undergird a decision about plans, benefits, and improvements. The scope and depth of an evaluation mainly depends on the type of decision to be made and the related issues of concern to stakeholders. Sometimes the evaluation scope is broad, as with a mandated accreditation review (which typically includes standards and guidelines for a self-study in preparation for an external review site visit). However, most adult and continuing education evaluations focus on one or a few aspects for which evaluation conclusions seem likely to be useful. Examples of such aspects include needs, context, goals, staffing, participation, materials, and outcomes. Chapters Four through Eleven focus on these aspects with examples, guidelines, and rationale. Thus you can focus on whichever chapters pertain to an evaluation project you are considering.

Of course, a continuing education agency or program can function without any formal evaluation. Loosely associated stakeholders can work together to make and implement plans based largely on precedent, which mainly reflects the values of those with power and resources. Each stakeholder makes evaluative judgments, but the explicit conclusions and their basis may not be shared. What actually occurs usually reflects negotiation among some stakeholders. Thus, if evaluation remains implicit then program decisions tend to reflect the interests of the stakeholders with power and resources, as when the expectations of adult learners are neglected in a subsidized program where their fees recover little of the costs.

There are various reasons for conducting evaluation:

- It may be a response to stakeholders whose interests are likely to be underrepresented in decision making. Such responsiveness can be reflected in assessment of unmet educational needs or identification of influences on participation and achievement of adult learners.

- It may be required by the parent organization (educational institution, enterprise, or association) as a condition of continued support.

- Planning by the provider agency may encompass evaluation findings which might help set priorities.

- Program improvement is aided when stakeholders who are expected to make changes also engage in the evaluation and hopefully gain commitment to the recommendations.

- Accountability prompts the evaluation to document extent of worth and benefits.

- The evaluation may contribute to a rationale for ongoing cooperation by stakeholders.

- It may inform explanations of program functioning; evaluation can contribute to feedback and reflection to help strengthen any aspect of the program.

An early stage of an evaluation project is to prepare a brief program description. This can build on and lead to decisions regarding the purpose and scope of the evaluation. For some evaluation approaches, this description contributes to specification of current features against which to compare desired characteristics. The recommendations that result from this discrepancy analysis can help stakeholders recognize potential improvements from what is to what should be.

A decision to make the evaluation process more explicit typically reflects an interest on the part of one or more stakeholders in improving, changing, or preserving the program in some way. Sometimes the evaluation findings lead to a change strategy. The issues and questions that interest such stakeholders in program evaluation make them the prime audience for a report of evaluation findings.

Evaluative feedback can contribute to the successive approximations by which educational programs evolve. Paradoxically, many new programs have limited resources; in combination with a sense of urgency, this contributes to neglect of plans and provision for evaluation. Even when a sound evaluation plan is followed, it is typically modified with experience, along with the program itself. Although it is desirable to include evaluation as part of early program planning, evaluation can be initiated at any stage.

The essence of most evaluations is making a judgment based on evidence about the worth and effectiveness of aspects of educational programs for adults in a way that encourages stakeholder use of conclusions for the purpose of planning, improvement, and accountability. There are evaluation models and approaches illustrated by examples throughout this book. Most of them recognize that evaluation uses many research procedures for data collection and analysis, but in evaluation the emphasis is on encouraging stakeholder use of conclusions in a specific context, in contrast to research emphasis on generalizability of findings.

A widespread evaluation question is, How much difference did an educational program make? This question has been explored at various and successive levels: learner satisfaction, achievement, improved performance, benefits to others, and return on investment.

Regardless of purpose, scope, and level, a formal explicit evaluation is usually coordinated, planned, and implemented. Such planning and coordination typically reflects some basic evaluation concepts. One is the helpfulness of specifying the main purpose of an evaluation to address issues of concern to stakeholders. A second entails selecting data sources, collection, and analysis procedures that fit the evaluation purpose and scope. Use of standards helps ensure the quality of an evaluation, especially data analysis, to produce useful conclusions. A third is to involve stakeholders and report findings in a way that encourages use of conclusions and recommendations. Additional concepts include using ongoing assessment to identify trends and relationships over time, assessing contextual influence such as economic conditions and other providers, and obtaining necessary resources and support for the evaluation.

Across the hundreds of thousands of educational programs for adults that occur on a given day in this country, there is enormous variety in the evaluations that occur. Many evaluations border on trivial because they address a small program fragment superficially. Is it any wonder that the greatest challenge to evaluation is underuse of conclusions? At the other extreme, some evaluations profoundly affect program planning, improvement, and accountability.

The usefulness of an evaluation project is not closely tied to its size and expense. Instead, it mainly depends on the focus and connection with issues central to the program and stakeholder expectations. At its best, evaluation can help people who plan and conduct a program clarify the connection between actual program decisions and the often-implicit rationale regarding program values and stakeholder expectations. In this way, evaluation can contribute to metacognition and reflective practice.

To take an example, in a variety of enterprises someone who coordinates staff development activities may be aware of some evaluations but unaware of others. An explicit rationale regarding program priorities and stakeholder expectations can enable a coordinator to identify high-priority issues on which to focus evaluation, along with implicit as well as explicit evaluative judgments germane to the selected issues. As a result of such focus, existing data from enterprise records can be combined with selected data from interviews or focus groups to form time series data regarding relations between learning, performance, and expectations. By collecting comparable data at successive times, time series data can document trends. The evaluation conclusions can guide decision making by learners, instructors, coordinators, and funders regarding their investment of time and resources in relation to benefit.

As another example, an association may launch an extensive educational effort for members, in which evaluation deals mainly with process to the neglect of evidence of impact and benefit. In response to member or coordinator concerns, meta-evaluation can help identify the extent and type of evidence of benefit that should be included in the overall evaluation effort.

These two examples illustrate a fundamental challenge facing those who seek to use evaluation in guiding reflective practice. It is to focus a feasible evaluation project on program aspects about which increased understanding is of high priority. The focus may be on learners or on the program. Evaluation feasibility can be enhanced by technical mastery of procedure. Attention to desirable aspects can be enhanced by responsiveness to stakeholder expectations. Feasibility and desirability should be interconnected when planning and conducting evaluations.

As with any complex practical activity, expertise evolves in part through rich experience. Familiarity with various evaluation reports affords valuable vicarious experience that can accelerate evaluation expertise. Unfortunately, detailed evaluation reports are inaccessible. Writings on evaluation typically emphasize guidelines and brief examples. Information analyses regarding evaluation do identify some detailed evaluation reports that could otherwise be located only with persistent searching (Knox, 1998a). Positive evaluations tend to be reported. However, some of the most instructive evaluation reports are not published because the conclusions were negative or the procedures were flawed. Fortunately, colleagues shared some such examples on condition that they be fictionalized for this publication. This enables you to learn from examples that are especially relevant to your own situation and to reflect on specific implications for strengthening your own evaluation. Thus you can deepen your understanding of your current evaluation rationale and procedures, in relation to the insights that you gain when you consider examples and guidelines.

If you have pretty well decided on aspects of your program on which to focus an evaluation, you can use this book selectively. Use the overview of basic evaluation concepts in Chapters One, Two, and Three to select one or more of Chapters Four through Eleven to obtain more detailed rationale, examples, and description of practical procedures. Each chapter also illustrates the interrelatedness of decisions. Chapter Twelve then summarizes the guidelines for conducting a successful evaluation:

1. Describe the program.

2. Estimate likely results through a small preliminary evaluation.

3. Specify the evaluation purpose.

4. Consider five levels of results.

5. Address value judgments.

6. Use ongoing assessment.

7. Assess system functioning.

8. Include contextual influences.

9. Arrange for a coordinator.

10. Involve stakeholders and obtain their cooperation.

11. Address differential stakeholder influence.

12. Obtain necessary resources and support.

13. Use various sources and procedures to obtain evaluation data.

14. Use standards to ensure quality of evaluation.

15. Analyze data to produce useful evaluations.

16. Include meta-evaluation where appropriate.

17. Use evaluation to enhance program vitality.

The main challenges to leadership on behalf of program evaluation are not technical but interpersonal; they regard planning, conducting, and especially using the evaluation. Resistance is commonplace. Another challenge is to help stakeholders revise their understanding of current and desired program functioning, with the help of evaluation conclusions. There are also ethical issues related to evaluation; sometimes meta-evaluation of the evaluation process on the basis of a broader view of such activity in various settings helps clarify issues.

As you reflect on the ideas in this chapter, consider these questions:

- How can you clarify the evaluation questions on which to focus?

- What resources and assistance are important for your evaluation project to succeed?

- How can you win and maintain cooperation from other stakeholders who are important to the success of an evaluation?

2

Approaches

Each evaluation project that you conduct is unique. Its success depends on your attending to the practical contingencies in the local situation: program characteristics and effectiveness, stakeholder concern about program improvement, and available resources and time for evaluation. A successful evaluation reflects cooperation among program stakeholders for the purpose of evaluation planning, implementation, and use of conclusions. Sometimes you must help stakeholders understand concepts and components of effective evaluation. Leadership of an evaluation effort entails use of basic evaluation concepts such as those in the Chapter One overview, in combination with an understanding of the local context and contingencies. Your goal should be a successful evaluation strategy or approach, especially if the evaluation extends beyond a single course or workshop.

As you read the three brief examples of evaluation approaches in this chapter, consider two questions. How would you characterize your likely approach to evaluation? What contingencies related to the educational project(s) to be evaluated should be considered?

This chapter contains only three case examples illustrating the basic concepts in Chapter One and foreshadows the detailed procedures for many types of evaluation approaches described in Chapter Three. The three examples are relatively ambitious; together they illustrate the basic evaluation concepts. These first three chapters present the main content of the book and enable each reader to select one or more of the eight core chapters in the second part of the book, which offer detail and examples on conducting evaluations on the program aspects that are of interest.

The first example (external review) emphasizes external evaluation for purposes of program accountability. In this approach, a statewide evaluation plan includes structured procedures and standards, self-study, and peer review by evaluator teams from similar programs in other parts of the state. At the conclusion of the site visit, commendations for major strengths and recommendations for improvement are shared with local stakeholders. By evaluating a quarter of the programs in the state each year, the cumulative results contribute to a collective benchmark against which to interpret local conclusions while respecting distinctive local features and conditions.

The second example (ABE guide) emphasizes internal evaluation for the purpose of program improvement. In this approach, an evaluation guide contains both rationale and illustrative data collection and analysis instruments and procedures. Users of the evaluation guide are urged to select and adapt its contents to conduct an evaluation that is attuned to local contingency.

The third example (action research) emphasizes use of conclusions to improve practice. In this action research approach, evaluation is integral to professional development; each learner selects a desirable type of improvement, receives assistance through a reflection seminar, plans and conducts an evaluation project, shares progress reports and conclusions with peers in the reflection seminar, and is encouraged to use evaluation conclusions to improve practice.

Review (External)

Some evaluations focus on a total system and benefit from cross-program analysis that avoids unfair comparison but uses a benchmark for interpretation. An example is a *community and family partnerships* adult education program evaluation (Lund and Mason, 1996). This external evaluation was conducted by the Northern Illinois University Office of Research and Evaluation in Adult and Continuing Education (RE/ACE). The office received a grant for this purpose from the Illinois State Board of Education (ISBE). Each year, it evaluated at least 20 percent of local programs in compliance with a federal plan.

This ongoing evaluation of the effectiveness of federal- and state-assisted local programs, services, and activities aimed to maintain and enhance program quality in accordance with federal, state, and local guidelines. The evaluator worked with various stakeholders, among them evaluation teams and program participants, to focus evaluation questions, interpret results, and apply findings.

The evaluation was based on eight indicators of program quality:

1. Educational gains

2. Program planning

3. Curriculum and instruction

4. Staffing and staff development

5. Support services

6. Recruitment

7. Retention

8. Program coordination and institutional support

There were three components of the evaluation. One was *self-evaluation*, conducted at twenty-one adult education programs statewide, based on survey forms sent to almost five hundred staff members and more than seven thousand participants. A second component was *external* evaluation, at eight adult education programs, conducted by twenty-three peer team members and two observers. The third was a participant *follow-up survey*, sent to a total of more than twenty-five hundred participants from nine programs. The follow-up from more than two hundred respondents yielded information about ethnicity, reason for enrollment, the program's effect on the participant's life, reason for attrition, and current educational activity.

External evaluation team members were carefully selected; team composition was based on expertise and background, along with serving outside their region to promote impartiality. There was broad cooperation, in part because team members appreciated their contribution to strengthening programs and what they learned from the process. A follow-up questionnaire from team members yielded responses to questions about how the evaluation team experience affected them professionally, the resulting changes they anticipate making in their own program, interest in serving on another team, and other comments on improving the onsite evaluation process.

Two RE/ACE staff members coordinated the overall evaluation. For the external onsite evaluations this included scheduling site visits, selection of team members, local arrangements, and distribution of materials. Peer team members received an orientation booklet and worksheets to guide observation and questioning. The local program director was asked to assemble documentation and examples related to indicators of program quality. Each director also offered his or her perception of program strengths and weaknesses. Peer team members reviewed the requested information; observed classes; and interviewed administrators, staff, instructors, volunteers, participants, and external stakeholders who interacted with the program.

The evaluation exit reports were guided by such standards as utility, feasibility, propriety, and accuracy. At the end of each evaluation visit, the team compiled both commendations and recommendations. A reading of the report was shared with the program director, some staff members, and sometimes a regional representative of ISBE. This informal meeting gave everyone a forum for discussion and questions. At the formal exit interview, the list of commendations and recommendations was presented verbally by the team leader to the institution's top official or representative, with the director of adult education and ISBE regional representative also invited to attend. Each annual report summarizes the process and conclusions for the local programs reviewed that year.

ABE Guide (Internal)

Many evaluations occur at the program level and emphasize improvement. This example illustrates an evaluation approach for adult basic education (ABE) teachers and administrators (Knox and others, 1974). The detailed evaluation guide recognizes that *informal* evaluation is widespread but that *formal* evaluation can increase the likelihood that (1) important evaluation questions are asked, (2) judgments are based on evidence, and (3) conclusions are used for program improvement. The essence of the evaluation guide's approach is comparison of intended and current practice, to identify gaps to be narrowed by program improvement. This approach reflects an action research rationale at the level of the provider agency.

The guide contains rationale and draft data collection forms to assist the stakeholders who plan and implement the evaluation in clarifying the purpose, scope, and procedures of the evaluation. The rationale explains the importance of and ways to involve stakeholders early to increase their understanding, commitment, cooperation, and utilization. Coordination of the evaluation effort might be done by the ABE director, a staff member, or an external consultant.

Coordination and planning an evaluation entails some initial organization. Designating an evaluation coordinator and providing necessary resources and released time are a start. Initial organization also entails broad staff involvement, which can increase communication, recognition, and utilization. Other organizational concerns include making adequate resources available; conducting periodic review; and especially matching evaluation purpose, scope, and resources. Early recognition of local contingencies helps with preparation of a realistic initial plan. Attention should be given to recent program history, available data, evaluation experience, focus on selected program aspects, scope of evaluation effort, contributions to planning, and encouraging use of conclusions.

A preliminary survey is recommended to help the evaluation committee decide on the program aspects on which to focus in the main evaluation. Illustrative steps in conducting a preliminary survey encourage each committee to develop its own plan. Preparation of a survey plan entails assigning responsibility, clarifying purpose, conducting initial review, estimating resources, reviewing and adapting the guide, and agreeing on a plan. Data collection and analysis involves identifying gaps between current and intended practice, using other information, and applying external standards. Use of survey results means deciding on the focus and extent of the main evaluation, selecting people to help with the evaluation, and setting a realistic timetable.

For the main evaluation project, preparing a detailed plan entails deciding on the focus, detail, and precision; adapting instruments and procedures; sampling; and arranging for external evaluation. To help decide who should help collect data, the guidelines list typical advantages and disadvantages of having the data collection done by the ABE director, a staff member, a staff committee, an internal evaluation specialist, or an external evaluation consultant or team. Data collection also encompasses ways of recording data, reporting distribution, obtaining information about current practice before intended practice, and increasing reliability. Guidelines for data analysis and interpretation cover analyzing intended practice, analyzing current practice, comparing intended and current practice, and comparing with external standards.

Evaluators are encouraged to analyze a combination of quantitative and qualitative data that allow cross-validation on the basis of multiple indicators for key variables. They are also encouraged to minimize program disruption and involve stakeholders to foster utilization. The guidelines have illustrative items for collection of data about six program components: recruitment of participants, staffing, in-service education of staff, instruction, collaboration, and goal setting. Draft instruments are also included: preliminary survey guide, staff interview guide, director questionnaire, teacher questionnaire, program statistics form, and student data form.

Action Research (Utilization)

Evaluation is sometimes an integral part of adult participation in an educational activity, as with action research at the level of the individual practitioner. A prime example is practitioner research as a vehicle for teacher professional development (Zeichner, 1999). Action research activities and reports are increasingly prevalent in adult and continuing education generally, such as CASAS (Marion and Zeichner, 1999). In addition to anecdotal reports, there are some systematic studies of practitioner research regarding rationale, structure, process, conditions, and impact (Zeichner, 1999). The example given here reflects conclusions from such studies of action research projects.

Practitioner action research opportunities by school teachers can be arranged by teachers themselves, a school district, union, university, state education department, regional lab, association, or various other sponsors and cosponsors. Teachers can conduct their action research project alone, in a collaborative group, or with colleagues drawn broadly from a school district. Teacher practitioner research projects that have been systematically studied and reported recently span one to two years.

The typical rationale was made up of a praxis model of knowledge and action, teacher initiative, understanding an aspect of teaching, conclusions that could benefit students, and implications for school culture and improvements. Features of professional development planning were being participant-driven; building on teacher proficiency, emphasizing problem formulation and focus; acquiring inquiry ability; collecting and analyzing data (evaluation); reflecting with colleagues in some depth and regularly (released time or after school); sharing results of projects; action planning for program improvement; and ongoing monitoring. Incentives included reflection time, graduate study credits, and professional advancement.

Conclusions regarding desirable features were collective responsibility for reform, voluntary participation and project ownership, respect for knowledge, continuity of participation for a year or two, manageable focus, supportive climate, facilitation and consultation, site-specific data, sharing with colleagues, benefits to students, implementing program improvement, and balance between individual teacher focus and organizational priorities.

Various outcomes and benefits of practitioner research by school teachers were reported, on the basis of systematic studies of such programs. Here are illustrative benefits:

- Flexible, proactive professional development that is self-directed

- Recognition of a gap between current and desired proficiencies to help solve one's own problems

- Critical reflection and redefinition of curricular, teaching, and learning practices and assumptions

- Increased collaboration and colleague communication

- Enhanced student learning and student-centered teaching

- Strengthened inquiry, research, and evaluation abilities

- Clarification of practice goals and influences, including double-loop learning (about goals as well as procedures)

- Increased validation and self-esteem

- Enhanced confidence and participation in energizing activities

- External benefits for school system and community

Some difficulties and deterrents were noted. For example, conducting practitioner research was harder than many teachers expected. Additional barriers were competing time demands, arranging for released time and substitute teachers, and achieving a fit between an individual project and school district priorities.

This approach to action research addresses the major challenge to evaluation: utilization (Patton, 1980). In practitioner research, evaluation is an integral part of the process of professional development and planned change. The teacher's early exploration of a practice problem helps focus on the evaluation topic and procedures. An inquiry seminar for teachers, along with related facilitation and consultation, enhances their ability to use such evaluation procedures as data collection, analysis, and reporting. Planning, conducting, and discussing a practitioner research project makes more explicit the rationale for improvement that undergirds evaluation procedures. Site-specific inquiry entails consideration of local problems, conditions, and stakeholders that also pertains to acceptance and utilization of conclusions, solutions, and improvements. Colleagueship with other teachers in joint projects and inquiry seminars strengthens teacher motivation; practitioner research projects; and utilization of conclusions for the benefit of student learning, teacher enhancement, and curricular improvement.

The main focus and benefit of an action research project occurs when practitioners use evaluation to analyze and reflect on their effort to improve practice. However, sharing their results is also beneficial. A recent guide to practitioner research identifies reports of action research by both school teachers (continuing professional education) and adult basic education teachers (where the learners are also adults; Marion and Zeichner, 1999). Additional sources on action research and reflective practice are Calderhead and Gates, 1993; Evans, 1991; Lewis and Dowling, 1992; Stringer, 1996; Tabachnick and Zeichner, 1991; Valli, 1992; and Zeichner and Liston, 1996.

Some summaries of action research in adult education are available online. An example of a collection of such online action research (OAR) reports is CASAS OAR (www.casas.org/oar.htm; Marion and Zeichner, 1999). An additional example that includes a print-based publication such as *Focus on Basics* or *Review of Adult Learning and Literacy* is the Practitioner Dissemination and Research Network of the National Center for the Study of Adult Learning and Literacy; its Website is http://hugse1.harvard.edu/~ncsall (Marion and Zeichner, 1999). Marion and Zeichner (1999) also report networks such as the Adult Education Teacher Inquiry Projects of the University of Rhode Island, and the Adult Literacy Staff Development Project of the University of Georgia.

Here is a summary of a May 21, 1996, online action research report on correctional education ESL tutor training in a Pennsylvania prison by Sue Klopp, from CASAS OAR (Marion and Zeichner, 1999). Her project focus was learning from reports and from local students and staff how to improve her tutor training. One benefit from her initial training was interaction with other action learning participants. For her, the essence of action research was identifying a local practice problem, studying it and ways to solve it, implementing a solution, and assessing progress and results. Support, accountability, and meeting deadlines influenced her initiating and completing this project. Completing the project and related reflection contributed to specific worthwhile improvements. She also appreciated peer collaboration and had suggestions about how to improve interaction among practitioners conducting a similar action research project. The experience was also motivational; it introduced her to the potential of the Internet. Student journals revealed that they appreciated improved performance by the tutors.

These three examples illustrate some of the various though ambitious evaluation approaches that can be taken. How similar are they to your past or future evaluation activities? What questions do these examples raise for you? Chapter Three is intended to address these questions. Each approach has both advantages and disadvantages. These three emphasize, respectively, external evaluation, internal evaluation, and utilization. Together they also illustrate many of the concepts and procedures that are presented in Chapter Three.

As you reflect on the examples, consider two questions: What are the main similarities and differences between each example and an evaluation project you are likely to undertake? What are the main implications for your role in an evaluation project, and desirable contributions from other people associated with the evaluation project?

3

Rationale and Procedures

The three examples in Chapter Two illustrate the basic concepts and practical evaluation procedures that are developed further (along with examples) in Chapters Four through Eleven. This chapter presents a general rationale for evaluating any aspect of any type of educational program for adults. Practical procedures are briefly noted but are not illustrated in detail by various examples until subsequent chapters.

As you read the overview of evaluation concepts and procedures here, consider these questions: What are some of the basic decisions you would expect to make in planning and conducting any evaluation project? As you read each section in this chapter, what are your reflections on how these concepts and procedures apply to an evaluation project you are likely to undertake?

The rationale and format of this chapter parallels that of the ERIC monograph on evaluating adult and continuing education (Knox, 1998a). Basic evaluation concepts and procedures applied to adult education are also presented in Boulmetis and Dutwin (2000) and in Burnham (1995). Other program evaluation overviews are Worthen, Sanders, and Fitzpatrick (1997) and Patton (1997).

This chapter consists of sections that reflect generic decisions made when planning and conducting any evaluation project:

evaluation purpose, stakeholders, planning, coordination, sources, data collection, analysis, and utilization of conclusions.

As you read each section, reflect on implications for whatever type of evaluation that interests you. This may also help you decide which aspects (presented in detail in Chapters Four through Eleven) focus on your specific concerns. The organization of this book reflects a combination of generic decisions that most evaluations address (purpose, stakeholders, planning, coordination, data sources, analysis, utilization) and program aspects on which specific evaluations are typically focused (needs, context, goals, staff, participation, program, materials, outcomes).

The organization of each chapter (Four through Twelve) reflects distinctive features of each program aspect on which an evaluation project is focused. Thus the sequence and detail related to each decision area varies from chapter to chapter. Also, in the long Chapter Four on needs assessment, the middle portion, on data collection and analysis, is applicable to other program aspects. Furthermore, these decision areas are not separate steps but are instead interrelated components. Consequently, each chapter indicates some of the ways in which decisions are connected. Extensive use of varied examples also illustrates this interconnectedness. This organization should enable you (especially if you have some evaluation experience) to reflect on and enrich your specific evaluation strategies.

Purpose

Initiating an evaluation project typically reflects one or more purposes for doing so, however implicit. An early task for the person or group guiding the project is to clarify the purpose of the evaluation.

This was illustrated in each of the three examples in Chapter Two. In the first example—the RE/ACE review guide for self-studies and external review teams—the evaluation purpose reflected expectations of federal and state funders. In the second example—the adult basic education (ABE) guide—the evaluation coordinator or committee was encouraged to decide on the purpose, perhaps aided by a preliminary review. In the third example—action research for professional development of school teachers—the main aim of the reflection seminar in the early months was to help each teacher or team decide on the improvement focus and related evaluation procedures.

Many program aspects could be included in an evaluation, and they are interrelated. Usually, there is insufficient time and money to evaluate everything, so priorities are necessary. Focusing on high-priority concerns typically entails value judgment related to both program characteristics and stakeholder expectations. The review guide indicated the general focus; the ABE guide encouraged evaluators to select program aspects on which to focus.

Sometimes the purpose is to identify discrepancies between desirable and actual program characteristics; this was fundamental in the ABE guide. There may be a choice of relative focus on program benefits for the individual participant versus other people in their organization or community. Program and evaluation objectives may be set at the beginning and serve as a reference point for evaluation planning, or later in the program to allow participants to help decide on their valued intended outcomes. In the review, the main objectives were set at the beginning to reflect federal and state expectations, whereas in the action research example participants set their own objectives in the early months of their project and the objectives continued to evolve.

Early identification and involvement of major stakeholders allows attention to stakeholder issues and expectations, which many evaluations address. This contributes to utilization of conclusions. Effective evaluation is responsive to stakeholders and seeks their continued cooperation. In the review, there were multiple stakeholders: federal expectations tied to funding, state IBE staff participation in review sessions, local program staff participation in each self-study and site visit, and reporting to parent organization administrators. In the ABE guide, the evaluation coordinator or committee was encouraged to involve participants, instructors, administrators, and collaborators.

Another way to focus an evaluation so that it is manageable and beneficial is to identify program characteristics that warrant attention. Illustrative symptoms that may suggest an evaluation focus are unclear goals, insufficient learner achievement and satisfaction, inadequate feedback, complaints about teaching, and outmoded educational materials. The ABE guide suggested a preliminary review to identify symptoms and pertinent program characteristics as a way to select a focus for the main evaluation.

Chapters Four through Eleven present program components that can be the focus of evaluation and program improvement: needs, context, goals, staffing, participation, program, materials, and outcomes. Evaluation of any one component may benefit from conclusions related to other components.

Clarification of the evaluation purpose and scope can guide selection of procedures that fit. For example, adult learning is a developmental process that includes participants and people associated with them before, during, and after they are engaged in an educational program. The ABE guide suggested ways for an evaluator to clarify this fit between purpose and procedure. For this reason, ongoing evaluation (needs assessment, time series data to identify trends, follow-up studies) is especially valuable.

The specific content and characteristics of an educational program can suggest criteria to use for data collection and analysis. For example, the review helped clarify the program characteristics. Such criteria might pertain to enhanced proficiency, program relevance, level of difficulty, learner engagement, and opportunity for practice and application. Clarification of the evaluation purpose can also help decide on a desirable level of evaluation. Purpose might be participant satisfaction, achievement gain, improved performance, organizational benefit, or return on investment in the educational program. The ABE guide used the preliminary review and selection of program aspects to help clarify the evaluation purpose. The action research example depended on teachers' planning and implementing their own projects with assistance from the reflection seminar to help clarify the evaluation purpose. Traditional suggestions regarding evaluation purposes are available from Worthen, Sanders, and Fitzpatrick (1997); Caffarella (1994); Queeney (1995); and Bennett and Rockwell (1995).

Various stakeholders can help clarify the evaluation purpose, through evaluation planning committees, focus groups, survey responses, and phone interviews. In the review example, external review team members from similar programs in other parts of the state helped implement the external evaluation, but they also gained valuable insight for their own program. The next section explores ways to involve stakeholders, which may entail negotiation of agreed-upon evaluation purposes when differing expectations exist.

Stakeholders

A successful evaluation reflects attention to both technical procedures and cooperation from stakeholders. Generally, cooperation in the evaluation process and use of conclusions is especially important for participants, instructors, and funders. Such involvement was important in the review and the ABE guide. In specific instances, other stakeholders should be involved (administrators, accreditors, materials developers, collaborators). If an evaluation coordinator contacts potential stakeholders early, this helps select which people should be involved and the optimal extent and type of involvement. This was emphasized in the ABE guide.

Stakeholder involvement in an evaluation project is aided by a convincing rationale, attention to issues they value, specific guidelines, interacting with able people, important but not burdensome contributions, and ongoing encouragement. Stakeholder involvement and commitment is especially important if they are to use evaluation conclusions for purposes of planning, improvement, and accountability. In the review, stakeholder involvement was encouraged especially by an effective guide that contained rationale and guidelines and focused on improvement and accountability purposes. Involvement was further encouraged by important and reasonable contributions. In the ABE guide, stakeholder involvement was encouraged by rationale, guidelines, and illustrative procedures focused on improvement on the basis of local staff commitment to reduce discrepancies between current and desired program features. In the action research example, the main stakeholders were school teachers who were sufficiently committed to improvement that they initiated action research projects and who received assistance from students, colleagues, administrators, and consultants who conducted reflection seminars.

A perspective on the educational program before, during, and after the assessment period can help stakeholders assess and appreciate the benefits of an evaluation. This is essential to their commitment to use the conclusions. Such assessments are more feasible through use of time series data, comparison with other programs, and a rationale for conclusions and their basis. The review used all of these means to help local staff members gain such a developmental perspective. Additional suggestions regarding evaluation stakeholders are available from Patton (1997); Knox and Associates (1980); Quigley and Kuhne (1997); Grotelueschen, Gooler, and Knox (1976); Braskamp and Ory (1994); and Knox (1985).

Planning

Leadership and planning are important for any evaluation project, especially those that are large and complex (such as the review). However, informed planning can enhance even a modest evaluation effort and save time and money. Usually, one evaluation coordinator or a small committee helps to make sure that satisfactory decisions are made regarding who contributes to the evaluation and its extent and focus, resources, and use of conclusions. Other people who typically contribute to planning are instructors, agency administrators, and evaluation specialists. In the action research example, seminar consultants and colleagues engaged in similar improvement efforts, which were especially helpful for planning.

One early planning decision is the extent and focus of the evaluation project. The ABE guide included a preliminary review to help decide on extent and focus of the main evaluation. In the action research example, the early months of the reflection seminar were devoted to focusing on a manageable project. A number of considerations affect making a decision on focus and feasibility: assumptions about program quality, stakeholder concerns about the urgency of issues on which the evaluation would focus, local contingencies, and available resources for evaluation. The ABE guide reflected such suggestions. A preliminary review or a pilot study can contribute to planning decisions regarding issues, goals, scale, timing, and feasibility. Negotiation of a prior agreement on evaluation guidelines can reduce conflict regarding ethical issues and differing stakeholder expectations and values.

Many planning decisions revolve around the fit among the evaluation purpose, scale, and resources. The fit was a major function of the review guide. This is distinct from attention, in the conclusions, to the fit among program goals, participant characteristics, program resources, the educational program, and contextual influences in the service area.

Evaluation planning can be enhanced by an overview of evaluation concepts, which can guide decisions by using suggested standards, criteria, and guidelines. Examples of such guidelines are focusing on issues important to stakeholders, obtaining sufficient expertise, keeping it simple, considering timing, minimizing disruptions, addressing stakeholder perspectives on benefits, building on earlier cooperation to encourage utilization, and obtaining sufficient resources. Most of these considerations were reflected in the review guide.

A major reason for early planning is to select a desirable and feasible evaluation approach, as illustrated in the early action research seminar resources (example three). General features of an evaluation approach are methods of identifying issues important to stakeholders, specification of evaluation purpose and scope, required expertise, balance of quantitative and qualitative data collection and analysis, and ways of encouraging utilization of conclusions. In a specific instance, the basic elements of the evaluation design are selected from among many alternatives. Examples of such alternatives are self-assessment, self-study, case analysis, practice adoption, systems analysis, follow-up study, quasi-experimental, experimental study, and external review. These designs are defined and illustrated in the second part of the book.

The three examples in Chapter Two cover many features of evaluation approaches and designs. The review emphasized self-study, external review, and case analysis in an approach that addressed expectations of major stakeholders, and use of conclusions based on both quantitative and qualitative data. The ABE guide emphasized systems analysis, self-study, and case analysis in an approach that addressed staff concern about issues, scope, and utilization on the basis of quantitative and qualitative data. The action research example emphasized self-assessment, case analysis, and review and reflection with colleagues in an approach that addressed issues, scope, and utilization by each teacher as the main stakeholder, inclusion of both quantitative and qualitative data, and use of expertise from colleagues and consultants through the reflection seminars.

Additional suggestions regarding evaluation planning are available from Worthen, Sanders, and Fitzpatrick (1997); Brinkerhoff (1987); Knox (1986); and Flagg (1990).

Coordination

Early selection of a person or small committee to coordinate evaluation planning and implementation is crucial. They can help formulate and use a checklist to coordinate the several parts of an evaluation (preparation of the plan, self-study, external review, use of conclusions). The guidelines can also address acquisition of expertise, cooperation from stakeholders, dealing with conflicting expectations, acquisition of resources, ensuring confidentiality, monitoring progress, ensuring rapid conclusions, and responding to requests. This coordination role was performed in each of the three examples—by the review staff; the coordinator or committee for the ABE guide; and the individual teacher who engaged in the action research project, with assistance from the reflection seminar consultant. Fundamental to such coordination guidelines are effective interpersonal relations, negotiation of differences, and appreciation of contributions. This is desirable in part to minimize distortion occurring because of unequal power among stakeholders. In the review, there was potential conflict to be negotiated between federal and state funders, local staff of the program being reviewed, administrators from their parent organization, and external reviewers from other programs.

Additional suggestions regarding coordination of evaluation are available from Kirkpatrick (1994); Green and Associates (1984); Duning, Van Kekerix, and Zaborowski (1993); and Rothwell and Kazanas (1993).

Sources

There are various sources of information for evaluation purposes. Consideration of such sources can contribute to decisions about data collection and analysis. Among the role perspectives to consider are instructors, counselors, program coordinators, policy makers, experts, participants, and people associated with them. In the review and in the ABE guide examples, such a range of data sources was addressed.

Various records and documents can also contain information useful for evaluation: provider agency records, external review reports, reports from similar evaluations, and writings about evaluation that identify common themes and distinctive perspectives (which can be useful for planning and for interpretation of findings). For evaluation of a specific program aspect, data and conclusions from similar evaluations can sometimes be useful. The documents included in the review were agency records, external review reports, and reports from many similar evaluations in an overall summary form. The ABE guide addressed agency records and writings about evaluation generally, as well as specific evaluation reports to use for planning and interpretation. The credibility of evaluation conclusions can be enhanced through cross-validation by inclusion of multiple sources of quantitative and qualitative data about program inputs, processes, and outcomes. The review and the ABE guide each included quantitative and qualitative data about inputs, processes, and outcomes.

Additional suggestions regarding sources of evaluation data are available from Merriam and Caffarella (1999), Brinkerhoff (1987), Davis and Fox (1994), and Naisbitt and Aburdene (1990).

Data Collection

Decisions about desirable and feasible data collection procedures are typically influenced by prior decisions as to the purpose and scale of the evaluation project. The preliminary review served this purpose in the ABE guide, as pilot projects generally do. An overview of the program aspects to be evaluated and symptoms of needed improvement can also contribute to decisions about data collection context and procedures. The individual teachers in the action research example, and the evaluation coordinator or committee in the ABE guide, were each encouraged to review program characteristics and needed improvements. There are many procedures for data collection to consider, each with its strengths and limitations. Typically, several are selected for use in combination, which allows cross-validation. For example, in the review various types of data were collected from participants and staff for the self-study; interviews (and observations) yielded supplementary and confirmatory data for the external review site visit after reviewers read the self-study report. The ABE guide suggested a variety of data collection procedures to provide cross-validation.

Various criteria can help you select the specific data collection procedures for an evaluation project: purpose of evaluation, program objectives and content, cooperation related to sources of data, simplicity, credibility for stakeholders, and availability of resources. For example, prominent criteria for selection of data collection procedures in the review were evaluation purpose, program objectives, credibility for stakeholders, and availability of resources. Prominent criteria for selection of data collection procedures recommended in the ABE guide were evaluation purpose, program objectives and content, fit with sources of data, and simplicity.

Procedures available for collection of quantitative and qualitative data include a questionnaire, test, observation, rating scale, rubric, interviews, focus group ideas, self-assessment, portfolio, program records, performance audit, case study, simulation, and unobtrusive measures. The review included questionnaires, observations, rating scales, interviews, self-assessments, program records, and case studies. The ABE guide included questionnaires, tests, rating scales, interviews, and program records. Collection of qualitative data usually entails a passage of text to be content-analyzed to identify themes (Miles and Huberman, 1984; Strauss and Corbin, 1990). Collection of quantitative data usually entails ratings such as scores on a test or a rating scale (Gall, Borg, and Gall, 1996; Salant and Dillman, 1994; Krathwohl, 1993).

Analysis

Analysis entails making judgments and drawing conclusions related to the purpose of the evaluation. Judgments reflect both facts and values. Even the selection of a procedure is influenced by the assumptions and beliefs of program stakeholders and evaluation coordinators. This was reflected in the standards for the review:

issues important to stakeholders, evaluation goals, type of data to be analyzed, and the intended form of reporting. Such influences were also reflected in the action research example.

Analysis procedures differ, and are separate for, quantitative and qualitative data. Even so, the combination of both contributes to cross-validation. This was reflected in the ABE guide especially. Typical procedures for analysis of quantitative data include frequency distribution, cross-tabulations, level of significance, and multivariate analysis. Typical procedures for analysis of qualitative data include inductive classification to extract themes from a natural language passage, coding, confirmation checks, and use of representative quotations.

An evaluation coordinator can contribute to sound data analysis by monitoring the process, using conclusions from a pilot test, assisting people who help with data analysis, comparing conclusions with those from similar evaluations, and making value judgments explicit in reports. These contributions were reflected in the review. It is helpful to include both commendations and recommendations in an evaluation report; this was the format of the external review reports. In the interest of utilization of conclusions, data analysis and interpretation should reflect sound and valid conclusions, ethical procedures, and responsiveness to the evaluation issues and goals (Guba and Lincoln, 1989; Hopkins, Glass, and Hopkins, 1987; Strauss and Corbin, 1990; Knox and others, 1974).

Utilization

Unfortunately, many evaluation reports are unused. Here are guidelines giving a rationale for involving, in the planning and implementation process, key stakeholders who are supposed to use the conclusions—that is, participants, instructors, program administrators, policy makers, funders, and materials developers. Involvement means they understand and commit to the conclusions and thus are more likely to use the conclusions for program planning, improve-

ment, and accountability. This ongoing cooperation in the evaluation process can be strengthened if the evaluation coordinator also
encourages stakeholders to use the conclusions, if the coordinator
is responsive to the key issues of concern, if important program features are addressed, if credible conclusions are produced, if unnecessary complexity is avoided, and if evaluation reports communicate
effectively. Among the criteria that stakeholders may use to judge
the soundness of evaluation reports are relevance, accuracy, usefulness, and clarity. The review and the ABE guide illustrate similar
ways in which the coordinator can encourage stakeholders to use
evaluation conclusions.

There are additional ways to encourage stakeholders to use conclusions as they make decisions. A modest assessment, in which the
main stakeholders are actively involved throughout, is one way, in
part because they develop a sense of ownership; this was illustrated
by the action research example. Another way to encourage utilization, even for stakeholders who were little involved in the evaluation process, is to ensure that the content and channels of
communication for each type of stakeholder are responsive to their
interests and style of information seeking. This was emphasized in
both the review and ABE guide examples. Another way is to offer
feasible recommendations that fit decisions they can make, along
with a clear rationale regarding why this is desirable (the case with
the review). Utilization is also aided by recognizing barriers as well
as facilitating recommended improvements, as occurred in the
action research example. Evaluation recommendations sometimes
generate resistance because people in powerful positions are apprehensive about negative consequences—a possibility in the review
approach.

One way to strengthen utilization is through meta-evaluation,
which consists of assessing and critiquing the evaluation process
and conclusions. The ABE guide includes suggestions about meta-
evaluation. In the action research example, a function similar to
meta-evaluation is served by sharing reports with colleagues and

discussing process and findings toward the end of the reflection seminar.

Standards to guide meta-evaluation include attention to matters such as feasibility, propriety, and utility. Findings from meta-evaluations following an evaluation project can strengthen utility of recommendations, recognition of limitations, response to criticism, reporting procedures, and planning of future evaluation. Feedback from the reflection seminar to teachers who reported on their project typically strengthened utility of recommendations, responses to criticism, and reporting procedures.

Findings from meta-evaluation concurrent with an evaluation project can contribute to acquisition of sufficient resources and expertise, as well as to a critique of preliminary data collection and analysis. These benefits were suggested in the ABE guide. Participants, instructors, colleagues, and consultants can all contribute to meta-evaluation. Additional suggestions about meta-evaluation and utilization generally are available from Patton (1997), Sanders (1994), and Brinkerhoff (1987).

Conclusion

The three approaches given here illustrate but a few of the many types of evaluation projects that occur in adult and continuing education and are reflected in Part Two. This overview of rationale and procedures is intended to enhance the decisions that you make as you plan, strengthen, and implement a specific evaluation project. In this chapter, the overview began with decisions about the purpose of an evaluation project that is important to you and your major stakeholders. Subsequent sections reviewed guidelines for planning and coordinating an evaluation project. This was followed by sections on data sources and collection and analysis. The concluding section explored decisions related to use of conclusions, which returns to concern about purpose and program stakeholders.

Potentially, program evaluation could address any aspect, or all, of a continuing education provider agency program. In practice, it is usually focused on one or more aspects for which decisions and choices are to be made. Each of Chapters Four through Eleven focuses on one such aspect (needs, context, goals, staff, participants, program, materials, and outcomes) and presents practical examples of provider agency types in which the aspect is especially salient. Each chapter also includes a rationale based on evaluation writings, suggesting why a combination of evaluation procedures is likely to be effective in a specific instance. Chapter Twelve, on how and why, discusses guidelines and future directions for strengthening evaluation.

As you reflect on the rationale, consider these questions:

- Which of these concepts and procedures seem most pertinent to your future evaluation plans?

- On which of the program aspects in the next eight chapters are you most likely to focus?

- Given the likely focus of a future evaluation project, which concepts and procedures would you like to better understand?

Part II

Applications to Various Program Aspects

4

Needs Assessment

The most familiar form of evaluation for planning adult and continuing education is educational needs assessment. Needs assessment has all of the basic features of evaluation: planning purpose, data-based conclusions, evaluative judgments, program development applications, and a baseline for assessing progress. This chapter contains four sections: concepts and purposes, planning and implementation, data collection and analysis, and coordination of needs assessment. Each section includes an overview of concepts and procedures, references to specialized readings on the topic, and brief examples that illustrate how to conduct needs assessments under specific circumstances. The chapter concludes with a listing of summary guidelines.

As you read this chapter on needs assessment as an aspect of evaluation, consider these questions:

- How familiar are you with needs assessment concepts, procedures, and approaches?

- What issues related to needs assessment most concern you?

- What indications have you noticed that attention (more of it, or redirected) should be given to needs assessment?

- How can you connect needs assessment more closely to other components of program development?

- How can needs assessment encourage learner participation without raising unrealistic expectations?

- How important is it to strengthen some of your current capability regarding needs assessment?

Concepts and Purposes

Needs assessment is important for various reasons, notably enhancing program planning and responsiveness to potential participants. Conclusions from needs assessment can also help us identify problems and opportunities to explore.

The concept of adult education needs assessment tends to be vague, and writings on this topic reflect varied meanings. Fortunately, a recent book by Queeney (1995) has a helpful overview and rationale for the range of needs assessment procedures from which to choose. Her Chapter Five, on methods for beginners, covers self-report, focus group, key informant, supervisor evaluation, and procedures such as nominal group process and the Delphi method. Subsequent chapters explain surveys, assessing performance, simulation, and assessment centers.

It seems useful to define an *educational need* as the discrepancy between current and desired proficiency. Discrepancy analysis is also useful for ongoing evaluation. Proficiency is the combination of knowledge, skills, and attitudes that constitute the capability to perform well when presented with an opportunity. In needs assessment, the focus is on adult learning, but findings are often aggregated to characterize widespread educational needs within a group, organization, or community.

The process of adult education needs assessment combines collecting and analyzing data with making value judgments. Pertinent data include experience level, current knowledge, topic interest, method preference, and career direction. Value judgments are included in conclusions regarding priorities for topics to be offered, learning methods to be used, scheduling options, and categories of adults to be served (Monette, 1977, 1979).

A feasible needs assessment entails projecting unmet educational needs and type of potential participant likely to fit the agency mission. The necessary focus for the scope of the needs assessment and the conclusions reached reflect judgments about relative importance. Such judgments are easier to make and defend if there are explicit criteria, which usually reflect the provider agency's mission and values.

Various needs assessment models and strategies have evolved with differing scales, complexity, perspective, and formality. There is substantial overlap between needs assessment and market research when the intent is to understand client needs for purposes of responsiveness. If there is a change agent, as in organization development or a community development program, needs assessment is closely connected with broader efforts to establish rapport and secure contributions to early program planning. Early involvement of potential participants can encourage their participation in the program and subsequent use of enhanced proficiencies. Engagement can also help reduce resistance to evaluative activity (including needs assessment). Both needs assessment and contextual analysis can address the influence of social trends, which may entail use of educational and social indicators (Queeney, 1995; Pennington, 1980; Posavac and Carey, 1992).

Examples of Planning and Implementation

At some point, adult and continuing education practitioners may decide to plan and conduct a needs assessment as a diagnostic form of evaluation. In practice, this process is typically informal and without an explicit plan. It is often the case that a program coordinator senses a new program direction is warranted and explores the notion with a review of pertinent writings on the topic and a few conversations with experts, potential participants, or a counterpart practitioner at a similar provider agency.

Sometimes, though, it is important to have a more explicit and detailed plan—if, for instance:

- Suggested participants differ from the adult learners with whom the practitioner has been working, an intuitive feel for their educational needs may be unreliable.

- Proposed content lies outside the experience and expertise of the expert or practitioner who has conducted previous programs.

- A pilot program is initiated, the success of which may greatly influence subsequent efforts.

- Early involvement of potential participants in planning a new program is a form of market research that can result in "satisfied customers" whose word-of-mouth comments may be influential in encouraging participation in a similar program in the future.

In addition to the basic decision to conduct a formal needs assessment, there are some related decisions that can be enhanced by deliberate planning. These decisions pertain to audience, context, scope, coordination, standards, and ground rules. The overview of such decisions and related examples given here present practical guidelines and a rationale for planning needs assessments for various types of adult educational programs.

Audience

One early planning decision is specifying the target audience of potential participants whose educational needs are to be assessed. Related considerations are familiarity, diversity, and accessibility. In particular, assessing the educational needs of a type of adult you have not previously served requires more effort than exploring how to better serve a familiar audience (as in the example here of an early needs assessment report focused on older adults). Conducting a needs assessment can pose special challenges for some populations; some of the difficulties and ways in which they have been addressed are illustrated in the example.

Assessment of educational needs of aging adults was an innovative project of a continuing higher education division in the Southwest, aimed at involving both university and community resources in exploring this topic. Twenty-five older men and women participated in an eight-week course about aging and survey research. They also helped design the interview guide they used during about thirty hours of interviewing urban adults over age sixty during the subsequent two weeks. They were highly motivated and attendance was nearly 100 percent.

More than five hundred randomly selected housing units were contacted; eighty-six half-hour interviews were completed with people over sixty who agreed to be interviewed. In addition to preferred content, format, location, and timing of educational activities of interest, the interview questions were on perceived influences on participation, and awareness of educational opportunities. A range of topics were of interest: health, current affairs, environment, psychology, languages, arts, humanities, and social sciences. The adults preferred daytime classes in the neighborhood; discussion groups were favored, though radio or television programs were also acceptable. The likelihood of participation was associated with access to transportation, lower age, higher level of education, and program subsidy.

Recommendations in the needs assessment report identified program characteristics likely to be attractive to older adults; broader ways in which the continuing higher education division could serve older adults (notably, by combating stereotypes of aging); and provision of information, counseling, and volunteer opportunities. By including university experts on aging and survey research and older course members who helped design the needs assessment process and complete interviews, the needs assessment process and use of findings were both strengthened, along with other benefits for course participants and the continuing higher education division.

Assessing the educational needs of a diverse population (such as a community survey) can be more complex than for a category of adults with similar characteristics (such as members of a professional association). This complexity reflects diversity of relevant topics and methods required to obtain information. Audience accessibility includes geographic location and willingness to cooperate with data collection.

Context

A related planning decision regarding needs assessment pertains to the context of the provider mission, resources, service area, and directions. Typically, the scope of a needs assessment matches the current and anticipated mission, resources, and service area of a provider agency in terms of subject matter content and potential participants to be served. The resources that providers typically devote to needs assessment reflect their commitment to serving new participants and better serving current participants. A provider agency with high-quality programs and overflow enrollment may be satisfied with a modest needs assessment to fine tune its efforts.

Scope

Preliminary decisions about the audience and content for a needs assessment can help you make the major decision about scope and content to be included in the data collection and analysis. In addition to deciding on necessary background information to collect to identify important subpopulations of potential participants, there are scope-related decisions which deal with topics, needs, obstacles, and incentives. Clarification about which data to collect and questions to be answered also suggests the most appropriate data collection methods and the requisite resources.

Coordination

For all but the most modest needs assessment, it is helpful to designate someone to coordinate the effort. For needs assessment related to the next offering of a course or workshop, coordination may be easily handled by the coordinator or the instructor. For a major needs assessment on behalf of one provider agency or a combination, serving as coordinator of the needs assessment may be a formal designation accompanied by released time, allocation of resources, and assurance of cooperation. It is helpful if the coordinator develops the proposal or plan and explores potential cooperation and expectations.

Here is an illustration of a collaborative approach to coordination of a needs assessment. The chair of a health occupation association committee on continuing education initiated a joint effort with the director of a university center engaged in continuing education research and outreach. The association had concluded that conducting a needs assessment was of high priority for planning continuing professional education activities for members of the association and for people in related health care occupations. There were early commitments to collect data from various sources and to produce findings relevant to the objectives and activities of an educational program by a number of continuing education providers that entailed various ways of learning. Joint coordination by an association committee chair and a university center director contributed to a needs assessment useful to both association members and practitioners in related health occupations, any of whom might be served by continuing education providers.

The needs assessment plan they prepared specified the contributions that they and other people would make to conducting the needs assessment. Included in the plan were the intended recipients of the needs assessment report (members of the health occupations, association leaders, educators, and potential providers of continuing education) and the decision types (priorities regarding topics, learning methods, special emphases, and attention to both acquisition and application of enhanced proficiencies).

The plan also included data collection by mailed questionnaire from members of the association and related occupations regarding their characteristics, past educational participation, interest in topics and arrangements, and perceptions of what would facilitate and what would impede participation. In addition to specifications for interviews with members and others and data analysis procedures, the plan included specifying the recipients of the report, encouraging completion of the questionnaire, and promoting dissemination and use of findings to improve continuing education opportunities.

Standards

As with other forms of program assessment, there are evaluation standards that can help ensure the soundness of a needs assessment that results in useful conclusions. If the coordinator and other people who help plan and conduct the assessment do not know about such standards, perhaps one or more people with understanding of such standards can be recruited.

Ground Rules

It is useful in a needs assessment plan to have some basic ground rules regarding objectives, resources, division of responsibility, methods, and access to and use of conclusions. Understanding regarding such guidelines can increase cooperation and reduce misunderstanding.

A plan for a needs assessment should consider some broad issues that underlie specific planning decisions and that become even more important during implementation of the plan: feasibility, timing, scale, involvement, self-assessment, obstacles, and administration.

The feasibility of a needs assessment reflects more than the scope of the effort and the complexity of the data collection and analysis methods. Other interrelated influences are organizational expectations, available resources, willingness of colleagues and potential participants to cooperate, and in particular the ability of the coordinator to persist until useful conclusions are actually put into practice. A pilot project to implement a small part of the needs assessment on a limited scale is a worthwhile investment for many purposes, among them increasing the feasibility of the total effort.

The timing of a needs assessment can vary greatly with scope, complexity, resources, commitment, and urgency. To assess the educational needs of current participants in a course or workshop may take but a few minutes, with the conclusions guiding the teaching and learning that occur in the following hours and days. By contrast, it may take more than a year to plan, conduct, and share conclusions to assess the educational needs of adults generally in a service area, on behalf of various provider agencies initiating new programs to address the unmet needs of underserved adults. In either instance, it is important to develop a realistic timeline for each stage of the process, provide for unanticipated delays, and recognize the importance of creating and sustaining momentum so that the effort moves to a successful conclusion. Many a worthy needs assessment or other evaluation effort runs out of steam owing to insufficient attention to timing as an ingredient in winning and maintaining cooperation.

The scale on which a needs assessment is conducted is a similar issue. With an ambitious needs assessment, availability of resources such as money, technical services, volunteers, and in-kind contributions can be crucial for successful implementation. Sound planning can help match the needs assessment plan with necessary resources.

As with many evaluation projects, involvement by key stakeholders is crucial not only for completing the assessment but also for encouraging use of conclusions (Patton, 1980). There tends to be a desirable window of involvement below which the sense of ownership necessary for cooperation is lacking and above which there is a sense of burden that also discourages cooperation.

Self-Assessment

An important aspect of needs assessment is provision for self-assessment. The conclusions are valuable for creating program responsiveness to learner motivation. Self-assessment helps make explicit the learner's perception of a gap between current and desired proficiencies. The procedures discussed here show various assessment methods, based on the type of evidence used to make a judgment.

As one example, a largely open-ended procedure asks potential participants to express in their own words their current and desired proficiencies related to the topic. This questionnaire approach works well with experienced and well-educated respondents.

Another self-assessment began with a checklist of proficiencies, based on such procedures as literature review, task analysis, focus group, and pretesting with representative potential participants. A checklist of one-sentence statements typically groups similar proficiencies. Respondents are asked to rate each one on a four-point scale of current proficiency from low to high, and sometimes a second rating of desired proficiency or of how important it is to enhance the proficiency. Checklists have been used with many populations: hospital staff, attorneys, continuing higher education administrators, graduate students, and others. Sometimes each proficiency area is also rated by the respondent as to the likelihood of enrollment for an educational activity on that topic. A checklist might assess perceptions of generic abilities—verbal (writing, speaking, negotiating), social (social ease, criticism), numerical (interpreting numerical data, computational accuracy), investigative (curiosity, technical procedures), manual (authority, stamina), creative (being artistic or imaginative), managerial (planning, deciding), and others (coaching, counseling).

Another approach to self-assessment uses a set of multiple-choice or similar questions that potential participants complete before an educational activity. They may use a scoring key, or have someone else score the inventory and give participants a summary of responses to each item (the answer sheet has a number to permit returning it to the corresponding person). Inventories have been used with engineers, school teachers, continuing medical education coordinators, and other professionals. Similar procedures have been used for members of emerging occupations (new specialties for judges, engineers, or lawyers) in which they are asked to describe their current practices, rationales, and concerns on a questionnaire. The summary of responses was distributed at the outset of the educational activity and discussion of their varied responses (along with assumptions and implications) was the main program content. With each response, the process and results of completing a self-assessment were educationally valuable to the individual learner and an important guide to program content.

A fourth approach is performance review (especially in workplace settings, but also in athletics and the performing arts), useful when the potential participant and someone else (work supervisor, coach, mentor) each review the learner's performance and then discuss growth areas on which to focus. The focus can be on actual performance, simulated performance, or an assessment checklist regarding typical performance. Sometimes (as with microteaching or medical diagnosis with a coached patient) the performance is videotaped for later review, reflection, and discussion. A valuable feature of this type of self-assessment is the selection of growth goals to which both the learner and another person are committed. This motivation to use the results of the needs assessment to guide and focus efforts to change is the special benefit of self-assessment using most procedures.

Using a self-assessment helps overcome one of the main obstacles to needs assessment: adult learners' resistance to using findings. As noted earlier, other obstacles are inadequate resources, insufficient cooperation, lack of persistence, and lack of expertise regarding the process of needs assessment.

One way to reduce such obstacles and increase the success of the effort is to develop a plan that is manageable. This can be done by reviewing writings on needs assessment to guide development of the plan, securing cooperation and assistance from other people who together have the ability to conduct the needs assessment, selecting a scale of effort that fits expectations and resources, and conducting a pilot project to fine-tune the plan in the case of a larger needs assessment.

By contrast, assessment centers and in-depth practice audits are among the most complex and expensive forms of educational needs assessment. Typically, they demand one to three days and a variety of assessment procedures to yield a comprehensive evaluation of needs and potential professional development (Moses and Byham, 1977; MacKinnon, 1991). This approach (which requires much time, expense, and expertise) was used at Penn State in the practice audit model for continuing professional education (Queeney, 1981, 1990, 1995), which assessed continuing education needs in six fields (pharmacy, accounting, architecture, clinical dietetics, clinical psychology, nursing). The practice audit model had seven phases, which evolved during work with pharmacists, as a systematic way to develop practice-oriented continuing professional education programs.

Phase one entails organization of a team to guide program development; it is composed of instructing faculty members, professional association representatives, and continuing education professionals. This makeup allows complementary contributions and avoids any one stakeholder having to assume the complete burden. Phase two is identification of professional proficiencies and practice standards, through use of such procedures as role delineation, task analysis, and occupational proficiency assessment. Phase three is construction of assessment materials, both the content related to specific occupational practice standards and techniques allowing professionals to demonstrate how they perform in practice situations (which reflect knowledge, skills, and attitudes). In phase four, these materials are used in an assessment workshop. Phase five sees analysis of the assessment results to identify individual needs by comparing current proficiency (from the assessment process) with desired proficiency (from practice standards). Phase six is provision of continuing education activities that are responsive to the identified needs. Phase seven involves ongoing evaluation of the programs regarding meeting needs and improving practice.

Data Collection and Analysis

Usually, writings about needs assessment tend to focus on the type of information or data to collect and the procedure for data collection and analysis.

One starting point for decisions about data type is noting indicators or "symptoms," which suggest that unmet educational needs may exist among the adults the provider agency seeks to serve. Such symptoms include a request for an educational program that the agency does not offer but that is within its mission, a comment by an instructor about ideas for a future program, projection of emerging trends related to adult role performance, reflection by counseling staff about themes regarding unmet needs that emerge from advisement, and a report of a high-demand program in a similar agency or service area. By scanning such symptoms, you can identify starting points for potential needs assessment.

There are three major sources of data for educational needs assessment. The first is potential participants, who can be asked about their views on the gap between current and desired proficiencies. The second is other people (instructors, experts, associates, helping professionals) who are in a position to know about the educational needs of potential participants. The third is materials and reports that address problem areas and trends that can illuminate such needs—reports on occupational performance, family functioning, community problems, new technology, health conditions, and research related to problems and opportunities among the potential participants.

Sometimes a review of pertinent writings about the target audience of adults can be useful as early information about likely needs and ways to assess them. Such writings are available for adults generally (Merriam and Caffarella, 1999), young adults (Darkenwald and Knox, 1984), middle-age adults (Knox, 1979a), and older adults (Okun, 1982). These writings analyze developmental trends and individual differences for adults; learning abilities and interests; and performance in major life roles in family, work, and community. An overview gives background to guide specific needs assessment for a category of adults in a geographic area.

A valuable and efficient source of information about educational needs of an intended audience of potential participants is a review of pertinent publications. The ease with which such a literature review is accomplished depends on how clearly the target audience has been specified and how familiar someone associated with the needs assessment is with literature review procedures. Reviewing pertinent publications can serve several purposes: recognizing basic generalizations about the intended participants to help interpret the collected needs assessment data, considering methods used in previous needs assessments, and identifying useful questions for planning a needs assessment. Publications also vary, from those generalizing about a broad range of adults to those focusing on a specific intended audience.

A sourcebook edited by Pennington (1980) typifies publications that emphasize assessment procedure but also include reports on needs assessments for a specific population (professionals, the underprivileged). Houle (1992, pp. 110–113) presents an overview of books that can guide selection of what should be reviewed for a specific needs assessment effort. An especially valuable source to review early in the process is a recent book on adults as learners that indicates the type of information on which a specific needs assessment might focus. *Learning in Adulthood: A Comprehensive Guide* (Merriam and Caffarella, 1999) is an excellent example, with perspectives on educational needs of adults that include concepts and influences. Major concepts are characteristics associated with differential participation rate, adults' reasons for participation, developmental influence such as a change event, and interplay of personal and situational influences. Some publications focus on developmental stages of adulthood, such as young adults.

Review of pertinent recent books and articles can contribute to the content and the process of a needs assessment effort. Reading them can clarify major concepts and terminology as well as suggest content and procedures to use. The indexing terms listed in the Library of Congress cataloging-in-publication data (on the copyright page of a work) can be used to select descriptors for a database computer search (such as ERIC) to locate pertinent publications.

Some publications focus on select populations of adults, by discussing widespread educational needs, ways to assess them, and use of conclusions to plan and conduct responsive programs. For example, Kasworm (1983) illustrates responsive programs for several populations (rural, undereducated, women, marginal, and older). Some publications focus on understanding and being responsive to specific populations; examples are minorities (Cassara, 1990; Ross-Gordon, Martin, and Briscoe, 1990; Hayes and Colin, 1994); hard-to-reach and low-literacy groups (Darkenwald and Larson, 1980; Sissel, 1996); and professionals (Baskett and Marsick, 1992; Boice, 1996; Curry, Wergin, and Associates, 1993; Davis and Fox, 1994).

Beginning the review with the most recent major publications facilitates locating additional pertinent books and articles that were cited and seem promising, along with selection of the most useful descriptive terms for broader searches. The result can help guide a needs assessment and interpret the findings. Information for purposes of needs assessment varies in regard to accessibility. It may be easier to obtain information from potential participants with a higher level of formal education who previously participated in an agency's educational programs than from harder-to-reach adults. Agency instructors, counselors, and program coordinators may be more accessible sources of information about the educational needs of potential participants than a more remote expert or colleague at a similar provider agency. Agency records may be more accessible than similar information from libraries and other organizations. Books and articles located in personal or agency collections may be consulted more easily than an electronic database or publication in a special collection.

Accessible sources of information are an efficient and convenient way to estimate unmet educational needs; more remote sources can supplement them and permit cross-validation. Themes can be identified by reviewing similarities and differences across information from potential participants, other people familiar with them, organizational records, and pertinent writings at various levels of accessibility. These widespread themes can yield the basic conclusions for the needs assessment; distinctive generalizations from one or a few sources can then furnish refinements.

A consideration in selecting or emphasizing some potential sources of information about unmet needs is credibility in the eyes of the main stakeholders or decision makers likely to use the conclusions from the needs assessment. For example, market research emphasizing the likelihood that potential participants will actually enroll in sufficient numbers to justify the expense of offering a program may be especially persuasive to funders and administrators in the parent organization. By contrast, information from potential participants about specific discrepancies between current and desired proficiencies may be most useful to the instructors and other experts who will design the program and related materials.

Procedures for data collection, for the purpose of a needs assessment, are similar to those in the social and behavioral sciences generally, but there are some distinctive features. For each needs assessment, relatively few data collection procedures are typically selected from the many available. When doing so, keep in mind the practical purpose of the needs assessment, especially encouraging use of findings. The overview presented here suggests some guidelines for data collection.

Early clarification of the sources and populations from which data are to be sampled and collected can facilitate the actual process of doing so. This pertains to obtaining cooperation as well as such considerations as how large and representative the sample is, or how a questionnaire, interview guide, or checklist for observation or review of records is worded.

There are many techniques and procedures available for obtaining information about the unmet educational needs of adults. Two excellent sources of examples and guidelines are Queeney (1995) and Angelo and Cross (1993).

Perhaps the most valuable information for an instructor is the learner's current proficiency regarding content. A brief diagnostic test may probe background knowledge, requesting answers to multiple-choice questions and brief responses to open-ended ones. This diagnostic inventory previews for participants the main concepts to be learned; for the instructor, it helps specify the range of participant backgrounds, the most helpful starting point, and a baseline for assessing subsequent achievement. The instructor should indicate that participants' thoughtful responses contribute to instructional decisions. A summary of responses can be shared with participants individually or in groups (Angelo and Cross, 1993).

Educational needs can emerge as an educational program progresses. In addition to assessment of programs and unmet needs, it is helpful to discover the ideas that participants find unclear or confusing so that the instructor can address these emerging needs in the next program segment. Following a reading, discussion, presentation, or case analysis, participants are asked to write, in a few words or phrases, the main points or ideas that they have found most unclear. The instructor (or several participants) can read the comments and sort them into piles of related comments. This summary helps the instructor recognize the diversity of understanding—and confusion—among the participants, so that in the next program segment some time can be devoted to clarifying the most confusing concepts (Angelo and Cross, 1993).

To use a brief self-assessment of preferred ways of learning, the instructor should select a framework for describing preferred learning styles and the main categories or types within that framework. This self-assessment could yield a profile such as one of the formal learning style inventories that address such distinctions as preference for the abstract versus concrete, seeing versus hearing, active versus passive, structured versus unstructured. A summary of responses can be used to discuss with participants various ways of learning, their pros and cons, and implications for teaching and learning in the program (Angelo and Cross, 1993).

Other Techniques for Data Collection

Here is an overview of highlights regarding other data collection techniques. Focus groups and surveys are described in some detail, followed by brief description of additional techniques that are covered elsewhere in the book.

Focus Groups

Sometimes a temporary group of potential participants meets for the sole purpose of discussing examples, priorities, and rationales for their educational needs.

Focus groups are increasingly used as a procedure for data collection and encouraging commitment to use findings for purposes of needs assessment and other forms of market research. They are especially applicable when potential applicants are at a location where a small group can readily meet for a session of an hour or two.

To illustrate: in a large enterprise with staff in multiple locations, the director of training conducted an assessment, which included nearly two dozen focus groups in almost ten regions in which staff members were located.

The total needs assessment obtained information from several sources, in addition to focus group members. External information included benchmarking with data from similar organizations and an opinion survey; both contributed to formulating some preliminary goals or production goals for individual roles and workgroups. Because explicit goals and global measures were lacking, the focus groups were an opportunity for staff members to comment on the preliminary goals, which could increase their acceptance as part of performance review and staff development activities.

Coordinating use of focus groups was difficult and occurred during several months of planning and implementation, with the focus group meetings covering several weeks. A survey would have taken less time and money, but the likely response rate and buy-in by staff members were low. Commitment of adequate resources was essential. The director served as facilitator of several focus groups, coordinating selection and supervision of other people who served as facilitators and recorders. The director worked with an external vendor for the equivalent of one week and helped prepare guidelines for the focus groups.

Overall, the director devoted the equivalent of about one month to the focus groups. In addition, several people spent about twenty hours scheduling and coordinating them. The facilitator spent a day or so on each focus group; a recorder put in about ten hours. The decision to use focus groups for needs assessment should be based on the conclusion that it is an appropriate method, and on a commitment of sufficient time and money to plan and conduct the focus group so that it is effective.

Survey

The mailed questionnaire survey is a widespread type of data collection used with various categories of adults (community residents, hospital staff, engineers, and so on). Mailed questionnaires capable of generating useful findings are sent to appropriate and current mailing lists; they are designed to encourage a satisfactory rate of representative response (Salant and Dillman, 1994).

The effectiveness of a questionnaire to collect needs assessment information depends on the characteristics of the people surveyed as well as the design of the questionnaire items and format. In an earlier statewide survey of educational needs of hospital staff members, almost all of the respondents had sufficient interest, familiarity, and literacy to complete the questionnaire. The contents of the eight-page questionnaire included name and location of hospital, respondent's department and position, a four-point scale for rating extent of perceived need (as expressed in lists of phrases dealing with supervision and general abilities for all respondents), and specific items to be completed only by staff in separate departments.

The questionnaire concluded with a listing of broad areas of instruction (with illustrative topics noted) for which respondents were asked to rate their likelihood of enrollment (definitely, probably, might, would not). Responses were tabulated by department and hospital, which helped interpret the information for a specific department, in particular both widespread and unique patterns of perceived needs and relative interest. Summaries from personnel records could describe current staff characteristics to help interpret survey findings.

Statewide surveys of adult educational needs are seldom conducted because of the high cost in time and money. One example from New York State during 1975–1979 was reported by Veres (1980); the entire article has many details regarding plans, procedures, and rationale, with special emphasis on encouraging use of findings.

The New York State Education Department's Division of Continuing Education conducted the needs assessment, funded under the Federal Adult Education Act, Title VI. The purposes involved assessing the educational needs of adults statewide, state provision of continuing education opportunities, and in-service education needs of continuing education faculty and administrators.

A department staff member served as manager of the overall project (and encouraged use of findings), working with directors of three subprojects: a survey of adult needs (conducted by Cornell University's Institute for Occupational Education); a similar study for New York City (conducted by City College of New York, Office of Research and Evaluation Services); and a staff development survey and project information workshops (conducted by the State University of New York at Albany Two-Year College Development Center). As project sponsor, the State Education Department worked with local school districts, intermediate BOCES districts (Boards of Cooperative Educational Services), and two-year community colleges. This alliance contributed to project planning, implementation, and encouragement to use findings. Separate arrangements were made for the project in New York City because of its population characteristics (it has almost half the state's residents).

In the fall of 1975, the multiple-choice questionnaire on adults' perceived learning needs was developed and field-tested by Cornell University. These interview guides covered background information, past participation, expressed interest, obstacles, preferred conditions, and interest in advising services. The questionnaire was reviewed by continuing education professionals and pilot-tested with fifty adults in half-hour interviews. The survey instrument was modified and translated into ten languages for use in New York City. Training and supervision were provided for twenty-two hundred volunteer interviewers. More than twenty-eight thousand usable interviews were completed for the survey of adult learning needs portion of the total project.

In each region, a committee representing various stakeholders was formed to help with all stages of the project. The data was analyzed and reported for each district, and statewide. Reporting included written reports, consultation, meetings, and workshops to explore implications within the region and local adult education programs. A broad range of local decision makers and continuing education practitioners were involved.

By far, most of the adults surveyed (94 percent) expressed interest in further learning, but the specifics varied greatly. The survey findings resulted in profiles of interest by subpopulation of adults with differing characteristics.

In 1997, interviews were conducted with a number of people who had been centrally associated with the needs assessment twenty years earlier, to discuss subsequent use of the needs assessment findings beyond dissemination reports. One result was increased awareness of unmet educational needs, especially among less advantaged and underserved adults, many of whom were not aware of many current adult education opportunities. The reporting, publicity, and dissemination meetings helped increase the visibility of local adult education directors and provision of staff development for adult education teachers and administrators. Some of these collaborative staff development activities continue to the present; some have encouraged cooperation between educational institutions and enterprises on behalf of continuing education and training. Another benefit was increased attention to the less advantaged, such as a work-related educational program for unemployed adults, with support from federal funding.

A number of the adult education programs in New York City seem to have made little use of the statewide needs assessment findings because various adult education providers were already working together in the face of pressing inner-city problems, had their own detailed indicators of educational needs, and were using a community development approach to staff development and supervision that served various providers.

This example yields some useful conclusions regarding statewide assessment of needs. A well-designed and coordinated needs assessment is complex and expensive. Use of detailed findings for planning specific programs tends not to occur. However, there can be various related benefits, such as increased awareness of underserved populations, increased collaboration, staff development for adult education practitioners, and connections with policy makers. In weighing the costs of extensive surveys, always consider such benefits.

Here is a brief summary of additional techniques:

- *Committee*. Advisory, consultation, and planning committees can help identify educational needs to the extent to which the members are representative of and associated with the potential participants whose needs are to be assessed.
- *Interview*. Both survey and in-depth information can be obtained by interview. Interview procedures might range from a highly structured survey research phone interview to a flexible, lengthy, focused interview conducted in person.
- *Observation*. Especially in workplace and voluntary association settings, observation is a valuable technique, especially when an observation guide helps focus on relevant performance and when supervisors, preceptors, and associates are in a position to make such observations to a sufficient extent. An interview guide can help them record pertinent and comparable information.
- *Performance samples*. In family, work, and community settings, adults sometimes engage in activity that leaves a record useful for needs assessment purposes; examples are family expenditures, health records, occupational production and innovation, and recreational participation. Performance samples can also be obtained solely for the purpose of a needs assessment, as by having potential participants demonstrate their ability to perform a procedure.
- *Nominal Group and Delphi*. Two procedures enable a group to contribute and refine suggestions on any topic, including educational needs. In the nominal group technique, members list suggestions independently, then take turns adding those that were not mentioned to the master list. They then clarify, consolidate, group, and prioritize the suggestions. The Delphi technique is similar, but instead of listing suggestions in a meeting, the panel members do so in successive rounds using mail or e-mail.

• *Simulation*. Performance-oriented assessment is especially realistic and useful in the form of a simulation, which can range from an in-basket simulation for administrators to discussion of a trigger film by a group of social workers, or a computerized simulation of a diagnostic procedure for physicians.

As you reflect on using any combination of techniques for gathering information about educational needs, remember that there are overarching guidelines for doing so effectively. The main purpose of data collection is to obtain information that is valid, realistic, and relevant to the unmet educational needs of the potential participants. This is the main criterion for selecting techniques to be used. Including informal techniques can encourage use of conclusions by major stakeholders (learners, instructors, coordinators, policy makers). A varied combination of techniques (such as interviews and performance samples from potential participants, surveys of coordinators and instructors with experience in similar programs) allows cross-validation and identification of major conclusions with implications for program development decisions. It is especially efficient to use existing pertinent information, if it is available. (Consider using organizational records and previous evaluation reports that contain information regarding needs.)

Often a combination of quantitative and qualitative data is most useful. Quantitative data (such as scores on tests and rating scales) allow convenient summary and comparison. Qualitative data (such as interview responses and comments in response to open-ended questionnaire items) help reveal respondents' reasons and concerns, which can answer some of the *why* questions and suggest how to use conclusions on quantitative relationships.

Because a needs assessment typically occurs in a naturalistic setting, it is important to minimize intrusion on program activity from the data collection techniques that are used. Doing so increases cooperation on the part of participants and staff with data collection, especially their use of conclusions. It is also important not to raise unrealistic expectations. Without some caution or disclaimer that only some of the identified needs can be addressed, some respondents will expect their suggestions to be used and thus be disappointed if they are not.

This is only one of the unintended aspects of a needs assessment. Some unintended outcomes can be beneficial, as when enrollment by potential participants contacted for needs assessment purposes increases as they hope that the subsequent educational program will be of high relevance and quality as a result of their input. One way to anticipate some of these aspects is to review pertinent writings on needs assessment and evaluation and then reflect such insights in the planning for a needs assessment.

There are many ways to analyze the data collected in a needs assessment. The specific analysis procedures to use in a particular needs assessment depend on the type of data and the purpose of the needs assessment. For example, when deciding on next year's topics for the tenth annual program for a familiar clientele, an experienced planning committee might find a summary of frequencies and comments on a questionnaire listing potential topics sufficient. By contrast, in charting new directions regarding content, methods, and learners, it may be a worthwhile investment to compare the conclusions from analyses of several quite different types of data and give special attention to common themes that emerge—say, trends from analysis of recent publications, frequency distribution of preferences for potential topics on a questionnaire by major subpopulations of potential participants, highlights from phone interviews with experts and instructors in similar programs, and a detailed evaluation summary from a pilot educational program designed to explore the potential responses to the full-scale program. The main justification for such a detailed needs assessment is that the investment is preferable to the risk of proceeding to offer the program without assessment and having it fail.

There are many publications on analysis of needs, evaluation, and research data of all kinds (Cook and Reichardt, 1979; Glaser and Strauss, 1967; Grotelueschen, Gooler, and Knox, 1976; Hopkins, Glass, and Hopkins, 1987; Lincoln and Guba, 1985; Miles and Huberman, 1984; Patton, 1980, 1990; Phillips, 1991). The overview here gives guidelines for data analysis that can aid in locating sources of more detailed information about specific data analysis procedures. This overview covers quantitative and qualitative data analysis procedures, triangulation for cross-validation on the basis of multiple sources, criteria to consider when drawing conclusions, and comparison of findings with those from similar studies. The general purpose of data analysis is to organize and summarize pertinent information as a basis for conclusions about high-priority educational needs to address.

For quantitative data (such as numbers selected on rating scales and scores on tests), a usual early stage of analysis is a frequency distribution (the result of listing the number of people who responded to each option). There is typically some effort to verify that scores correspond to the phenomenon (knowledge, skill, attitude, performance, influence) that the scale or test is intended to assess. The reliability of a test or scale tends to be more satisfactory when each item (question) is clearly worded and there are a number of items for each concept. There are additional ways to analyze data early on to find out how validly a scale or test assesses what it intends to; scores can be compared with the behaviors to be predicted (actual participation rates), with scores on similar scales, or with features of the phenomenon to be assessed.

After such preliminary analysis, a typical analysis procedure is cross-tabulation by comparing frequency or percentage of response for several categories of respondents (often in a matrix or grid). All of these analyses can contribute to data reduction, which allows focusing on those relationships among variables that appear to be most important for purposes of the needs assessment. For more complex analysis, there are many forms of multivariate analysis of statistical data that allow precise prediction.

For qualitative data (comments about a rating, responses to an open-ended interview question, a transcript of a recorded conversation, notes from an observer), a usual early stage of analysis is to make an inductive classification of responses by reading through the data related to an item, noting a word or phrase that summarizes the comment, and doing so for all respondents by adding a new summary phrase for each additional comment and by recording the frequency of respondents who made comments similar to ones already on the list. The resulting inductive classification of qualitative data can then be used for coding themes. Such coding can be used to identify relationships of interest, such as between topic interest and learner characteristics (work specialty or years of experience). Quotes of actual words used can illustrate the meanings expressed by the respondents. The process of analytic induction from qualitative data typically includes reviewing data to identify themes; forming a working hypothesis to be tested by reference to specific passages; and by a confirmation check and triangulation, with further validation by considering rival explanations and exceptions, and placing conclusions in the context of other indicators of need (Worthen and Sanders, 1987; Guba and Lincoln, 1981; Patton, 1990).

Sound conclusions about educational needs depend on more than analysis of each source of data. Cross-validation or triangulation on multiple sources and types of data is fundamental. For example, quantitative data from performance samples and simulations, qualitative data from observations and interviews with experts, and combined data from a survey of potential participants each have a bias. The themes that emerge from these five sources and types of data in common are likely to be valid and useful for needs assessment purposes.

Data-based conclusions about educational needs reflect interpretation based on both facts and values. It is also important to minimize misinterpretation, as in imputing causation where there is only evidence of association, or confusing statistical significance with practical significance as viewed by various stakeholders. There are additional criteria for judging the soundness of conclusions regarding needs:

- Relevance to the purpose and scope of the needs assessment

- Usefulness of the findings as estimates of unmet educational needs, which can guide other program development and instructional decisions

- Extent of detail and precision in the conclusions that is warranted, taking into account the intended use of findings and the costs of conducting a needs assessment

- Importance of including key stakeholders in the interpretation process, for purposes of validity and use of findings

Another aspect of analysis is comparison with conclusions from a similar needs assessment. Similar findings can provide reassurance; differing findings prompt critical questions about the needs assessment procedure, findings, and further analysis that may be warranted. As with data collection, the depth and complexity of data analysis depends on the understanding of unmet educational needs that already exist and the price of program failure. In many instances of high familiarity and low risk, the most cost-beneficial approach may be just to proceed with a program on a small scale and use evaluation to guide improvement, justification, and planning of subsequent programs.

Coordination

For most needs assessment, one or a few people have the main responsibility for coordination and management of the process. In addition to planning and implementation of data collection and analysis, coordination can include at least three other responsibilities: reporting, meta-evaluation, and continuous assessment.

Reporting findings and encouraging their use is essential for effective needs assessment. Without this, it becomes difficult to obtain cooperation for future assessment. An early decision when planning a needs assessment is, Who should decide what to do with the conclusions? Specifying early the main stakeholders for a needs assessment allows involving them in the process and ensuring that the reports are responsive to them and encourage their use of findings. Reporting also includes broader forms of dissemination. Patton offers a succinct list of guidelines for reporting findings:

- Involve stakeholders in the process.

- Hold early interpretation sessions to increase utility, facility with data analysis, realistic expectations, and commitment to use findings.

- Establish standards early to guide interpretation and reporting.

- Make the analysis and reporting process interesting for stakeholders.

- Help stakeholders separate reporting regarding analysis, interpretation, judgment, and recommendation.

- Organize and focus reporting so that stakeholders can deal with the report.

- Offer balanced conclusions that reflect multiple indicators and interpretations.

- Make sure that comparisons are sound.

- Use multiple process and content reporting strategies to address various stakeholder interests and capabilities.

- Help stakeholders assess findings regarding understand-
  ability, relevance, believability, accuracy, practicality,
  and utility.

- With stakeholders, plan strategies for utilization by
  intended users and perhaps dissemination to additional
  audiences.

- Develop recommendations carefully so they will be
  taken seriously (1997).

Such involvement can encourage stakeholder use of conclusions, as they make program development decisions to increase program responsiveness. Needs assessment conclusions can also be disseminated to additional audiences who may not use them for program development decisions but find such conclusions useful nonetheless. Two examples are a human-interest story from the needs assessment that can encourage potential participants to enroll, and a report to policy makers and funders that can strengthen their support because of increased appreciation of the needs that a program addresses.

An aspect of coordination occasionally encountered is meta-evaluation (assessment of the needs assessment process and conclusions). Needs assessment is a form of evaluation for planning purposes. Standards for judging the soundness of an evaluation project can be used as guidelines for needs assessment planning and meta-evaluation (Worthen and Sanders, 1987; Worthen, Sanders, and Fitzpatrick, 1997). The standards address issues of utility, feasibility, propriety, and accuracy. Each needs assessment is evaluated informally by people associated with it. However, more formal involvement by stakeholders in meta-evaluation can provide increased benefits, notably, more informed confidence in the relative soundness of the needs assessment process and conclusions, and a clearer basis for deciding the extent of cooperation that is warranted.

Meta-evaluation can also clarify aspects of the general approach used for a needs assessment, as a basis for future planning. Examples of general methodological approaches are experimental (analyze causal relationships between predetermined variables as a basis for a go–no go decision), descriptive (portray holistically potential participants' expectations to which the program should respond), eclectic (combine causal relationships with information about process and context as a basis for program improvement), and cost-benefit (assess costs and benefits from potential participants' viewpoint, as a basis for a judgment about offering a program). Some of these approaches combine needs assessment findings with those from contextual analysis.

Another contribution of coordination pertains to the connection between needs assessment (as a form of evaluation for planning purposes) and ongoing evaluation for purposes of program improvement and accountability. Such continuous assessment includes monitoring and institutionalization. Monitoring entails use of evaluation during program planning and implementation to guide decision making. Needs assessment conclusions and recommendations that are used to decide on program objectives and methods can also contribute to a baseline of initial proficiency that can be monitored by ongoing evaluation to assess learner progress. Continuous assessment can contribute to institutionalization by specifying organizational changes within the provider agency to increase responsiveness to the clientele and their unmet educational needs. Such organizational changes might include mission, staffing, content, methods, resources, and technology so that participants are better served.

As you reflect on this overview of needs assessment, consider these questions:

- Which of your existing ideas and information regarding needs assessment is it most important to build upon?

- How can you best strengthen the combination of data collection and analysis procedures that you use for needs assessment?

- What are promising next steps you can take for planning and coordinating a future needs assessment?

Summary Guidelines

Here is a checklist reviewing the basic guidelines for planning and conducting a needs assessment. The extent of detail that is applicable depends on the scale of the needs assessment. As you plan or strengthen a needs assessment, such guidelines can help enhance your rationale and procedures.

Concepts and Purposes

1. Clarify the purposes of each needs assessment. This usually includes increasing program responsiveness and learner participation.

2. Understand educational needs as the discrepancy between current and desired proficiency.

3. Consider various available needs assessment procedures.

4. Recognize that value judgment is included in any conclusion regarding priorities.

5. Involve potential participants in the needs assessment process to encourage commitment and application.

Planning and Implementation with Stakeholders

6. Consider formal needs assessment:

   Do so if there are unfamiliar participants and objectives.

   Decisions about the extent of a needs assessment effort reflect resources to invest and procedures to use.

   Designate a coordinator to guide needs assessment planning.

Know about standards for conducting a sound needs assessment.

Clarify ground rules to increase cooperation.

7. Use a pilot project to increase feasibility, notably with decisions about timing and scale.

8. Involve stakeholders to strengthen the process.

9. Include provision for self-assessment by adult learners.

10. Obtain needed support and assistance.

Data Collection and Analysis

11. Recognize indicators of unmet educational needs.

12. Include multiple sources (potential participants, others, written reports) to identify common themes and distinctive perspectives.

13. Review writings about adults as learners.

14. Start with accessible sources, but supplement them.

15. When selecting sources, consider credibility with major stakeholders.

16. Use guidelines to select data collection procedures:

Understand features of various sources and populations (focus group, survey, interview, committee, self-assessment, observation, performance sample, simulation, assessment center).

Select a combination of techniques to obtain valid, valuable, and relevant information, and to allow cross-validation and encourage use of conclusions.

Use existing information when available.

Include both quantitative and qualitative data.

Minimize intrusion on program activities.

Recognize unintended results.

17. Analysis procedures vary with the type of data and the purpose of the needs assessment:

From various types of data, identify common themes to specify needs and reduce risk of program failure from unresponsiveness.

For quantitative data, use such procedures as frequency distribution, validity check, cross-tabulation, data reduction, and multivariate analysis.

For qualitative data, use inductive classification, code themes, form working hypotheses, test concepts with specific passages, make confirmation checks, and use quotes to illustrate insights.

Use cross-validation across multiple sources to identify common themes.

18. Recognize that interpretation combines facts and values.

19. Criteria for stakeholders to use when judging the soundness of a conclusion are relevance, usefulness, and precision.

20. Compare conclusions with those from a similar needs assessment.

Coordination and Utilization

21. Designate someone to coordinate planning and implementing of data collection and analysis.

22. Shape reporting with guidelines to specify key stakeholders; encourage their use of conclusions and recommendations.

23. Where appropriate, include meta-evaluation of the needs assessment process and conclusions, by use of standards regarding utility, feasibility, propriety, and accuracy.

24. Encourage continuous assessment for monitoring and organizational change and responsiveness to learner needs.

5

Contextual Analysis

A relatively recent form of evaluation for planning adult and continuing education is contextual analysis, also referred to as situational analysis. As with needs assessment, contextual analysis is sometimes unrecognized as a form of evaluation, but it shares all of the basic features, with an emphasis on input instead of process and outcome. This chapter contains five sections: concepts and purposes, planning, data collection and analysis, implementation, and coordination of contextual analysis. Each section has an overview of concepts and procedures, references to specialized readings on the topic, and brief examples. The chapter concludes with a listing of summary guidelines.

As you begin this chapter, what issues and decisions related to contextual analysis are likely to be important? When reading each section of the chapter, think of implications for your evaluation activities. Likely issues to consider are suggested by these questions:

- What trends and situational influences are especially important to understand for program planning and assessment of change?

- What would help clarify the main purpose and desirable timing of a specific contextual analysis?

- Which stakeholders should be involved in the process?

- How can contextual analysis build on the management information system, environmental scanning, and strategic planning?

- What would help focus contextual analysis so that it is manageable?

- How can you make the contextual analysis more explicit and connect it to program development decisions?

Concepts and Purposes

Increasing attention to contextual analysis reflects recognition that long-standing use of needs assessment findings to set program objectives was insufficient. High-priority program goals and objectives also reflect provider priorities and societal influences, and such variables are typically included in the contextual analysis form of evaluation. Conclusions from contextual analysis are usually combined with needs assessment findings to guide selection of program objectives that are responsive to both learner needs and priorities in the setting. Examples of such conclusions are the mission of the provider organization; expectations from the participant's family, work, and community settings; broad societal influences (such as economic conditions and demographic trends); and relations with other providers of educational opportunities for adults.

Initiation of a contextual analysis usually occurs when an adult and continuing education practitioner concludes that greater understanding of situational influences would enhance program development and coordination. The impetus may be from various sources related to the provider agency and service area. Many practitioners have tacit knowledge of such influences, such as provider mission and economic conditions. It is a recognition of the importance of more explicit and systematic analysis of situational influences on program development that is likely to prompt contextual analysis.

The typical focus of contextual analysis is the mission and resources of the provider organization and the parent organization with which it is typically associated. This is most evident for practitioners associated with an enterprise where funding and cooperation in support of human resource development (HRD) activity greatly depends on the perception that such investment contributes to the enterprise mission (production of goods and services). However, changing demands, constraints, and expectations can lead to analysis of parent organization mission and resources, along with priorities in other organizations in which educational activities are provided for members (associations, labor unions, religious institutions). Parent organization priorities also influence adult and continuing education offerings of an organization that offers educational opportunities for the public, as with libraries, museums, community agencies, and other educational institutions.

The potential value of conclusions from contextual analysis may become apparent as you are making program development decisions. For example, recurrent requests for educational activities beyond the scope of previous offerings may prompt reconsideration of program guidelines and organizational priorities. Formal analysis of parent organization mission and priorities may also occur as part of strategic planning, priority setting, and goal clarification (Knox and Associates, 1980; Patton, 1997; Green and Associates, 1984).

A less frequent form of contextual analysis is environmental scanning. By focusing on relevant topics and likely sources of information, it is possible to identify societal trends and influences (economic conditions, recent legislation, occupational performance, pertinent practices, technological innovation). The evolution of program evaluation generally reflects social influences on the theory and practice of evaluation as well as the educational programs that have been evaluated (Madaus, Scriven, and Stufflebeam, 1983). Some trends, such as changes and expectations related to occupational performance, tend to be monitored and reported for various purposes and have direct implications for continuing education (Curry, Wergin, and Associates, 1993). Some broader societal trends and influences are more difficult to identify; fortunately, though, such analysis occurs from time to time in the form of megatrends and analysis of decennial census data (Naisbitt, 1982; Naisbitt and Aburdene, 1990). International comparative analysis of adult and continuing education can help practitioners in each country clarify societal influences and address them in their strategic planning generally and contextual analysis specifically (Knox, 1993).

Here is an approach to environmental scanning for continuing education at the University of Georgia. The scanning and futures forecasting procedures used to understand relevant emerging trends in the state sought to identify early signals to guide program planning and organizational relations. Planning for environmental scanning by the continuing education division was characterized by administrative commitment to costs and benefits, clarification of organizational mission and the purpose of scanning, and provision of a coordinator whose role included reinforcement of staff commitment to the process. An early orientation workshop emphasized voluntary and open staff involvement as the participants discussed the mission of the division, the value of environmental scanning, trial use of scanning procedures, and their willingness to volunteer to help with the scanning effort.

The detailed design of the scanning process (beyond broad, voluntary participation) included explanation of responsibilities and procedures for use of a taxonomy to select and code content of publications and media. The four major taxonomy categories were social, technological, economic, and political (STEP) trends and events. Each scanner reported on specific media and prepared single-page abstracts that also assessed implications for the division. At least three times a year, interested staff members reviewed abstracts to identify a manageable number of themes (about six to ten) and to discuss ramifications for planning. The analysis procedures included Delphi procedures, cross-impact analysis, and scenario development.

In addition, there was documentation of resultant action taken in the division and feedback to staff to encourage use of conclusions and continued cooperation (Simerly and Associates, 1989). Today, computer searches are replacing review of print materials.

For many providers, a major situational influence is other providers with similar programs in the service area, which can be a source of cooperation and of competition. Contextual analysis can identify such providers, clarify their distinctive features, and suggest desirable relationships. An example is provided by "An Evaluation Guide for Adult Basic Education Programs" (Knox and others, 1974). The section on collaboration includes illustrative questionnaire and interview items on relationships with other organizations that could be readily adapted for use in contextual analysis by any type of provider. Included are extent and type of cooperation, benefits and contributions, and disadvantages and difficulties.

Contextual analysis is sometimes part of a periodic assessment or accreditation review. Especially for a provider associated with an educational institution that goes through accreditation self-study and external review every five or ten years, situational data typically include availability of qualified students, staff, and faculty members; demands for graduates; external relations; public image; and level of external support (Davis and Fox, 1994).

Some providers have management information systems that include data on situational influences and relationships. For example, in Chapter One of *Continuing Education for the Health Professions* (Green and Associates, 1984), more than one hundred quality elements are listed to guide planning and evaluation. Here are the quality elements, by number and phrase, most relevant to contextual analysis:

2. Identify expectations of parent organization and external groups.
5. Obtain approval of the mission from external and parent organizations.

12. Identify professional concerns related to health care standards.

14. Promote provision of time, resources, and incentives for health care professionals to participate in continuing education.

15. Obtain practical data for detection of potential problems and evaluation of impact.

16. Designate people responsible for collaborative analysis of practice problems.

18. Influence the health care setting to encourage application of learning to practice.

19. Identify people in external groups and organizations who can contribute to achievement of the provider mission.

20. Establish and maintain such external relationships.

21. Assess the goals of such external groups and organizations, and consider implications for the provider.

52. Use practical data to identify potential concerns.

53. Consider changing knowledge, technology, and social attitudes, to identify potential concerns.

55. Use aggregate data on populations, health problems, and health care practices to identify potential concerns.

56. Corroborate debated concerns by using data from more than one source.

66. Ascertain potential environmental influences that would assist or hinder meeting identified needs.

75. Assess resources available for educational activity.

92. Identify organizations with an interest in program evaluation.

These items illustrate the type of information that can be included in contextual analysis, which can be especially valuable for decision making if it is collected periodically to monitor trends and guide planning.

There is a potential reciprocal relationship between contextual analysis and a management information system of a continuing education provider agency. The foregoing example is for a large provider agency with many educational programs to be served and monitored, as well as smaller providers with a few staff members (Green and Associates, 1984). Because most continuing education administrators are in a power-poor position in a continuing education agency (which is usually part of a parent organization with another mission), it is important that their organizational and societal context be understood. A management information system should support decision making related to external and internal dynamics.

A management information system should be one source of information for use in conducting a specific contextual analysis, especially because a major use of such a system is for planning, including identification of external threats and opportunities. The results of each contextual analysis can augment and enrich the overall information system. Because of this reciprocal relationship, both should evolve and be improved over time.

The rationale for goal-centered information systems involves recognition of the external environment as a major source of information about trends and conditions for formulating mission and strategy for responding to external constituent expectations. For example, to address the success factor and an appropriate mission and strategic plan, an information system might contain as evidence expectations of parent organization and external groups, forecast of future directions and events that could influence the success factor, external relationships that are appropriate, and expectations that are met. Additional suggested evidence is having a list of external organizations with whom relationships are critical; defined expectations of external organizations; and periodic assessment of current external relationships to decide which are satisfactory and just need monitoring and which are unsatisfactory and should be changed.

Regardless of whether the origin pertains to provider mission, environmental scanning, external cooperation, or periodic assessment, decisions must be made on the purpose and coverage of a contextual analysis. The extent and type of potential information to collect can be overwhelming, so focus and selection are essential. As with evaluation generally, it is important to be responsive to the specific situation and to address issues of major concern to the main stakeholders. The purpose of contextual analysis can be past-oriented to justify the program, present-oriented to improve the program, or future-oriented to plan the program. Selection of one or a combination of these orientations can guide choice of topics, data sources, and coverage. The coverage of a contextual analysis can also focus on program goals, design, implementation, or outcomes. Each of these program perspectives suggests some questions to include in the contextual analysis:

For Justification Purposes

- Were the attained *goals* educationally important?

- Does the *design* optimize available resources?

- Was the *implementation* of this program timely?

- Was the impact of *outcomes* appropriate?

For Improvement Purposes

- Does our current knowledge of context suggest a change in *goal*?

- Is the *design* of the program appropriate in its setting?

- Does the selection of participants (*implementation*) comply with equal opportunity expectations?

- How might impact of *outcomes* in the learner's setting be increased?

For Planning Purposes

- Are the proposed program *goals* consistent with the parent organization image?

- Does the *design* reflect awareness of setting differences of program offerings?

- Is instructional planning *implementation* consistent with program philosophy?

- What kind of impact (*outcomes*) will the anticipated goals have on the parent organization?

There are other approaches. Here are evaluation procedures that seem especially appropriate for contextual analysis (Brinkerhoff, 1987):

- An action research study combines inquiry with action to solve a problem in ways that have direct application in the work setting. For example, such a project could pertain to collaboration.

- Case study generally uses various data collection methods to assemble both qualitative and quantitative data to understand specific groups or events that are complex and highly influenced by the context. An example is benchmarking studies of similar providers to use for comparative analysis related to an accreditation self-study.

- Expert review occurs when the opinions of people with exceptional expertise are obtained through correspondence, questionnaires, personal or telephone interviews, panel discussion, or Delphi technique. This procedure is especially appropriate for identifying emerging trends, such as technological developments or public policies, that have direct implications for a responsive educational program.

• Literature review can be an efficient procedure for identifying key traits and characteristics related to work performance. Database computer searches can identify relevant reports.

These suggestions can help focus the contextual analysis on content and information sources that are feasible, given available commitment and resources (Knox and Associates, 1980; Patton, 1997).

Planning and Stakeholders

Several planning considerations can prepare the way for detailed
plans regarding data collection and analysis. They pertain to responsiveness to stakeholders, general strategy, and guidelines. When
planning a contextual analysis, early identification of the main
stakeholders to receive program reports (along with the issues
related to the program that concern them) has several benefits. One
is that the resulting understanding is the basis for deciding on the
appropriate extent and type of stakeholder involvement in planning and conducting the contextual analysis. A related benefit is
that understanding the perceived issues related to situational influence allows deciding on the extent of effort in contextual analysis
that is warranted, in light of anticipated benefits and likely costs.
As a result, there should be a good fit between stakeholder expectations and the scale and focus of the contextual analysis, which
can contribute to their use of conclusions. This is a fundamental
consideration for program evaluation generally (Patton, 1997;
Worthen, Sanders, and Fitzpatrick, 1997).

The importance of early clarification of stakeholder expectations is especially evident for staff development and training programs that an enterprise may offer its members. The main focus of
such expectations is usually on results and organizational benefits
from the enterprise's investment in training and development
(Kirkpatrick, 1994). Because such staff development is embedded
in the enterprise, contextual analysis can clarify problems and

opportunities, assess the worth of staff development to the enterprise, and indicate whether a problem is worth solving (Brinkerhoff, 1987). Contextual analysis can use data from an enterprise information system and contribute to its enhancement (Green and Associates, 1984).

Evaluation of management development programs is critically important because the connections between education, performance, and benefits to the enterprise are indirect (Rothwell and Kazanas, 1993). Contextual analysis can contribute to the rationale and justification for such programs. Five potential obstacles are reluctance to evaluate, lack of resources, lack of know-how, low credibility, and difficulty in using traditional research methods. Several strategies are suggested for management development specialists to overcome these obstacles:

- Overcome reluctance to evaluate by making a commitment to such evaluation, and letting people know why and how it is done and the benefits related to the organization's strategic plan and individual career development.

- Overcome lack of resources by publicizing results, adapting methods to available resources, and finding out what stakeholders want to know to make decisions, and then providing it as cost-effectively as possible.

- Overcome lack of know-how by increasing knowledge about evaluation among management development specialists and stakeholders, through reading and visiting excellent management development programs to find out about their evaluation procedures.

- Overcome low credibility by involving stakeholders in the evaluation process, and in producing and using conclusions.

- Overcome difficulties with traditional research methods by matching methods to stakeholder requirements, in part by working with them to select and use methods and results they find worthwhile.

The second early planning consideration pertains to the general strategy and design regarding the scale, scope, and goal of the contextual analysis. This is especially important because of the potential complexity of contextual analysis owing to the great variety of types and sources of data. As with evaluation generally, contextual analysis begins with an initial explanation that seems to be inadequate in some respects; the purpose of the evaluation is then to produce a more satisfactory and useful explanation. For contextual analysis, this explanation typically addresses situational trends and expectations in the parent organization and service area, which in conjunction with needs assessment findings have direct implications for goal setting and other program development decisions regarding current and new programs.

Sometimes the purpose of a contextual analysis is clear and specific, with evident sources of data:

- Review of recent changes in legislation and appropriations likely to affect a current subsidized adult education program

- Review of recent innovations likely to affect occupational performance by current and potential program participants

- Analysis of compatibility and complementarity of potential cosponsors for a proposed program

- Benchmarking comparison of the current goals, programs, arrangements, and outcomes with those of similar provider agencies, as part of a periodic accreditation self-study

By contrast, sometimes the purpose of contextual analysis is to discover expectations, satisfaction, resources, and other external influences when the issues and sources of information are unclear at the outset. In this instance, it may be best to use an open-ended exploratory approach, based mainly on qualitative data, for the purpose of discovering an explanation instead of testing preconceived ideas (Guba and Lincoln, 1981, 1989; Lincoln and Guba, 1985; Patton, 1990).

Sometimes, contextual analysis is part of a summative evaluation with multiple purposes, one of which is to explore interagency cooperation, with implications for planning similar programs in the future. This is illustrated by an evaluation report of a family English literacy network program conducted in South Florida during 1986–1989 (Garcia, 1990). The network project and the summary evaluation were funded by the federal Department of Education. Questionnaires and interviews by evaluation staff, along with achievement testing by program teachers and information from program records, were used by evaluation staff to make preassessments and postassessments of the achievement of process and outcomes objectives. The contextual analysis portion of the evaluation pertained to interorganizational cooperation.

Among the agencies that cooperated with the Florida International University family English literacy network program were public school systems, libraries, churches, and community agencies. Contributions from cooperating organizations included encouraging participation; provision of training sites, instructors, and transportation; and experience working with minority families. Project services to cooperating organizations encompassed increased parental involvement, literacy, library use, employability, and community service.

The family English literacy evaluation report cites benefits of interagency cooperation (increased range and quality of services, reduction of duplication, fiscal advantages through cost sharing, and increased organizational support and advocacy) and suggestions for

replication (agency policy flexibility can foster cooperation, conflicting and changing organizational arrangement can deter cooperation, and contextual analyses can promote cooperation). This
collaborative approach emphasized capacity building; the curriculum guide was disseminated through a national clearinghouse, and
the parent involvement training component was useful for teacher
in-service purposes. As often occurs for such a large, externally
funded project, this one was neither continued nor repeated to
assess long-term impact.

The third early planning consideration is use of guidelines and
standards as criteria for planning and assessing contextual analysis.
Several of the criteria discussed and illustrated in the second edition
of *The Program Evaluation Standards* (Sanders, 1994) directly address
contextual analysis: context analysis, stakeholder identification, and
political viability. For example, the context in which the program
exists should be examined in enough detail so that its likely influences on the program can be identified. The overview notes that the
context includes location, timing, political and social climate, competing activities, and economic conditions. Among the benefits of
context analysis are helping the evaluation be realistic and responsive, helping audiences interpret the evaluation, and helping stakeholders judge similarity with other settings in which findings might
be applied. Suggested guidelines are using multiple sources of information, noting unusual circumstances and influences, and analyzing
contextual influences likely to affect replication of the program.

Brinkerhoff (1987) characterizes stage one evaluation as focused
on reasons and goals for education and suggests that these conclusions be compared with stage six evaluation (focused on benefits
and criteria for success). Using human resource development as an
example, he lists as useful information for contextual analysis items
such as productivity, morale, supervision, commitment, and
involvement in development activities. He urges that contextual
analysis (to specify reasons for education and likely fit with criteria
for success) should precede HRD program planning.

Data Collection and Analysis

As with needs assessment, a range of procedures for data collection and analysis are available from which to select those that best fit a specific contextual analysis. Three sources and related data collection methods seem especially appropriate: documents, individuals, and groups.

Because there are many documents in the form of books, articles, and records, it helps to select sources and specific documents that are representative of the type of information most relevant to the purpose and focus of the contextual analysis. Espoused and actual characteristics can be included. This is readily seen in environmental scanning. Generally, beginning with secondary sources (such as reviews and recent reports of environmental scanning on a pertinent topic) is an efficient way to obtain useful substantive generalizations and methodological suggestions. Organizational records can be especially useful; they may be in the form of inquiries, enrollment trends, and market research reports. Time series data on demographic, economic, and social indicators (which occur periodically with similar content and format) help to identify emerging trends. A major source is the decennial U.S. census reports by census tracts, which allow local application. Almanacs compile such information. In regions where adult and continuing education providers have pooled information about program offerings, enrollments, and participants for purposes of educational counseling and brokering through libraries, community colleges, and other arrangements, summary information can also be useful for purposes of needs assessment and contextual analysis.

A major critique of many research reports on an aspect of continuing education, in a form useful for contextual analyses, is evident in a 1994 book by the American Medical Association (Davis and Fox, 1994). Two North American conferences assembled scholars associated with continuing medical education to identify broad topics, assemble teams to review scholarly writings on the topics, share their critiques, and report their critiques in the book, titled *The Physician as Learner*.

The Introduction of that work is an overview of forces in the external environment that affect continuing medical education. Notable among them are patient characteristics and expectations, new medical knowledge and technology, recertification, government, insurance systems, managed care, and variety in providers of continuing medical education. This Introduction offers a broad perspective for analyzing the context of a specific continuing medical education program, and it suggests and clarifies variables likely to be pertinent. Chapter Five of that work, on developmental perspectives on learning (especially the section on life span theory), explains how career development and learning is shaped by a person's environment related to family, occupation, and community.

Chapter Eleven, on participation in continuing medical education, notes the breadth of learning activities and the transactional nature of participation, reflecting the participant, provider, and societal context that facilitate and deter initial and ongoing participation, persistence, and application. The proposed model includes external influences and the context of medical practice (patient characteristics, technological change, managed care, and continuous quality improvement).

Especially knowledgeable people are a second major source of information for contextual analysis. They may be experts on technological innovation, economic trends, consumer behavior, or community problems. Data collection can be by personal or phone interview, questionnaire, or Delphi technique (as I describe in Chapter Four, on needs assessment). Sometimes the same experts can be consulted early regarding contextual analysis, and subsequently for other program development decisions. They can also help identify and interpret pertinent documents and their program implications.

Groups can make distinctive contributions to the data collection process, as when a focus group is assembled for the purpose (which may use the nominal group technique, described in Chapter Four), and brief sessions with groups of pertinent experts who may assemble for other purposes. Such a group can bring together people with varied viewpoints who can enrich analysis and interpretation of situational trends and conditions, especially program implications. This combination of document reviews and group analysis has been used to identify megatrends (Naisbitt, 1982; Naisbitt and Aburdene, 1990). Additional data collection and analysis procedures are reviewed in the middle portion of Chapter Four of this book, on needs assessment.

Varied types of data are typically included in contextual analysis, but qualitative data are usually an important part. Such data can take the form of descriptive or speculative comments by experts or other respondents and written interpretation of trends and implications for program development. Effective collection of such data occurs in forms that facilitate the data analysis to follow.

In addition to publications on social science data analysis generally, there are useful works on analysis of data for evaluation purposes (Cook and Reichardt, 1979; Glaser and Strauss, 1967; Guba and Lincoln, 1981; Miles and Huberman, 1984; Patton, 1990; Posavac and Carey, 1992; Smith, 1981; Spindler, 1982; Thompson, 1980). Several themes from these writings can be especially useful for analysis of data regarding contextual analysis: combination of quantitative and qualitative data, interpretation as part of analysis of qualitative data, and inclusion of stakeholders in the data analysis process to increase utilization of conclusions.

Implementation

Contextual analysis entails more than planning and then activating the plans. Primary issues regarding implementation are cooperation, resources, timing, and feasibility.

Cooperation is an essential ingredient in most types of evaluation. For contextual analysis, it is especially important in relation to three roles: staff, sources, and stakeholders. Cooperation among staff associated with the continuing education provider agency addresses both variety of information sources and cost containment. This is seen in environmental scanning or situational analysis for an accreditation self-study, in which a number of staff members divide up the tasks and pool the results.

An evident requirement is cooperation from people who provide data for the contextual analysis by identifying and sharing documents, or agreeing to be interviewed or participate in a focus group. Such cooperation is enhanced if people appreciate the value of the contextual analysis as it relates to goals important to them. Cooperation from stakeholders is valuable because it enhances the quality of the contextual analysis process and conclusions, as well as encouraging stakeholders to use findings (Patton, 1997; Knox and Associates, 1980).

Resources for conducting contextual analysis include expertise, time, money, and in-kind contributions. Expertise can come from publications and people with knowledge related to conducting this type of evaluation, which can help guide implementation. Time can be the most important and scarce resource of all for staff, experts, stakeholders, and other people who can provide pertinent information. An important implementation decision is how much time should be devoted to a contextual analysis by people in each of these categories. A related consideration is how best to encourage such contributions. Allocation of money for contextual analysis can be aided by a rationale dealing with likely benefits to justify the cost, and by accurate estimates of cost. Sometimes in-kind contributions (such as volunteer assistance or services by a cosponsor) can reduce the amount of money to be allocated. A proposal can be a useful way to obtain internal as well as external funding for a contextual analysis (Buskey, 1981).

An effective way to obtain requisite support for a contextual analysis is to prepare a proposal for any combination of external funding and internal support. Chapter Four of Buskey (1981) offers a detailed rationale for involving stakeholders in preparing a persuasive plan of action likely to obtain and use support. The rationale suggests beginning with related goals, objectives, and activities (which allows a succinct statement of need that justifies the goals) and then program narrative, internal and external relationships, time line, and evaluation plan. Such an organized process for proposal preparation can be especially useful given the diffuse nature of situational influences to be analyzed.

Coordination and Utilization

In addition to planning and implementation, coordination of a contextual analysis includes attention to power, reporting, and meta-evaluation. The people associated with a contextual analysis usually vary regarding power and values. In such instances, those who coordinate the effort should recognize this and try to minimize the extent to which the results are greatly distorted as a result of those with the most power overemphasizing priorities that they value (Patton, 1997; Abrahamson, 1985).

As an open system, an enterprise or educational institution is affected by its external environment (Rothwell and Cookson, 1997). Technological, regulatory, economic, and social conditions and trends are situational influences. To survive, the HRD and continuing education agencies associated with such an organization must contribute to the mission of the parent organization, which in turn must benefit the larger society.

There are many ways to monitor and appraise external change, so that an educational program is vital and responsive: reviewing print and electronic media, surveying or networking with colleagues, benchmarking with exemplary providers, participating in associations, meeting with advisory committees, and so on. As an example, in their environmental appraisal, practitioners in continuing higher education emphasized regulations, demographic, and economic conditions. HRD practitioners appraised similar conditions, but also scanned the environment to identify likely future changes.

Attention to reporting and using the results of contextual analysis is important throughout the process. When identifying stakeholders, you should find out about the issues that concern them and the forms of reporting most likely to promote utilization of findings. Recognize that appropriate involvement in the evaluation process can increase stakeholder commitment to use conclusions. Given the broad nature of information typical of contextual analysis, major trends, relationships, and implications should be highlighted so that reports are not daunting. In addition to graphic displays for written reports, oral reports can enable recipients to contribute to interpreting and exploring implications.

Contextual analysis can be a major part of a comprehensive analysis of a pilot project (Jones, 1988). This was illustrated in 1986 when a visual artist served for four weeks as a community arts developer in Southeastern Colorado, funded by the state Council on Arts and Humanities. The author, with some staff assistance, conducted the evaluation on behalf of the Center for Community Development and Design of the University of Colorado at Denver. Resources for the evaluation were merely staff support, a minimal budget, and some in-kind contributions.

The project included preparation of fifteen murals in a main street studio open to the public and mounted on local buildings, workshops for various community groups, and a show of work by local artists held in conjunction with a centennial week celebration.

The goals in the council's request for proposals were that the artist and community should be mutually challenged and enriched, that the artist serve as a catalyst, and that the arts contribute to community development. The evaluators looked for possible change among multiple systems: the artist, arts council, local artists, and the community.

The evaluation employed triangulation using six approaches: twenty interviews with key participants, surveys of representative households before and after the residency, informal interviews on the street, direct observation of arts activities, a short questionnaire left in local businesses, and monitoring the local newspaper.

The evaluators concluded that all systems were affected. The artist learned about the community development role. The local arts council was energized, accepted more ownership for the project, gained leadership development, and received increased support. The local arts community enjoyed increased exposure, support, and appreciation. The general community benefited from collective action, enhanced sense of community, and capacity building.

The evaluation report indicated that much insight into the setting of a community development project can be gained from a modest investment in evaluation.

Meta-evaluation refers to evaluation of the evaluation process and conclusions. This can occur in successive stages. Evaluation standards can be used to critique the plan for contextual analysis. Familiarity with similar evaluations can be used to assess implementation and make adjustments. Stakeholders can review a draft report and share comments that might strengthen the report and increase its utilization. Special attention can be given to people engaged in program development (Knox and Associates, 1980; Sanders, 1994; Stufflebeam, 1974).

As you reflect on this overview of contextual analysis concepts and procedures, consider these questions:

- Which of these ideas seems most pertinent for conducting a future contextual analysis?

- What data collection and analysis procedures seem most promising?

- Who should help plan and coordinate future contextual analyses?

Summary Guidelines

Here is a checklist reviewing the basic guidelines for planning and conducting contextual analysis. The extent of detail that is applicable depends on the scale of the contextual analysis and how unprecedented it is. These guidelines can help you enhance your rationale and procedures as you plan or strengthen your contextual analysis.

Concepts and Purposes

1. Recognize that contextual analysis usually complements needs assessment to select program objectives that are responsive to stakeholder expectations and situational conditions.

2. The impetus for contextual analysis may be from various sources related to the provider agency, parent organization, and service area.

3. Contextual analysis is infrequent, but typically it occurs in relation to program development decisions as they relate to provider mission and parent organization expectations.

4. Environmental scanning is useful in identifying emerging societal trends and influences.

5. Contextual analysis can identify other providers in the service area, clarify their distinctive features, and suggest desirable relationships.

6. Contextual analysis is sometimes part of a periodic assessment or accreditation review.

7. Some providers have management information systems that include data on situational influences and relationships.

8. Focus and selection are essential for contextual analysis because the extent and type of potential information to collect can be overwhelming.

Planning

9. Early involvement by stakeholders contributes to decisions on the extent of effort and stakeholder involvement, along with encouraging their use of conclusions.

10. Early planning pertains to the scale, scope, and goal of a contextual analysis.

11. Guidelines and standards can serve as criteria for planning and assessing contextual analysis.

Data Collection and Analysis

12. Documents, individuals, and groups are especially appropriate sources of data for contextual analysis.

13. Useful documents for contextual analysis are reviews, organizational records, time series data, almanacs, and educational brokerage databases.

14. Experts can contribute their insights through interviews, questionnaires, or Delphi technique.

15. Focus groups and expert panels can use their varied viewpoints to interpret situational trends and conditions, as well as implications for program development.

16. Themes regarding data analysis include combination of quantitative and qualitative data, interpretation of qualitative data, and inclusion of stakeholders in the process to increase utilization.

Implementation

17. Cooperation is especially important for contextual analysis in relation to agency staff, information sources, and stakeholders.

18. Resources to conduct contextual analysis include expertise, time, money, and in-kind contributions.

Coordination and Utilization

19. Try to minimize distortion of contextual analysis conclusions due to great differences in power among stakeholders.

20. Reporting should be responsive to stakeholders and audiences, avoid unnecessary complexity, and encourage utilization.

21. Evaluation standards can be used for meta-evaluation to critique and improve the contextual analysis.

6

Goals and Policies

The vision and mission of a provider agency, and the goals and objectives of each educational program for adults, are often assumed to be the desired standards against which actual performance is to be compared to produce evaluative judgments. This chapter addresses goals and policies as the focus of evaluation. The rationale for evaluating the desirability of the goals, and of the process by which they are formulated, is in four sections: concepts about goal setting for evaluation purposes, influences on goals, planning and assessment of goals setting, and use of policy decisions.

Program goals and the process by which they are set are seldom evaluated. This deters assessment of the desirability of goals and ways to strengthen them. Goals, policies, and standards are an essential part of the evaluation of all other program aspects. As you read this chapter, consider issues likely to be important as your evaluation activities pertain to goals. These questions suggest decision points on which to reflect:

- What are the main sources of your program goals, and influences on the process of setting priorities?

- What indications suggest increased attention to evaluation of goals?

- To what extent do program stakeholders accept program goals?

- What are the main sources of resistance to evaluation of goals?

- What are potential uses of conclusions from evaluation of goals?

Concepts About Goal Setting

Probably the least frequently evaluated aspect of program development is the goals, including their desirability and the goal-setting process. Agreed-upon goals and policies can greatly influence a provider agency and individual programs and facilitate evaluation of all of the other program aspects. Goal setting seeks to set priorities regarding desirable future directions; such goals can be reflected in stated or implicit indications of mission, values, objectives, policies, and standards (Worthen and Sanders, 1987; Patton, 1997). This focus for evaluation can entail meta-analysis and attention to values and power. Efforts to evaluate the desirability of goals in educational and social programs generally have been controversial (Argyris, Putnam, and Smith, 1985; Shadish, Cook, and Leviton, 1995; Posavac and Carey, 1992; Patton, 1997).

At least three broad and contrasting approaches have been taken regarding goals and evaluation. They emphasize acceptance, critique, and goal-free as the basic approaches. For each evaluation project, consider which approach seems to fit best.

In most evaluations, stated goals are accepted to guide the evaluation features, with only cursory evaluation of the goals themselves. It is usually assumed that stated goals reflect outcomes desired by stakeholders. In actuality, stated goals may be minimally related to outcomes desired by stakeholders and the aims implicit in program emphasis and budget allocation (Cervero and Wilson, 1994, 1996). However, evaluators may decide that stated goals and standards are satisfactory for evaluation purposes and then devote minimal effort to evaluating the goals themselves (Brinkerhoff, 1987; Green and Associates, 1984).

Sometimes, evaluators and stakeholders decide that it is important to critique program goals and the major influences on goal setting. This may entail analyzing assumptions, exploring alternatives, and seeking agreement on goals as a part of the evaluation process if such agreement does not already exist. It may be difficult to achieve agreement because goal setting is abstract and viewpoints may be diverse. Critique of goals and consensus building may include procedures such as values clarification, Delphi technique, and affinity diagrams (Knox and Associates, 1980; Patton, 1997; Shadish, Cook, and Leviton, 1995; Posavac and Carey, 1992; Madaus, Scriven, and Stufflebeam, 1983).

When a group of stakeholders or advisory committee members have many and diverse ideas about program goals, an affinity diagram process can be used to identify major themes that connect related ideas, with a minimum of discussion. In practice, there is some variation when the basic process has been used with a number of groups, though these are the basic ingredients:

1. Assemble a group of stakeholders appropriate for the purpose of formulating goals.
2. Select an issue that is important, complex, and uncertain, for which resolution and implementation is highly desirable.
3. State the issue generally enough to encourage creative and forward-looking ideas about future goals.
4. Brainstorm many ideas related to the issue, clearly and briefly stating each on a Post-it note, until there are no additional suggestions.
5. On several large sheets of paper, place all the Post-it notes in random locations; allow enough space in front for group members to walk around to read and move Post-its around.

6. All group members can help identify two or more similar ideas and move Post-its to a row, with little discussion.

7. Single Post-its or groups can be moved to form a row, and subgroups can be separated from a larger set.

8. Some ideas can be copied or modified to fit into two or more sets; sometimes a single idea will stand alone.

9. Keep the process moving until group members are satisfied with the process.

10. Write a concise statement that summarizes the meaning of each set of Post-its, sufficiently clearly so that people who did not participate will understand it; place the phrase at the head of the column of Post-its.

11. Rewrite all unclear Post-its so that people who did not participate will understand them.

12. The result is the affinity diagram of proposed goals, which can be duplicated for sharing, consensus, and implementation.

A contrasting approach is goal-free evaluation, which rejects stated goals as useful for evaluation purposes and instead advocates an open-system analysis of what is actually emphasized and valued in a program to identify implicit goals and intended outcomes. As a result, better understanding of actual goals and priorities may occur toward the end of the evaluation process instead of as a precondition (Patton, 1997; Posavac and Carey, 1992).

Whether the focus is on explicit or implicit goals, it is important that evaluation explicate connections between goals and action plans for program development and implementation. Such conclusions enable stakeholders to make sound decisions for program planning, improvement, and accountability. These decisions may entail modification of goals as well as action plans. The rationale for evaluation of goals suggests standards to use as criteria in meta-analysis of the relative desirability of explicit and implicit goals, including influences on their formulation.

In an integrated approach to planning and evaluation titled Targeting Outcomes of Programs, societal conditions are a focus for assessment related to both program development and impact evaluation (Bennett and Rockwell, 1995). Current baseline social, economic, and environmental conditions are compared with desired conditions to identify discrepancies in needs and opportunities that should be addressed. Assessment of goals considers the priority of societal needs and opportunities regarding importance and the likelihood that specific conditions will be improved through an extension program. By envisioning desired conditions and understanding discrepancies with current conditions, specific practices can sometimes be identified that would help achieve such desired conditions; related practice adoption would be among the highest aims of an extension program. Assessment questions related to goals include:

- What present conditions will the program help improve?

- What describes the situation once the condition has been improved?

- How will you know if the condition has been improved?

- How will your program target public interests but also consider the private needs of individuals?

Responses to these questions could be used to decide on the relative importance of various societal conditions that an educational program for adults might address. The conclusions could be used in several ways. One would be to initiate a series of planning decisions regarding practice, proficiency, reaction, participation, activity, and resources. A second would be to guide evaluation of impact on the societal conditions reflected in the selected goals.

Influences on Goals

To evaluate influences on goals, it is important to understand some of the typical dynamics associated with formulating program goals and relationships among goals, program activities, and stakeholder expectations. Explicitly stated goals and priorities tend to reflect the values of the more powerful stakeholders, such as funders and policy board members (Cervero and Wilson, 1994, 1996, 1998). Goals that are implicit in programs that are emphasized, clients that are served, and resources that are allocated tend to reflect the values of stakeholders who decide how to spend their time and resources. One question to ask when evaluating goals is, Whose goals? (Patton, 1997).

This list of quality elements related to goals were among more than one hundred developed for use in planning and evaluating continuing education for the health professions (Green and Associates, 1984). The numbers in parentheses following the statements are the original quality element numbers.

1. Identify relevant expectations of the parent organization and important external stakeholders (2).

2. Define the mission of the continuing education provider, considering expectations, capabilities, limitations, and constraints (4).

3. Obtain approval of the mission from external and parent organizations and agreement on the mission within the provider unit (5).

4. Identify professional concerns by applying health care quality standards (12).

5. Identify external stakeholders whose actions and attitudes can affect the provider agency's achievement of its mission (19).

6. Review provider mission, goals, objectives, structure, policies, plans, and procedures periodically and as needed (22).

7. Identify the proposed accountability requirements for the provider (27).

8. Develop a strategic plan, policies, and procedures to enable accomplishment of the mission (31).

9. Develop a set of goals and objectives that reflect the mission and strategic plan of the provider unit (32).

10. Negotiate a resolution if constraints placed on the provider by its parent organization conflict with provision of high-quality continuing education (33).

11. Set standards to assess the accomplishment of provider plans and implementation of policies (50).

12. Assess the severity of the health care problems associated with an identified educational need (61).

13. Estimate the health care benefits likely from meeting each health-related educational need (62).

14. Estimate the relative potential for meeting the identified needs through education (63).

15. Establish relevant, achievable, and assessable objectives related to identified learning outcomes (74).

In assessing influences on goals, an early stage is to identify the range of stakeholders who are likely to have influenced stated goals and policies, have expectations related to implicit as well as explicit goals, and care about achievement of program goals (Worthen and Sanders, 1987). This means the stakeholders whose commitment to such goals is important for utilization of conclusions from program evaluation generally, including assessment of the desirability of goals and policies (Patton, 1997).

One way to assess program goals is to compare them with expectations of the parent organization (Vicere, 1996). Here are questions that can be asked about organizational expectations for an executive education program. The conclusions could be used to modify or interpret goals to organization members, to improve the fit between goals and expectations.

- Does your organization recognize executive education as a competitive capability that can assist in developing and revitalizing both individual leaders and the overall organization?

- Do your organization's executive education programs focus on building both the individual talents of leaders and the collective knowledge base of the organization?

- Do your organization's executive education programs blend experience, training, education, and other forms of challenge into a learning process?

- Does your organization use real-time discussion of real-life business issues as part of your executive education process?

- Does your organization recognize the power of executive education as a force for individual and organizational development?

There are other major influences on goals: legislation, funding availability, participant interest, characteristics of similar programs in the service area, formal plans (such as by the parent organization), and even evaluation itself. Early identification of likely influences enables the people who coordinate evaluation of goals to begin answering some basic questions:

- What are the explicitly stated goals?

- What have been the main influences on the goal-setting process and resulting goals?

- Do any implicit goals exist? How are they related to stated goals?

- How much agreement is there among stakeholders on the implicit and explicit goals?

- What alternative goals might be considered?

- How satisfactory is the current goal-setting process, and what modifications, if any, seem warranted?

- From a preliminary review, how much and what type of in-depth evaluation of goals is warranted?

For a vital and effective program, satisfactory answers to these questions might result from a few informal conversations with people familiar with the main stakeholders' perspectives. For a large and complex program with evidence of major disagreement, answering these questions might be an expensive and politically charged process to be undertaken with care, sensitivity, and commitment to follow through so that the situation related to goals is likely to improve. This is a usual focus of action research and organization development, when an organization development consultant performs a crucial role (Argyris, Putnam, and Smith, 1985).

It is important to decide how much effort to devote to assessing goals. Here are two examples regarding human resource development in enterprises differing considerably in the level and pace of assessment (Brinkerhoff, 1987):

- *Airline example.* An airline was put on probation by a regulatory agency because of maintenance procedure violations. If more violations occurred in the next six months, the operating license might be suspended. The airline hired a consulting firm to study guidelines and procedures, along with employee knowledge, skills, attitudes, and actual practices. It became evident that inadequate supervision was the likely root problem. Worker proficiency was adequate; resources, procedural guides, and training were also adequate and comparable to airlines not having problems. However, there was evidence of unsatisfactory supervisory monitoring and feedback, and poor worker morale and motivation. Thus a supervisory training program was proposed; specific objectives for improved supervisory performance were agreed upon by supervisors and their managers.

• *Fastener example.* A metal fastener company was doing well, with strong sales and secure budgets in various departments. The HRD manager noticed increasing mention in trade publications of new types of fasteners. At a meeting of other department managers, he discussed this, and they agreed that the company was doing well, but its product line was limited and no one had read up on emerging trends. They decided to list likely trends for discussion at their next meeting. At that time, they prepared a set of expertise goals for key personnel. They then asked the HRD manager to identify learning opportunities on emerging trends and fastening systems.

These two scenarios suggest quite different approaches to assessing goals. The airline confronted an urgent operational problem that threatened its existence, one that warranted an early, comprehensive, and accurate assessment of potential goals to ensure an effective educational program. By contrast, the fastening company was functioning well; this warranted a systematic but more modest and leisurely approach to exploring future directions to maintain organizational health.

Evaluation should be continuous and included in the planning phase when goals are being formulated, reviewed, or revised (Caffarella, 1994). The goals can pertain to a specific program or to the mission of the entire provider agency. Assessment of goals can focus on policies and intended outcomes and their desirability, as well as on goals as a basis for assessing impact. In either instance, it is important to have criteria upon which evaluative judgments are to be made; this may be difficult if much of the evidence is qualitative, as is typical when assessing goals.

Some examples illustrate evaluation of goals and policies. A hospital department supervisor arranged for an external consultant to conduct three sessions for all nurses on her service. She questioned the proposed plan in talks with three key staff members who were likely to provide frank feedback on the plan. Their responses confirmed her hunch, so she used the informal assessment to decide whether to either modify the plan substantially or to phase out the arrangement with the consultants. A director of volunteers and others associated with the volunteer effort were asked if the new orientation program was satisfactory; the themes from the interview notes were used to decide on the goals for the subsequent orientation program.

In another example, an HRD director concluded that a recent staff development program did not improve a high staff turnover rate, so evaluation was used to assess influences on turnover as a basis for planning goals for alternative intervention. Sometimes the criteria for evaluation cannot be stated at the outset. When a new president was selected for a community college, and respected instructors complained that poor communication and distrust among staff was negatively affecting students and the program, it reaffirmed a staff development goal of improved trust and communication. Informal evaluation activity helped clarify various viewpoints related to this goal and suggested ways to proceed. An organization development approach could be used to monitor staff viewpoints and reactions, with the periodic conclusions used to guide the staff development effort.

Planning and Assessing of Goal Setting

In the case of even a modest assessment of goals for a successful program, it is usual to have someone coordinate the process and include various stakeholders. If the initial review of goals suggests a modest assessment, it might be coordinated by a program administrator. If the initial review indicates that the review is likely to be complex and controversial, it seems prudent to involve some of the stakeholders in planning the evaluation, perhaps arranging for an external consultant to guide the process. As with many major evaluations, interpersonal relations tend to be more crucial to the success of the evaluation than are technical procedures (Patton, 1997).

Long-range organizational plans and individual plans of work should include attention to goals, which can be assessed by various stakeholders regarding desirability and feasibility. This was illustrated by the Texas Agricultural Extension Service in its assessment of the quality of county plans of work, in the context of assessment of Extensions' long-range planning for the 1990s (Marshall, 1990).

During the mid-1980s, changing economic and demographic conditions in the state prompted expansion of the stakeholders in the 1987–1990 county planning cycle (which was titled "Programming into the 90s"). In each county, staff, program council members, and other leading citizens participated in study groups to analyze critical issues of high priority for county extension programs, so that time and resources would be devoted to the issues of greatest concern. District directors reviewed the selected issues, and a statewide summary was prepared. The four most frequently mentioned issues were agricultural profitability and competitiveness, rural revitalization, struggling families, and youth development. Statewide staff development programs were instituted to help implement and evaluate the 1987–1990 long-range, issue-based extension programs to help ensure that the programs would be in the mainstream of a changing society. This included help in preparing annual plans of work to indicate goals, procedures, time, and resources to be devoted to address the selected issues.

In December 1989 and January 1990, a Texas A & M professor and extension program development specialist surveyed district extension directors and county extension agents to assess the quality of county annual plans of work. Questionnaires were returned from all 28 district directors and 72 of a representative sample of 100 county agents who received them, which was generalizable to the 650 agent positions in the state. In the four-page, fifteen-item questionnaire for staff in each role, criteria related to goals and the quality of the plan of work were that the goal and subject matter to be taught are closely related, the situation is stated as a basis for goal and activities, and the program is relevant to a current critical issue in the county. Because people other than the specialist use annual plans for performance review, the response rate was high. The critique of the plans of work was part of a decade-long effort to improve reporting in relation to planning and budgeting, including sound comparisons from year to year. The findings from the survey helped improve reports.

The specialist had the main responsibility for planning and conducting the survey and reporting the results. The main resource was printing and mailing questionnaires, in particular more than a month of the specialist's time over a three-month period. Extension staff at the state, district, and county levels viewed assessment of reporting as important, so cooperation was forthcoming.

Among the decisions to include in a plan for assessing goals are:

- Extent and type of attention to implicit goals
- Relative emphasis on goals in relation to program planning, improvement, and accountability
- Specific data collection and analysis procedures

- Selection of sources of data

- Comparisons of goals to alternatives

- Timing of the evaluation process

- Resources for support of the evaluation

- Feasibility of an initial plan and necessary modifications

- Coordination roles related to the evaluation

If attention to implicit goals is warranted because stated goals do not reflect major stakeholder expectations, resource allocation, and program emphasis, then consider an open-systems analysis of the program. This entails inclusive analysis of program scope, vision, mission, and intended and actual outcomes, from the perspective of major stakeholders. The goals and priorities that emerge are interpreted partly within the context of the program as an open system in a service area, and composed of inputs and processes. The resulting understanding of implicit goals can then be compared with explicitly stated goals to identify those that appear to be influential but unstated as well as to discover the influences that contributed to these additional goals. Stakeholders can then consider the implementation of these conclusions for future goal setting. Qualitative evaluation and research methods are entirely applicable for this purpose (Patton, 1990; Argyris, Putnam, and Smith, 1985; Glaser and Strauss, 1967; Guba and Lincoln, 1989; Miles and Huberman, 1984).

As with evaluation generally, assessment of goals can be for purposes of planning, improvement, and accountability. Questions about the soundness of goals and desired modification can emphasize participants, instructors, topics, or contexts. The next example presents questions related to each purpose and element (Knox and Associates, 1980).

Perspective	Element	Question
Planning	Participants	Have various potential participants achieved their expectations?
	Instructors	How might desirable instructional goals be attained?
	Topics	Is a proposed topic relevant to proposed goals?
	Contexts	Are proposed goals consistent with the agency image?
Improvement	Participants	How could program goals better correspond to learner objectives?
	Instructors	Would a revision of some instructor aims better align them with related aims?
	Topics	Would other topics better contribute to achieving goals?
	Contexts	Does current knowledge of the setting suggest modification of the goals?
Justification	Participants	Are the educational goals appropriate for these participants?
	Instructors	Are the instructional purposes compatible with the program goals?
	Topics	Is this the best topic to achieve program goals?
	Contexts	Were the attained goals educationally important?

When assessing goals for planning purposes, the aim is to use the assessment to produce intended program outcomes that the main stakeholders accept as desirable and feasible. If explicit goals exist, the assessment can explore stakeholder acceptance, and probably add some goals that are currently implicit and thus update them. If not, an open system assessment can identify implicit goals on which the main stakeholders agree. The resultant goals can be used to increase stakeholder support and can guide other program development decisions.

When assessing goals for improvement purposes, the aim is to evaluate how well program goals are serving decision making related to participants, staff, program, and resources. This may entail monitoring actual use of goals and suggesting changes if indicated, and perhaps repeating the process in an effort to strengthen the ongoing program. When assessing goals for accountability purposes, the aim is to evaluate congruence between desired outcomes (goals) and evidence of actual outcomes. One result can be validation of goals, including justification of those that are beneficial and identification of those of questionable merit. The resultant conclusions can include assessment of stakeholders' expectations and satisfaction related to program goals.

A major evaluation of a continuing education program illustrates many issues, procedures, and benefits related to assessment of program goals (Umble, Cervero, Yang, and Atkinson, 2000). The focus of a multiphase evaluation of a continuing professional education course in traditional classroom and satellite broadcast formats was the course impact on adherence to recommended practice guidelines. The comparable content of the two course formats was prevention of vaccine-preventable diseases. The participants were health care professionals associated with vaccinations.

The evaluation included analysis of the series of negotiations through which decisions were made about the course purposes, content, audience, instructors, activities, and format. Power differences among stakeholders were apparent in the negotiation process, and stakeholder interests were shaped by their roles. However, because expectations about immunization were compatible and the sponsoring agency's influence on policy was accepted as legitimate by all stakeholders, there was little conflict. Some stakeholders who were directly involved in basic policy and planning decisions were more influential than others, such as field staff (Cervero and Wilson, 1994, 1996, 1998).

An early phase of the evaluation used existing data to analyze the course content, participants, staff, methods, achievement, satisfaction, and expenditures. This was followed by an evaluability assessment (Wholey, Hatry, and Newcomer, 1994), which begins by making major program assumptions and expectations explicit. Then stakeholders were asked about their program regarding expectations, experience, influence, evidence of impact, explanation of influence, and desired information to guide decisions. The resulting conclusions were used to decide specifications for the subsequent evaluation of impact.

Here are a number of conclusions based on survey responses from managers of national projects whose staff were served by the educational program on vaccination to be evaluated for impact:

- There was strong agreement on the value of the course for immunization projects.

- More than half wanted to receive the classroom (as opposed to satellite) version of the course in their area.

- Most wanted the satellite version offered once or twice a year.

- The course was tied for first place with one other option when ranked with other related courses regarding relative priority.

- Though endorsing the current course content, they did suggest improvements in course-related arrangements such as timing of publicity and costs of materials.

- The courses could better serve private health services providers through shorter and more focused courses at convenient times and locations.

These conclusions from the evaluability assessment of goals and expectations were used by a team to design the impact study. Interviews with stakeholders regarding their perspectives and expectations helped identify priorities related to the program and the impact evaluation objectives, procedures, and resources. The team then selected process and impact indicators, designed evaluation procedures and instruments, collected and analyzed evaluation data, and presented conclusions to the stakeholders. In the model that guided the impact evaluation, it was assumed that the course influenced knowledge and thus beliefs but also directly affected beliefs and self-efficacy, which in turn improved behavioral intentions and thus adherence. Setting factors can influence both behavioral intentions and adherence to recommended practices.

The main objective of the impact study was to evaluate the effects of a major federal immunization continuing education course delivered in both traditional classroom and satellite broadcast versions. The participants were nurses and members of other health care occupations related to vaccinations. The main course purpose was to increase adherence to a new sequential vaccination schedule and related recommendations. Such adherence depends on enhanced knowledge, agreement, and self-efficacy because it entails choosing, explaining, and justifying the recommended procedure. This is because administering the vaccine is straightforward—unlike the objectives of some other courses that entail performance tasks that may be difficult to master.

The evaluation design included comparative time series to assess course effects at the end and three months afterwards, comparison of the impact of classroom and broadcast versions, longitudinal surveys to test the model and explain how the course produced changes, and path analysis to explain how the variables were related to one another over time. Data were collected at the beginning, and at a three-month follow-up of the course.

To assess whether the classroom and broadcast courses produced significant results, paired sample t-tests were used with the mean composite scores from the three times of data collection. To assess whether there were significant differences between the classroom and broadcast versions, analysis of covariance was used to examine net differences in effects, while controlling for initial differences. To assess how the courses influenced adherence, path analysis was used.

There was no significant difference in knowledge gain for classroom and broadcast course participants, both immediately and three months after the course. Classroom course participants significantly increased knowledge, agreement, and self-efficacy during the course, and improvements were maintained three months afterwards. Agreement with the vaccination schedule declined after the course but was still significantly higher than before the course, as was adherence to general recommendations. Broadcast course participant achievements were similar (including significant increases in adherence to general recommendations) except that adherence to vaccination recommendations increased, though not significantly. The classroom version had a stronger effect on adherence to the vaccination schedule than the broadcast version. The findings regarding relations among variables were similar to those predicted by the model.

Throughout the total evaluability assessment and evaluation of impact, quantitative and qualitative data made valuable contributions. The quantitative data analysis allowed specification of associations among well-defined variables important to stakeholders and the model. The qualitative data contributed to selection and validation of quantitative variables; interpretation of findings; specification of contextual influences; and especially understanding of expectations about program goals, procedures, and benefits.

The evaluation findings support use of continuing education programs to facilitate implementation of clinical practice guidelines.

In this case, dissemination of information through media and publications was insufficient to ensure adherence; knowledge gain from
continuing education seems insufficient to improve performance
without attention to other model components such as self-efficacy
and setting factors (policies, resources). The findings also support
use of distance education.

This example illustrates why and how to assess stakeholder perspectives on educational program goals. Attention to stakeholder
expectations was pertinent for design of an impact evaluation of a
continuing professional education program, and for subsequent use
of findings. The example addressed issues, procedures, and benefits.
One issue was the influence of power difference among stakeholders on negotiation over program goals, procedures, and evaluation.

An evaluability assessment helped make stakeholder expectations explicit, which contributed to design of the impact evaluation. A model of likely relationships among program variables also
guided the evaluation plan and interpretation of findings. Qualitative data contributed throughout. The classroom and broadcast versions had comparable effects regarding the main program goal,
which was increased adherence to practice guidelines.

Data collection and analysis regarding goals and priorities can
reflect a variety of procedures, but the nature of goals and relations
among stakeholders make some procedures especially applicable.
Goals reflect people's values, assumptions, and aspirations. They are
also somewhat abstract and thus more difficult to think about and
discuss than concrete decisions about procedures and resources. This
is true as well for more tangible guidelines to action such as priorities, policies, standards, objectives, and future directions. As a result,
evaluation of goals tends to entail qualitative data and procedures
such as values clarification and nominal group technique.

Evaluation of goals can also be controversial. This is especially
so when stakeholders vary greatly regarding power or values. Agreement among people with differing viewpoints can be promoted by

use of a focus group or nominal group technique; another method is to have group members stand along a line to reflect their opinion related to some options and to observe the positions of other group members. It is sometimes desirable to approach evaluation of goals cautiously until there is a preliminary idea of stakeholder viewpoints, which may suggest evaluation procedures that emphasize consensus building and perhaps conflict resolution.

Sometimes it is difficult to judge which of a number of conflicting goals should be pursued. The conflict can reflect differing values among various stakeholders. More than two decades ago, a judicial or adversarial evaluation model was developed and tried; it was based on the process of judging in a court of law, with advocates for each position (Madaus, Scriven, and Stufflebeam, 1983). Chapter Eleven in the cited work presents the judicial model, and Chapter Twelve raises some cautions because of its use in practice. The emphasis in the first example was on formulation of educational policy and goals. Policy-level issues were characterized as public, consequential, complex, uncertain, and complicated. The stages of a judicial evaluation include issue generation, issue selection, preparation of arguments, clarification forum, investigative teams, use of an analyst to supervise each team, case presenter, forum moderator, and clarification panel moderated by a panel facilitator.

Example two was a study of policy formulation in a local school district. The process resulted in analysis of issues from the perspectives of various segments of a community, along with presentation of eleven recommendations, seven of which were adopted. Thus the evaluation process affected the goals that were selected. The cautions raised in Chapter Twelve of Madaus, Scriven, and Stufflebeam (1983) were disparity in proponent prowess, fallible arbiters, excessive confidence in the model's potency, difficulty framing the proposition in a manner amenable to adversary resolution, manipulation by biased decision makers, and excessive costs. Remedies were suggested for each deficit, but the authors—who were part of an adversarial evaluation—concluded that in practice the deficits far outweigh the benefits. This suggests caution and use of this approach only under circumstances in which it is appropriate.

Sometimes views on goals can be clarified by considering alternatives. Futuring workshops do this, as participants develop scenarios for alternative futures and then discuss the implications. As part of evaluation of goals, stakeholders can invent alternatives or be presented with alternative sets of goals from other programs, and then proceed to use such alternatives for comparison with their current goals.

There are some timing considerations in assessing goals. Because the conclusions tend to be useful for evaluation of other program components, it is useful to assess goals relatively early in a broad program evaluation. Because stakeholders typically experience difficulty with the abstract and value-laden nature of goals and priorities, and power relations can compound the process further, one is well-advised to allow sufficient time for evaluation of goals to help people work through these difficulties.

Time and expertise are the main resources for most efforts in evaluating goals. Assistance by people with experience conducting such evaluations can be valuable for planning purposes, with help in making estimates of training and specialized expertise likely to be required. Other planning decisions are selection of people to include in the evaluation process, topics to emphasize, and data collection procedures. Various data collection and analysis procedures are reviewed in the middle portion of Chapter Four of this book.

The person(s) with the main responsibility for coordinating evaluation of goals should have a solid understanding of this aspect of evaluation, basic management ability, effective interpersonal relations, and a good sense of both the desirability and feasibility of specific evaluation activities that are considered. In addition to producing a sound evaluation report, it is desirable that the process encourage stakeholders to use the conclusions.

Use of Policy Decisions

Conclusions from evaluation of goals, policies, and priorities can be useful in various ways. Examples are decisions about program emphasis, participant attraction, staffing, collaboration, community support, resource allocation, and organization. If the results of such evaluations encompass anticipated benefits and desired future directions valued by stakeholders, and if they at least suggest implications regarding likely cost and implementation, then utilization related to the subsequent decisions can occur gradually as stakeholders start to address action plans.

Comparison of a profile of goals that reflect the agency or program mission and vision for future improvements with current program goals and emphases helps stakeholders identify discrepancies on which to focus. The intended changes may pertain to topics and issues, participant and staff characteristics, methods of teaching and learning, resource allocations, or desired impact. Evaluation of goals and priorities can contribute in several ways to modification of relative program emphasis. One is to help achieve stakeholder agreement on major goals. A second is to compare these goals with the current actual program to identify desired changes so that the program is better aligned with these goals. A third is to value stakeholders in a process of evaluation that encourages them to use the findings and help modify the program. A fourth is to use ongoing evaluation of the process to provide feedback to stakeholders that they can use to guide their decisions about modification of goals and program.

Another use of conclusions from evaluation of goals and policies is for improvement in specifying and attracting the learners who will participate in the program. Even if a goal statement lacks explicit indication of the intended participants, it can be used by stakeholders to explore the characteristics of adults most likely to be served by the goals. This can be an early stage of market research and needs assessment. This use of evaluation related to goals can also entail statement of intended outcomes as one basis for ongoing evaluation of the process of participant attraction, progress, persistence, achievement, and application.

Staff selection and development is a similar use of conclusions from evaluation of goals and policies. Such priorities and intended outcomes can help stakeholders decide on characteristics, sources, and incentives to attract and retain instructional and administrative staff and volunteers. Including stakeholders in evaluation of goals can strengthen the assessment, their commitment to the goals, and their help in using the goals to guide staffing decisions. Evaluation conclusions and staff participation in the process can be especially valuable for purposes of staff and volunteer development so that they become increasingly committed and able to achieve the goals.

Collaboration and other forms of external cooperation provide a fourth use of conclusions from evaluation of goals. Sometimes a review of goals and priorities can identify certain ones that are better achieved in cooperation with an external organization. By beginning with the provider organization's own likely contributions to goal achievement, given its mission and resources, stakeholders can specify the complementary contribution expected from cooperating organizations with shared goals and appropriate capability. Conclusions from evaluation of goals can also be used to monitor and strengthen collaborative activities.

A fifth use of conclusions from evaluation of goals is to obtain support and resources (beyond participants, staff, and collaborative arrangements). Assessment of goals can include connection with such resources, such as influence of resources on goal setting and influence of goals on resource acquisition and allocation. The resultant goals and related connections can suggest guidelines for making a strong case for resources and the main stakeholders to include in the process. Cost-benefit analysis can also result.

Organizational decisions constitute a sixth use of conclusions from evaluation of goals. There are various ways in which an adult and continuing education provider agency can be organized, internally and in relation to its parent organization. In its broader context of parent organization and service area, there is the policy decision about the extent of centralization versus decentralization of the continuing education function. Within the provider agency, staff responsibilities can reflect attention to content, client, or format. Conclusions from assessment of goals can be used to guide such organizational decisions so that form follows function and intended outcomes.

As you reflect on this review of ways to evaluate the process of setting goals and priorities, consider these questions:

- What have been the main influences on goal setting and program priorities?

- How important is it to conduct evaluability assessment?

- What special challenges are associated with evaluating goal setting and use of policy decisions?

Summary Guidelines

The checklist presented here reviews the basic guidelines for planning and conducting an assessment of goals and priorities. You can use it to improve your procedures and rationale for assessment of goals and priorities.

Concepts About Goal Setting

1. Clarify agency mission and program goals as standards and priorities to guide decisions about desirable future directions.

2. Understand that assessment of goals and priorities is infrequent and can be controversial, in part because of various stakeholder values and expectations.

3. Consider various approaches to assessment of goals:

   Accept explicit goals to guide program evaluation, and reconsider goals mainly at the conclusion.

Critique explicit and implicit goals regarding assumptions and alternatives.

Ignore stated goals and use open-system analysis to clarify implicit goals as a starting point.

4. Involve stakeholders to ensure that goals contribute to implementation of the action plan.

5. Consider the feasibility of procedures to assess goals.

Influences on Goals

6. Recognize the influence of more powerful stakeholders on goal setting.

7. Consider the range of stakeholders who do and should contribute to goal setting.

8. In particular, involve stakeholders who are important for implementation of plans.

9. Analyze societal influences most related to program goals.

10. Decide on a feasible scale of effort.

Planning and Assessment of Goal Setting

11. Decide on the relative attention, in ongoing assessment of goals, to use of conclusions for planning, improvement, and accountability.

12. Consider open-system analysis of implicit goals, in addition to explicitly stated goals.

13. Decide how best to involve stakeholders in assessing goals.

14. Recognize that assessment of goals can be controversial, so consider procedures such as values clarification, weighing of alternatives, and consensus building.

15. Plan and coordinate assessment of goals so it proceeds in a timely fashion.

16. Ensure that sufficient time and talent is devoted to coordination of the assessment.

Use of Policy Decisions

17. Specify goals to clarify discrepancies between desired goals to be achieved and current goal achievement.

18. Obtain agreement from stakeholders on specific changes to make satisfactory progress toward goals.

19. Encourage use of conclusions for decision making on participants, program, staff, collaboration, resources, and organization.

7

Staffing Assessment

M ost educational programs for adults in the United States are
planned and coordinated by staff and volunteers associated
with a provider agency that is part of a larger parent organization.
This means an agency director or administrator, program coordinators, support staff, and various full-time and part-time instructors
from the agency, parent organization, and service area. They may
be paid or serve as volunteers. The performance of these staff members greatly affects program quality and benefits. This chapter
addresses assessment, appraisal, and evaluation of staff at various
stages related to selection, placement, monitoring, personal growth,
staff development, recognition, and retention. This rationale for
staff evaluation is in four sections: concepts, planning assessment,
organizational change, and coordination.

Informal evaluative judgments regarding potential and actual
staff performance are made by various stakeholders, especially program directors and coordinators who make decisions about hiring,
assignment, retention, and development. Assessment of each of the
other aspects of the overall program evaluation result in conclusions
that pertain to staffing. However, this chapter on staffing assessment
focuses on formal and informal evaluation of potential and actual
performance and satisfaction by all categories of staff and volunteers
at various stages of employment, for purposes of planning, improvement, and accountability. Thus employee appraisal is an integral

part of staffing assessment. However, it is important to distinguish between assessment for staff development and for merit, promotion, and retention.

In reading this chapter, consider issues likely to be especially important to you regarding evaluation of staff and volunteers. Reflect on examples and guidelines and note implications for your staff evaluation. These questions suggest likely issues to consider:

- How can you take into account both individual and organizational perspectives on staff performance?

- What are major relationships between staff assessment and other aspects of evaluation?

- What are the likely benefits of assessing staff and volunteers?

- What are the main categories of staff and volunteers for purposes of evaluation?

- What are the main deterrents to staff evaluation, especially when considering assessment for both merit and development?

- How should staff evaluation address the continuum of selection, placement, monitoring, growth, development, recognition, and retention?

- How can you best separate evaluation for accountability and for improvement?

- What parts of staff capability and performance should be emphasized in evaluation?

- Who should contribute to staff evaluation?

- What methods of data collection are especially applicable to staff evaluation?

- How can evaluation conclusions be used to improve
  staff performance?

Concepts

Staffing assessment is related to both individual performance and
organizational effectiveness (Braskamp and Ory, 1994). Various
stakeholders have expectations and perspectives on evaluation,
which creates problems and opportunities. The problems pertain to
the complexity of evaluating staff performance, which relates to all
other aspects of agency functioning, and to the difficulty of dealing
with a negative evaluation of performance. Opportunity pertains to
staffing assessment's potential contribution to organizational change,
quality, and benefits, if a developmental systemic approach is used
(Braskamp and Ory, 1994; Brookfield, 1995; Posavac and Carey,
1992; Pratt and Associates, 1998).

A specific evaluation project related to staff can begin with any
aspect of overall program evaluation. Conclusions from evaluation
of goals and policies, along with related needs assessment and contextual analysis, can help set expectancy for staff, and staffing assessment can contribute to such expectations and implementation of
plans. Staff members are major contributors to evaluation of participants, program, and materials and to strengthening these vital
program aspects. Conclusions from impact evaluation can help
assess staff contributions; staff assessment can suggest ways to
improve results and benefits. This complexity compounds the difficulty when providing feedback to a staff member about a negative
evaluation, because performance can be affected by the interrela-
tionships. In fact, the rationale for many quality improvement
efforts stresses that impediments to quality are generally structural,
not individual.

It is helpful to approach staffing assessment by understanding
staff members and volunteers as adult learners functioning in an

interpersonal context. Especially for those with instructional responsibilities, the teaching-learning transaction is central to assessment, but other staff and volunteers are only a step or two removed. Participants and instructors each evaluate the teaching-learning transaction for purposes of planning, improvement, or accountability. In addition, there are collaborative activities (such as action research and quality improvement) that entail cooperative effort at systemic improvement. Teaching itself is becoming recognized as a focus for scholarship, not just a process for sharing the results of scholarship (Boyer, 1990; Glassick, Huber, and Maeroff, 1997; Braskamp and Ory, 1994; Curry, Wergin, and Associates, 1993).

Staffing assessment decisions, criteria, descriptions, judgments, conclusions, and use of conclusions occur at successive stages. Included in staffing assessment are staff recruitment, selection, placement, monitoring, development, and retention. Past staff evaluation reports, along with agency expectations and goals, help to shape the position descriptions and criteria used to recruit and select staff. Past evaluations and future expectations also contribute to initial placement and orientation to enhance prospects for success. Ongoing evaluation of both individual and organizational functioning uses criteria for purposes of monitoring, development, and retention.

The entire staffing assessment and appraisal process is developmental in several ways, and the fit between appraisal and development is very important. Each staff member and volunteer has abilities and expectations, which affect motivation, performance, and satisfaction related to the work itself and to costs and benefits. Both paid staff and volunteers evolve in their proficiency, performance, and aspiration; evaluative feedback can make valuable contributions to this career cycle.

Provider agencies also change with time, both overall and for specific programs. The staff and volunteer proficiencies that are required can shift, sometimes in a major way in a short time period. Because of this, provider agencies largely depend on part-time and short-term staff and volunteer contributions. Ongoing staffing assessment can be used by program administrators and policy makers to strengthen decision making to the benefit of participants, agency vitality, and staff (Braskamp and Ory, 1994).

There can be a valuable symbiotic relationship between staff development and agency vitality; staffing assessment conclusions can contribute to a desirable fit. But there is potential conflict in such evaluation, between personal growth and external judgments as aims of a single assessment activity. This is why it is desirable to distinguish between evaluation for merit and retention and evaluation for staff development.

Planning Assessment

Planning and implementing data collection and analysis include obtaining sound conclusions and encouraging use of findings (Patton, 1997). This entails decisions about the type of data on staff and organizational performance to collect, the design of feasible data collection and analysis procedures to use, the focus on staff and organization development, and requisite resources. Some parts of the assessment deal mainly with staff selection and performance, while others principally address staff development activity. Many staffing evaluation activities should encompass both performance and development, even though assessment for each should be differentiated so that defensiveness regarding judgment about merit does not interfere with openness for development.

Early planning decisions relate to inclusion and emphasis on various categories of staff (instructors, administrators, volunteers, support). Other early decisions pertain to which aspects of staffing to include: general capability, content mastery, interpersonal style, effectiveness, innovation, and the like. Other desirable characteristics for teaching are clarity, organization, enthusiasm, responsiveness to diversity, and encouraging participant responsibility for learning (Grotelueschen, Gooler, and Knox, 1976).

Decisions about staff categories and aspects can help with selecting a desirable and feasible design for data collection and analysis. One way to focus evaluation of staffing is to select from the issues and questions of concern to stakeholders, those that are most important for assessing staff acquisition, performance, and benefits (Shadish, Cook, and Leviton, 1995). Both the importance of potential improvement in staffing and availability of time and money for assessment are likely to guide the scale of the evaluation so that it is feasible as well as desirable. This type of cost-benefit analysis is difficult, but a rough estimate can be made to avoid miscalculation that weakens or aborts the evaluation.

Some methods of data collection and analysis are applicable for both staff acquisition and development: self-assessment, review of past performance, rating of potential goals, interview, knowledge inventory, and simulation. Each method has distinctive features and conclusions. A self-assessment inventory enables an instructor to rate a list of proficiencies regarding the discrepancy between what is current and what is desired. The proficiencies listed may encompass components of program development, working effectively with others, negotiating stakeholder interests, using procedures to help adults learn, and setting priorities. Completing a self-assessment can help an instructor use and enhance his or her talents.

A review of past performance can be a descriptive resume, a portfolio, or letters of reference and other forms of external review (Diamond, 1987).

Ratings of potential goals by current or potential staff members and by others can be compared to identify the fit with provider agency expectations and priorities for staff development.

An interview with one or more people is a usual part of staff selection; it can also be a useful form of global assessment regarding staff development. The interview can be structured by categories of desired proficiency and other expectations and criteria.

A knowledge inventory can help a staff member and other people recognize areas of strong background knowledge and areas for which growth would be desirable.

A simulation permits robust assessment of knowledge, skills, and attitudes as well as estimates of a person's capability to perform well if given the opportunity.

Teacher assessment can help improve instruction, reward excellent performance, modify responsibilities, and promote staff development (Banta, 1985; Boice, 1996; Grotelueschen, Gooler, and Knox, 1976; Knox, 2001). It seems advisable to separate evaluation for accountability and for improvement.

There are various aspects of performance that can be assessed, and numerous ways of doing so. The examples presented here regarding evaluation of adult education teacher performance and development suggest items usable in a self-assessment form; they can be modified for guiding observation or interview with instructors in any type of educational program for adults.

A general form for an external evaluator to record ratings of the extent of supporting evidence and comments can include assessment of commitment to program goals, sensitivity to ethnicity, dedication, personality traits, understanding of participant background, subject matter competence, flexibility, and teamwork.

An observation guide can focus on how frequently instructional questions are used. Separate tabulations can be done for instructor use of initiatory, divergent, convergent, and redirecting questions.

A teacher might informally ask participants a number of questions regarding their satisfaction with aspects of instruction:

- Ways of teaching that help most

- Those that are least helpful

- Better types of help

- Enough feedback to know how well you are doing

- Helpfulness of learning materials

- Pace of learning (too fast, too slow, about right)

- Interest in subject matter

- A good place to learn

- Learning what you thought you would

A self-assessment form may include ratings on satisfaction with the variety of methods, preparation and organization, enthusiasm, encouragement of active participation, taking teaching seriously, thorough coverage of content, striving for mastery learning, and optimization of pace of learning.

Evaluation regarding staff development can pertain to assessing people's educational needs, view of development plans, satisfaction with results and benefits of development, and resource support for development. One way to assess staff development needs is to ask members to indicate their general role but otherwise respond anonymously to open-ended questions about aspects of their responsibilities on which they would like staff development help, topics of interest, preferred timing, and anticipated benefits. Development planners can use a listing of responses, grouped by role, to appreciate the variety of needs expressed and to decide on more structured needs assessment and likely types of in-service activity. An example is a listing of potential staff development topics, which members can rate regarding relative interest. Topics might be understanding participants, selecting and using materials, evaluating participant progress, working with volunteers, improving interpersonal relations, and varying teaching styles.

Once preliminary staff development goals and activities are drafted, staff members can rate each goal regarding the importance of the goal for themselves, the desirability of the proposed activity to achieve the goal, their current proficiency related to the goal, and the likely benefits from achieving the goal.

Another approach is assessment of satisfaction from the development procedures employed, such as usefulness of materials, quality of instruction, appropriateness of method, responsiveness of an activity to staff concerns, thoroughness of coverage, pacing of instruction, and sequencing of activity.

A follow-up opinionnaire on staff expectations enables staff to indicate their objectives for participating in a development activity, aspects of the activity that contributed to and detracted from achievement of their objectives, the extent to which their expectations changed as a result of the activity, and the extent to which their objectives were achieved.

Follow-up assessment of outcomes (if staff members had a chance to use what they learned) can include a rating of the extent of impact as well as respondent comments explaining a number of aspects: enhanced knowledge, insight on how to improve practice, greater appreciation of an aspect of teaching, actual use of new ideas, increased networking with other staff, and situational influences that helped or hindered application.

Some methods of data collection and analysis are especially applicable for selecting and supervising staff: observation of actual or videotaped performance, feedback from participants and peers, evaluation of a targeted aspect of performance, preparation of a case study, assessment of a creative innovation, and follow-up to assess impact and benefits. Each method has its own strengths and limitations.

When a program coordinator or experienced colleague observes an instructor or other staff member for assessment purposes, it is useful to have agreed-upon criteria and procedures to guide the evaluation of live or videotaped activity, and then to discuss reactions and suggestions.

Feedback from participants and peers can take various forms: a written questionnaire, oral comments from an individual or a group, letter of reference, and so on. The feedback may be direct to the staff member with the source identified, or it may be done confidentially to an assessment committee. Sharing detailed or summary feedback with the staff member is important for staff development purposes.

By targeting and assessing an important aspect of a staff member's performance, the ongoing and detailed evaluation results can be especially useful for improving performance.

A case study is another way of portraying an important aspect of a staff member's performance, including origins and setting, along with process and outcomes. This can be especially useful if the roots of a team effort were much earlier and assessment would be valuable for team members and other people in the future.

A creative innovation can be assessed as a targeted evaluation or case study; it can also be peer-reviewed. An innovation can also be the focus of an external review by a small committee or an expert on the topic.

Follow-up studies are especially valuable to assess the impact of staff performance if it takes some time for the benefits to other people to occur. Planning of a follow-up study during the staff activity contributes to assessment of the connection between process and outcomes (baseline information, time series data).

Some assessment methods are especially useful for evaluating staff development: needs assessment, evaluation of staff development plans, evidence of learner achievement, organization development assessment, and quasi-experimental designs. Each needs assessment procedure described in Chapter Four can be used to evaluate the educational needs of staff as well as participants. The plans that a staff member and perhaps other people prepare to guide staff development activity can be critiqued. Learner achievement and its connection to staff contribution can be portrayed in various ways, notably an achievement test, portfolio, simulation, or discussion of a product with an examination committee. It is important to obtain the rationale from participants, peers, and the staff member regarding his or her contribution to learner achievement.

Organization development assessment occurs as part of quality improvement activities, in which team or quality circle members use performance information to evaluate the impact of improvement efforts on the productivity of the team and the entire organization. Such an assessment takes into account structural factors and organizational dynamics, not just individual performance. Staff development activities in which a number of members can take part in various in-service activities during different time periods can be evaluated using quasi-experimental designs, perhaps with a time series assessment or a comparison group, or even random assignment to treatment. Additional procedures for data collection and analysis are included in the middle section of Chapter Four.

All of these evaluation methods can be used for assessing any aspect of staffing. An important consideration throughout is a focus on staff development. This means having the individual staff member contribute to planning and conducting the assessment. Such involvement helps to enhance the validity of the evaluation conclusions and commitment to use conclusions on the part of the staff member and people in related roles. This process can go well beyond individual development as explicit provision is made for staff members to learn from each other and to learn together to increase teamwork.

One major deterrent to assessment that is related to staffing is limited resources of time and money devoted to this type of evaluation. The most explicit allocation of resources for such evaluation pertains to staff selection and review. Early planning and adequate allocation of time and money for evaluation related to staffing is likely to result from recognizing the investment it represents in staff quality, satisfaction, and productivity with many resultant benefits for all concerned. The evaluation expertise of a staff member or consultant can contribute to an accurate estimate of resources and to a rationale to help justify their allocation.

Organizational Change

Especially in larger agencies that offer educational opportunities for adults, staffing evaluation can contribute to organizational vitality and change, to the extent to which there is attention to teamwork. This is similar to the basic rationale for quality improvement, with its emphasis on structural influences, data-based decisions, teamwork, and communication. In such quality improvement activity, staff members have responsibility for doing their job and learning how to do it better. There are many ways to evaluate aspects of staffing that take the societal and organizational context into account and that emphasize cooperation and organization development, instead of overemphasizing advancement of the individual staff member.

Evaluation for staff selection, performance, and development can include attention to both individual and group (Robinson and Robinson, 1995). This is illustrated by an example of discrepancy analysis of adult basic education staff performance and development. Assessment related to staffing entails attention to selection criteria, recruitment, selection, assignment, satisfaction, performance, retention, and development. Evaluation regarding this process can pertain to teachers, administrators, support staff, and volunteers. Many items used for data collection and analysis include information about both expected and actual characteristics, the basis for discrepancy analysis to guide improvements. The publication on which this example is based offers rationale and illustrative items to use in data collection forms such as questionnaires and interview guides (Knox and others, 1974). The format for items includes a space to indicate what the case should be and what it actually is:

- Percentage of budget and time allocated to staffing

- People having influence on staffing criteria

- Desirable criteria and sources

- People involved in staffing decisions

- Staff characteristics

- Considerations for staff assignment

- Importance of staff cooperation

- Level of satisfaction and commitment

- Staff turnover

- Ways to improve staffing

- Proportion of staff participation in in-service education

- Basis for selecting staff for in-service education

- Emphasis on various types of in-service education

- Main roles in planning in-service education

- Incentives to encourage participation in staff development

- Variation in staff development activity according to staff role

- Extent of participation in staff development activity

- Outcomes and benefits of in-service education

Information is obtained from people in various roles; discrepancy analysis of the gap between current and desired conditions contributes to planning for organization development in ways that promote cooperation and program quality.

Inclusion of items that assess complementarity of contribution and team effort, from the perspective of various staff members in related roles, is the basis for conclusions about collective contribution. The example presented here also shows how sharing and exchange can occur among adult workplace education programs statewide, not just within one provider agency.

In 1992, the New York State Department of Education, in cooperation with the AFL-CIO and an external consultant, helped practitioners with workplace education programs funded by the department review with how they could improve their program evaluation (Jurmo, 1993; Cichon, Sperazi, and Jurmo, 1997). In March and April, about sixty practitioners attended a day-long workshop in their region. They analyzed their current evaluation practices to identify what worked and what needed improvement. Their analysis of current evaluation concluded that they addressed a number of purposes: clarifying learner needs; assessing impact; encouraging continued support, program improvement, and information for funders; furthering labor and management monitoring; and responding to diversity.

An evaluation consultant devoted about twelve days to guiding the project and sharing experience from an earlier workplace education project in Massachusetts. The workshops identified improvements that participants wanted to make in their evaluation activity. During the subsequent month, participants revised the program and evaluation proposals for annual funding by the department. One outcome during the following year was action research by some practitioners, as they analyzed their planning and evaluation practices and shared what they learned with other participants.

In spite of competing job demands on state staff and local practitioners, some progress occurred in this one-year project. In addition to organizational benefits, individual practitioners gained understanding and expertise from and about program evaluation (Jurmo, 1993).

This evaluation and staff development was continued in a three-year project on collaborative learning for continuous improvement, which began in November 1994. It was funded by the National Workplace Literacy program (through the same department). Participants were from seven manufacturing companies and five cooperating evaluation agencies (Cichon, Sperazi, and Jurmo, 1997). These were the goals and features of the collaborative learning project:

- Create educational planning teams at each site, composed of major stakeholders (coordinator, educator, supervisor, worker, union representative), that used a continuous improvement rationale to set goals, oversee programs, and monitor progress through internal evaluation

- Develop and evaluate collaborative learning for a continuous improvement model, including workplace needs analysis, stakeholder planning and evaluation, problem posing curriculum, and portfolio assessment

- Demonstrate program impact on worker proficiency and performance, workplace productivity and return on investment, and enterprise or union commitment to workplace education

- Promote continuation and expansion of the program

The project achieved these goals to varying degrees. Evaluation was a major feature of many parts of the project, among them the planning team's attention to assessment, portfolio assessment, internal evaluation by project members, and assessment of outcomes by external evaluators.

A team-based evaluation approach was further assessed in seven case studies of workplace evaluation programs (three in Massachusetts, two in New York, one in New Jersey, and one in Nova Scotia; Cichon, Sperazi, and Jurmo, 1997). Key program stakeholders participated in a collaborative process that included building an education team; clarifying what information to generate in an evaluation and designing a strategy to do so; collecting, analyzing, and reporting findings; and taking follow-up action.

The project directors studied the use of this approach at the seven sites to explore its efficacy, in contrast to traditional evaluations in which program staff informally monitor the program while outside evaluation specialists conduct the forward-oriented evaluation. The collaborative approach seemed to be especially appropriate in workplace education programs that emphasized team decision making and continuous improvement.

The strengths of the team evaluation approach were its fit with team management and continuous improvement, stakeholders' focus on important outcomes, internal standards for use in evaluation,

stakeholders' caring about evaluation to warrant resource allocation for evaluation, opportunities for staff development, procedures
that can be replicated, and provision of an audience for stakeholder ideas.

One challenge of the team evaluation approach was that it takes
time, special ability, and discipline. Also, it can be skewed for the
benefit of one or two stakeholders, jeopardize confidentiality, and
complicate ensuring validity; introducing a team approach to evaluation in an enterprise not already team-oriented is also difficult.

A procedure that is often individually oriented, especially when
tied to merit and promotion decisions, is the use of a portfolio presenting tangible examples of performance. However, portfolio
assessment can also be team-oriented if the result of joint effort is
included and the rationale and critique are offered by people in various related roles in the spirit of improvement. Here is an example
of how HRD instructors could cooperate on preparing or revising a
worksheet for identifying critical instructor proficiencies; preparing
a profile of an ideal instructor; and using the results to select additional instructors, evaluate instructor performance, and list proficiencies to assess actual performance and staff development plans.

Appendix One of Rothwell and Cookson (1997) is a self-
assessment form for HRD instructors on which they rate how much
more they want to learn about each proficiency area listed (they can
also add other areas). For proficiencies that an instructor would
especially like to enhance, the participant is encouraged to read
about the topic, solicit feedback from peers, take a course, or conduct a learning project. Illustrative proficiencies on the list are program development procedures, working effectively with others,
analysis of external context, negotiating power interests, setting priorities, and planning evaluation.

For an educational program for adults conducted by a higher
education institution, staff assessment and development can occur
effectively through a peer-oriented arrangement sometimes referred
to as a teaching academy. Here is an example illustrating how effec-

tive teachers who are committed to improving teaching can assemble as a learning community to assess various aspects of teaching and learning related to outreach and continuing education along with resident instruction, and then to cooperate on implementing conclusions and improving staff practice generally.

In the mid-1990s, the University of Wisconsin-Madison established a teaching academy, composed of faculty members and instructional staff engaged in undergraduate, graduate, and outreach teaching. Excellent teachers are selected each year as fellows; for a three-year period they are active fellows and can then be renewed for a second three years. Over the years, this turnover results in about one hundred fellows, about half of whom are active. Several universities have set up a similar arrangement in which higher education teachers help each other strengthen teaching and learning. In 1998, the Carnegie Foundation for the Advancement of Teaching announced that it had received a large grant from the Pew Charitable Trusts and begun working with the American Association for Higher Education to coordinate a teaching academy campus program to establish such efforts at about eighty higher education institutions.

In the UW teaching academy, governance, planning, assessment, assistance, and dissemination are provided by the fellows themselves. This development is important for evaluation of continuing education, extension, and outreach teaching because faculty members with responsibility for outreach and extension are among the fellows and so benefit from and contribute to the mission of the teaching academy in major ways. Teachers from many fields and disciplines help explore issues and directions regarding excellent teaching and benefit greatly from this collaborative effort. As faculty members with extensive continuing education experience share ideas and practices that have been effective in helping adults learn in outreach activities, it increases the interest and capability of colleagues who might thus contribute to future outreach programs.

Some teaching academy activities entail assessment and evaluation for purposes of faculty development. A task force enables an interested fellow to assess aspects of teaching that lead to improved practice generally or on the part of an individual teacher. An example is assessment of student learning, which entailed reviewing practices at UW and in higher education generally for student feedback on courses and workshops, drafting a position paper on uniform procedures, and even posing questions to include in departmental student opinionnaires. Peer review is another example, in which pairs of faculty members in a department visit each other's class sessions and discuss rationale, procedures, results, and desirable improvements. One pair even arranged a comparison of their teaching styles for sections of the same course, with other faculty members in the field assessing student achievement to allow conclusions regarding the association between method and outcome.

When a report of this peer review project was shared at a monthly teaching academy meeting, two fellows from different departments decided to exchange visits; one faculty member made a videotape of a session that the two discussed afterwards, and from it each reported valuable insights. Another task group on celebrating effective teaching reviewed writings on higher education teaching, distributed a bibliography and highlights from publications, and then videotaped examples of effective teaching (along with a companion videotaped interview in which the teacher discussed the rationale regarding goals, decisions, outcomes, and teaching style generally). Reflections by these excellent teachers with quite contrasting teaching styles contributed to self-assessment by the faculty members and teaching assistants who viewed the videotapes, read selectively, and decided on desirable modifications. In yet another instance, a task group on instructional technology prepared a position paper and helped conduct a one-day workshop open to all interested teachers. Planning included assessment of facilities, review of sources of assistance, and review of approaches by teachers at various stages in their experience with instructional technology of many types.

The pertinent theme from the teaching academy regarding evaluation and staffing is the peer-oriented combination of assessment and improvement by university teachers with various degrees of interest and experience in outreach and continuing education. Informal interaction and shared enthusiasm among colleagues regarding important aspects of teaching and learning helped reduce the separation that sometimes occurs between evaluation and improvement, distance education and classroom use of instructional technology, and preparatory and continuing education.

The following example illustrates how a comparative database can be used to help evaluate effective extension teaching. In 1989, Ohio State University established a system for evaluating extension teaching for purposes of improvement, performance appraisal, and promotion and tenure (Spiegel, 1992). Data collection instruments were developed for use by participants, peers, supervisors, and subject matter experts. Widespread use of these standardized instruments contributed to cross-validation to reflect the perspectives of multiple stakeholders, and to interpretation of conclusions regarding performance by a staff member by way of reference to assessment summaries for other staff members.

For example, a nine-item questionnaire (at a seventh-grade reading level) was prepared to obtain feedback from groups attending cooperative extension programs. The items about the instructor pertained to topics such as good preparation, interest in helping, respect for all, stimulation of learning, clear answers, application of content, clear explanations, ability to hold attention, and helpful information. Participant responses were on a five-point agree-or-disagree scale. Participant responses were obtained for a number of extension staff members, which created a database that contributed to interpretation of summaries for a staff member, by allowing comparison with summary information for similar staff regarding role, content specialty, years of experience, and size of learning group. The instructor completed a form to accompany the participant questionnaires, giving background information about the instructor and session along with teaching methods.

Other instruments and feedback included assessment of one-on-one instruction and feedback from peers and experts. Extension instructor use of one or more of these standardized instruments, and normative information to help interpret tabulations, illustrates innovative use of evaluation for staff review and development.

Multiple influences on developing instructional strategies by clinical medical school faculty are illustrated by this example. Sometimes evaluation related to staffing includes both teachers and students as learners (Kazemekas, n.d.). Clinical faculty have major patient care and related research responsibilities, but they devote part of their time to helping medical students master the specifics of medical and surgical practice. The assessment focused on their teaching methods; it was based on observations, interviews, and documents.

The main goal for clinical faculty members was to help medical students develop their innate thinking processes in patient-oriented problem solving. The faculty members in this study were unable to express an explicit rationale for instructional planning on the basis of a learning theory. Instead, they relied on intuition to guide them in selecting examples of patient problems in the clinical setting, combined with a synthesis of basic science concepts and their own clinical experience. In this apprenticeship approach, they served as role models and used student observation of faculty patient care as a cost-efficient, person-centered way to help students learn about clinical practice. They also relied on listening, coaching, mentoring, Socratic dialogue, and small-group discussion. There were differences in teaching methods used by surgical and medical faculty.

Attention to teaching was influenced by the greater incentives for patient care and for research. Faculty satisfaction was less from the process of teaching than from student progress in clinical problem solving. Faculty decisions about teaching reflected their monitoring of student reactions to their instructional methods and materials, as part of an ongoing personalized process of socializing medical students into professional practice. Assessment of teaching methods provides feedback to help clinical faculty members analyze their own instructional decision making and increase self-understanding.

Here are questions that guided the assessment interviews and observations:

- What educational theories, models, or systems (if any) guide your clinical teaching?

- What are the best parts of clinical teaching? the most frustrating?

- How do you decide what to teach and what methods to use?

- What gives students the most trouble with learning? How do you address this in your teaching?

Harper College, in Palatine, Illinois, offers an example of a more comprehensive assessment of staff development related to outreach teaching (Mulcrone, 1997). In addition to procedures for periodic assessment of full-time and adjunct faculty, there is evaluation of support staff and overall program review, on the basis of information from people in each of these roles as well as students and administrators. Program quality reflects the contributions of people in various staff roles, so it is desirable for assessment to include multiple roles.

This excellent example includes the Adult Educational Development Department at Harper (Mulcrone, 1997). The professor who chairs the department has helped plan and coordinate comprehensive evaluation for her department, as part of a collegewide plan for ongoing staff evaluation. Included are an overall program review on a four- or five-year cycle, annual review for untenured full-time faculty members, review of tenured faculty members every three years, and annual review for adjunct faculty and support and supervisory staff.

Assessment booklets and forms explain the evaluation rationale and procedures, which help each staff member engage in self-assessment and appreciate the various contributions to staff and program evaluation in the interest of program quality. Data collection regarding staff performance and development included self-assessment, student feedback, peer review, and classroom observation and summary feedback to the staff member. The data analysis served several improvement purposes, in particular professional growth, instruction, and service.

As an indication of the effort required for this faculty and staff evaluation system, the department chair adapted the collegewide performance appraisal and program evaluation system to the contingencies in her department. The Adult Educational Development Department is part of a division, whose dean helps by assisting department chairs as needed, arranging for review committees, doing some classroom observations, and reviewing evaluation reports to identify implications for commendation and improvement.

The department chair coordinates the evaluation effort. This encompasses adapting forms and procedures, working with peer review committees, observing, preparing reports, and holding individual meetings to discuss conclusions. Each staff member completes a self-assessment. In addition to the program review on a four-year cycle, tenured faculty members are reviewed every three years (the chair does about three each year), and annual performance reviews are conducted for nontenured full-time faculty, adjunct faculty, support and supervisory staff. Aside from the program review, the department chair devotes at least 150 hours annually to staff assessment.

The full-time faculty and staff are accepting of the time and effort they devote to evaluation and assessment; the adjunct faculty welcome it because it helps to offset the sense of isolation that can accompany a part-time role at an outlying location.

The evaluation for full-time faculty includes self-evaluation, peer evaluations by at least three colleagues, the division dean's evaluation, classroom observation, student questionnaires, and coordinator evaluation by the department chair. The self-evaluation requests information about instructional service (active materials, teaching activities, student development, or learning resource center), institutional and community service, and professional development (such as taking courses and workshops). The peer's, dean's, and coordinator's evaluations covered the same staff responsibilities; each included both comments and an overall rating. Information from all sources were summarized in an evaluation grid, which was discussed with the faculty member, who could then add comments. All parties signed the summary form; disagreements could be discussed with the dean, who sent the summary to a vice president.

The evaluation procedure for adjunct faculty was less extensive—mainly classroom observation, student questionnaires, and review by the coordinator. The observation form had three to ten criteria to be rated for five aspects of teaching (classroom atmosphere, the lesson, variety of learning activities, student participation, and feedback). The observer also prepared a one-page narrative summary of activities observed and the observer's comments. The anonymous student questionnaires asked for rating of the teacher's explanations, preparation assistance, encouragement of questions, materials used, interest in student progress (along with what the student especially liked and disliked about the class), and general suggestions.

For support staff, a booklet for self-assessment included guidelines for preparation of a narrative report on performance, a list of the objectives and procedures for the employee performance evaluation process, and a list of job performance factors (along with a statement of the standard; a four-point scale for rating to indicate if the evaluator believed the employee exceeded, met, or failed to meet the standards; and a place for comments and examples). The employee also prepared a development plan. The evaluator and employee jointly reviewed the employee's accomplishment in relation to the development plan; each one completed sections of an overall summary, with sign-off and comments by the evaluator, reviewer, and employee.

These staff assessment activities occurred in the context of a program review covering about eighteen months and recurring every five years. The plan for this program review comprised a dozen steps, with target dates and staff responsibilities noted. A faculty and staff survey for the department was summarized according to responses. The survey included sections on program scope, curricular changes, staffing, strength of faculty and staff development, instructional approach, facilities, college and department support services, equipment, and feedback about student outcomes.

This sort of comprehensive evaluation effort related to staffing requires substantial institutional commitment, finances, and leadership. However, there are many benefits, which were heightened because of the leadership of the department chair in adapting the assessment to the distinctive features of her department and encouraging use of the conclusions for planning, improvement, and accountability. The findings were especially beneficial because they pertained to all staff roles and functions.

Self-assessment is especially valuable for professional development, as in the case of adult and continuing education administrators. An example was the self-assessment inventory, included as Chapter Seven of the UCEA *Handbook for Professional Development in Continuing Higher Education* (Johnson, 1990; see also Knox, 1990b). Forty-six proficiency statements allowed five-point ratings of current and desired proficiency and a difference score. The proficiency statements were grouped by perspective on the field (direction, institution, providers, influences), personal qualities (commitment, interpersonal relations, approach), program development (needs, context, objectives, activities, evaluation, assistance), and administration (participation, resources, staffing, leadership). Biographical information was also requested that allowed use of self-assessment profiles from similar practitioners to interpret self-assessment results. The chapter in the handbook begins with an essay on leadership challenges and concludes with suggested readings grouped by broad category of proficiency; this enables practitioners who complete the self-assessment to use the findings to guide a self-study plan.

Especially at a research-oriented university, there is growing attention to evaluation of assistant professors with *outreach* responsibilities, in preparation for decisions about promotion to associate professor with tenure. As illustrated by the next example, the main issue is clarification of the criteria and evidence to make such a judgment, for the benefit of the assistant professor and the people who help make the promotion decision. The stakes are high for a department that may be unable to replace someone who is denied tenure, as well as the assistant professor who must then seek a position elsewhere. If evaluative criteria are not explicit, it is difficult for a beginning assistant professor to set priorities. Ambiguous criteria also make it difficult for reviewers to justify their conclusions.

Meta-evaluation entails assessing the evaluation process. An example is a long-standing effort to clarify and gain agreement on criteria for making promotion and tenure decisions for university assistant professors having outreach and extension responsibilities. At many universities, the main basis for approving promotion has been quality of research and publication, with resident instruction a secondary criterion. In the 1970s, the University of Illinois initiated a series of efforts to gain institutional agreement on criteria for judging the quality of outreach teaching and scholarship. The conclusions were useful for assistant professors with continuing education and other outreach and extension responsibilities, and for the faculty members and administrators who mentored them or reviewed their packet of promotion materials and thus were part of the decision process (Hanna, 1981).

In recent years at seven similar universities, scholars interested in the outreach promotion process cooperated on a project designed to assess the evaluation criteria and process (Knox, 1998b, 2001). Permission was obtained to fictionalize eighteen packets that were actually reviewed at these institutions. The promotion packets were from several fields of study; they reflected great variation in the extent and type of outreach teaching and scholarship. Packets contained a nomination letter from the department chair with details on the promotion recommendation, the assistant professor's rationale for past performance and future plans, examples of publications, rating of teaching by peers and students, confidential external review letters that indicated the nominee's stature and promise nationally, and the letter of appointment or other document that stated the nominee's responsibilities and sometimes the proportion of effort devoted to extension and outreach.

At each university, faculty members and administrators with experience reviewing such promotion materials did so for some of the fictionalized packets as if the nominee were from their university. After completing each packet, the reviewers completed a questionnaire on which they recorded their recommendation regarding promotion, rating on various criteria and the relevant materials in the packet, and other pertinent comments. More than sixty questionnaires were completed, which allowed analysis of the criteria and other considerations associated with positive and negative overall recommendations on promotion. This analysis was completed for the entire set of ratings of promotion pockets, and for subsets of questionnaires according to individual nominee (assistant professor), broad content field, individual reviewer, and institution in which the reviewer was located.

The conclusions helped identify criteria and evidence of performance that were associated with strong recommendation for promotion to associate professor with tenure. They also pointed to variations among reviewers (and especially institutions) to be considered, and thus how important it is for a beginning assistant professor with outreach responsibility to discern early on the criteria and process for review of his or her promotion packet. Important criteria and even procedures and type of information to include tend to be implicit and not readily available in writing.

The conclusions from this assessment of criteria can help an assistant professor with outreach responsibility in any similar university engage in and document outreach teaching, research, and service (along with resident instruction, discipline-oriented research, and service to the institution and field) in ways that strengthen the promotion packet and ensure a valid assessment. The conclusions can also help colleagues who mentor assistant professors to guide their goals, activities, and assessment of the quality of their performance so that the promotion packet reflects that quality. This can enable reviewers to make a valid assessment that fairly evaluates the outreach portion of the nominee's role. The conclusions can help some reviewers clarify a rationale for outreach forms of teaching, research, and service, along with appropriate criteria and type of evidence to consider.

In the past, some reviewers have explained that they gave minimal attention to outreach and extension performance because they lacked a basis for judging its quality. The conclusions can also help university administrators and review committee members clarify written promotion policies, guidelines, and procedures at the department, college, and university level so that everyone associated with the promotion process has a similar understanding regarding performance by assistant professors with outreach extension and continuing education responsibility.

The middle portion of Chapter Four, on needs assessment, contains various examples of data collection and analysis procedures, some of which can be adapted for use in staffing assessment.

Organizational change and quality improvement is clearly affected by societal and organizational influences, which evaluation should address. However, individual staff members typically constitute the main impetus or resistance to change. A major example in

Chapter Two illustrated how an action research network of school teachers can identify people associated with desirable changes and include them in a process of evaluation, action, and reflection, in part to win their cooperation for such improvement.

Coordination of Assessment

Various people make decisions about staffing, which affects the coordination of assessment related to staffing. Staffing decisions are made by each volunteer or staff member, by the person(s) supervising, and by people in related roles. They are each a stakeholder who can provide information, make decisions, and help implement them in the interest of quality improvement and organizational change. A useful systemic perspective on staffing can pose a special challenge for coordination of assessment.

For self-assessment and the staff member's self-evaluation portion of performance review, it is important for the volunteer or staff member to understand and assume a major responsibility for coordination of this part of the process. Provision of guidelines and rationale enable many staff members to guide this assessment, and especially to use the evaluative conclusions. Because supervision and staff performance are so closely connected, it is desirable for the supervisor to help coordinate staff evaluation; in a small provider agency a program coordinator may do most of the coordinating of evaluation. For a larger agency, there may be a staff member or consultant with evaluation expertise who coordinates assessment related to staffing. The person in this role has oversight of the process, shares the rationale for why as well as how, and ensures that essential assessment tasks are well performed regardless of who might do so. An agency director who understands and appreciates the importance of staff-related assessment can also contribute to oversight (monitoring, delegation, and resource allocation for the purpose). Among the questions that can guide evaluation regarding staffing are:

- Why is the assessment being initiated?

- What are the sources and types of questions to guide the evaluation?

- What methods of data collection and analysis are most appropriate?

- How will use of evaluation conclusions be encouraged?

- What are the fallback options in case there are difficulties with the plan? (Shadesh, Cook, and Leviton, 1995)

In addition to reporting and sharing evaluation conclusions to encourage utilization, coordination of assessment can include some aspects of meta-evaluation. Evaluation standards can be used to critique and strengthen the assessment process. Findings from similar staff evaluation projects can be used to interpret findings. Also, action research or another type of evaluation study can focus on staff assessment procedures in an effort to strengthen the process. Coordinators can gain expertise in program evaluation (Knox and Associates, 1980; Sanders, 1994).

As you reflect on the concepts and procedures regarding staffing assessment, consider these questions:

- What are the main differences in staff assessment between people in instructional and coordination roles?

- What is the extent and type of attention that should be given to self-assessment?

- How can your staff assessment be best coordinated?

Summary Guidelines

This checklist reviews basic guidelines for staffing assessment. As you plan or strengthen your staffing assessment, the guidelines can enhance your procedures and rationale.

Concepts, Purposes, and Stakeholders

1. Staffing assessment by various stakeholders regarding potential and actual performance by paid staff and volunteers pertains to decisions about hiring, assignment, retention, and development for purposes of planning, improvement, and accountability.

2. Staffing assessment is related to both individual performance and organizational effectiveness.

3. Conclusions from other aspects of evaluation (goals, participants, materials, program) can contribute to staffing assessment.

4. Staff assessment can contribute to a developmental process related to the individual and other members of the provider agency.

Planning Assessment

5. Data collection and analysis procedures can foster sound conclusions and encourage use of findings.

6. Early decisions about staff categories and evaluation aspects can help with selecting a desirable and feasible design for data collection and analyses.

7. Selection of high-priority issues and questions can guide planning to focus on the most important potential improvements and allocation of sufficient time and money for the assessment.

8. The various methods of data collection and analysis from which to select for staff selection or development each have strengths and limitations.

9. Adequate allocation of resources for assessment of staffing typically reflects recognition of the investment it represents in staff quality, satisfaction, productivity, and many resultant benefits for all concerned.

Organizational Change

10. Staffing evaluation can enhance the vitality of the provider organization if there is attention to teamwork.

11. Assessment can include complementarity of contributions by staff, information from various providers, and profiles of desired performance.

12. In continuing higher education, a contribution to staff assessment can be made by a peer group, a comparative database, recognition of multiple influences, comprehensive performance review of multiple staff roles, and explicit assessment criteria.

13. Action research is an especially promising vehicle for assessment and improvement.

Coordination of Assessment

14. Assessment is closely associated with staffing decision making; coordination of assessment typically includes multiple roles.

15. Especially for self-assessment, the staff member can contribute to coordination.

16. Supervisors, evaluation specialists, and agency directors can also contribute to aspects of assessment.

17. Coordinators can use a checklist to guide planning and implementation of staff assessment.

18. Meta-evaluation can also strengthen staff assessment.

8

Participation

Adult learners participating in your continuing education program have various types of mostly formative evaluation and feedback that can benefit them and the program: perceived influences on initial and continued participation, expectations, preferred learning style, satisfaction with content and process, achievement, application, attrition, and self-assessment. Evaluation of such segments of participation and progress tends to be more useful if it is coordinated than if it is fragmentary.

The participants are the main sources and users of such information. However, other people can encourage and assist them regarding evaluation. Teachers, counselors, work supervisors, and members of their families or organizations can contribute to evaluation related to learner participation. Evaluation information regarding learner participation and progress can be gotten through tests, opinionnaires, interviews, observations, performance records, and practice adoption indicators.

Because learner motivation, achievement, and application are central to adult and continuing education, it is understandable that potential uses of evaluation related to participation are so extensive. A challenge to leadership on behalf of such evaluation is to select ways of doing that are desirable, feasible, and likely to be useful. This can occur with formal and nonformal programs. It is especially important when there is concern about satisfactory participant progress.

In formal preparatory education of young learners, evaluation related to participation tends to focus on grading student achievement. By contrast, this chapter on evaluation of adult participation in continuing education and training pays attention to assessment of participant progress before, during, and after program participation. Part of this progress is analogous to achievement testing in preparatory education. In adult education, though, progress also means attention to attrition and application of new learning in adult roles beyond the educational program. Evaluation of this continuum of participation is responsive to adult development and stakeholder expectations alike. Before proceeding with the chapter, consider the broader range of evaluation activities regarding participation in various educational activities for adults. Consider issues likely to be important and implications for your evaluation activity:

- How can you decide on the scope and focus of the evaluation?

- Who should contribute to evaluating participation?

- How should evaluation of participation consider relations among attraction, retention, and achievement?

- Which types of evaluation procedure best address persistence, achievement, and benefit?

- How should you connect evaluation conclusions related to the developmental process (enrollment, satisfaction, achievement, application)?

- Which types of evaluation design are most applicable to evaluating participation?

- What contribution can simulation make to evaluating participation?

- What contribution do standards and norms make to evaluating participation?

- Which types of coordination best fit evaluation of participation?

This chapter has three sections: concepts, stakeholders, and purposes; data collection and analysis; and leadership coordination and utilization. The chapter concludes with a listing of summary guidelines.

Concepts, Stakeholders, and Purposes

Several basic ideas pertain to evaluation related to learner participation and progress: the purpose of the evaluation, program characteristics, evaluation criteria (satisfaction, achievement, performance, benefits, return on investment), and stakeholder interest in influences on initial and continued participation.

Most assessment related to participation is in the form of feedback to learners about their progress, as well as formative evaluation to stakeholders for use in enhancing program responsiveness. The participant is an essential program element; learner persistence, achievement, and application are desirable program results. Learner participation reflects personal and situational influences before, during, and after the educational activity. Evaluation before the program assesses expectations and preparation (Pratt, 1988). Evaluation during the program assesses learning style, achievement, satisfaction with content and process, and persistence. Evaluation after the program assesses application and benefits. Needs assessment findings contribute to evaluation and market research regarding initial participation and program responsiveness. Evaluation of the teaching-learning transaction contributes to assessing continued participation, critical thinking, and achievement. Evaluation of outcomes and impact contribute to understanding of application and congruence between objectives and learner outcomes, which can be used for planning future programs that are effective and responsive.

In this chapter, the focus on evaluation related to participation emphasizes the developmental process in which a learner considers and decides to engage in an educational activity, persists or withdraws, and (to some extent) uses what is learned (Knox, 1990a). As instructors, program coordinators, and other stakeholders better understand this developmental process, they increase program responsiveness. They also enable participants to use self-assessment and other forms of evaluation to guide their self-directed learning activity (Knox and Associates, 1980; Brinkerhoff, 1987; Cookson, 1989; Blackburn, 1994; Moore, Bennett, Knox, and Kristofco, 1994; Rose and Leahy, 1997).

Evaluation procedures regarding learner participation vary with program characteristics. Formal educational programs for adults tend to be planned and conducted by instructors and program coordinators. Conclusions from formative evaluation regarding participation can be used for program improvement and responsiveness, which takes into account learner expectations, satisfaction, and achievement (Kasworm, 1983). For a nonformal program, formative evaluation enables participants to help make program decisions. Evaluation related to participation can take the form of self-assessment, which learners can use to guide their self-directed learning (Green and Associates, 1984).

Several levels or criteria may guide planning of evaluation related to participation. One is participant expectations and satisfaction with respect to program goals, design, implementation, and outcomes (Knox and Associates, 1980). Evaluation of participant expectations is evident in the example given here of adult religious education goals and topics. One way to assess expectations and preferences of potential participants is to have them rate their views of the importance of a list of likely goals on a four-point scale, from no importance to great importance (Knox and Associates, 1980). The goals for this instance of adult religious education are to:

- Development or maintainance of good moral character

- Leadership development for congregation members

- Examination of religious beliefs

- Understanding of religious traditions

- Enrichment of religious fellowship and experiences

- Enhancement of spirituality and the faith journey

Another way to assess participant expectation is to ask members to rate, on a five-point scale, their level of interest in possible topics for adult religious education. Topics might be study of religious writings, ethical and social issues, sharing views of personal spiritual journeys, and perplexing religious and philosophical questions. This rating of interest can then be used to increase program responsiveness and participant persistence.

A second level of education, educational achievement, is typically assessed by testing (Worthen and Sanders, 1987). This type of assessment is familiar in formal education instruction. A third level is assessment of participant application through performance in family, work, or community role; evaluation conclusions are useful to the program coordinator. A fourth level is follow-up evaluation of benefits to other people as a result of improved performance (Kirkpatrick, 1994). A fifth level is return on investment in the program. Focusing on one of these levels can suggest useful procedures for collecting and analyzing evaluation data, and encouraging use of findings.

Upcoming examples on education and family literacy instruction illustrate evaluation design decisions of this kind (Garcia, Hasson, and Younkin, 1992; Garcia, Hasson, and LeBlanc, 1997). Two consecutive demonstration projects on family learning were evaluated regarding process and impact, with findings relevant to encouraging participation. The objectives were to improve the English language proficiency of Hispanic parents with limited

English proficiency and of the elementary school students, increase their adjustment to a new society, and enable parents to become more active in their children's education. The program of sixty to seventy hours included instruction related to literacy, life skills, parenting, school involvement, and communication. Learning activities were interpreting a report card, parent-teacher conferences, and experiential learning activities with their K–6 children.

In the 1989–1992 project, the evaluation included review of program and ongoing evaluation of records, interviews with project staff, a demographic questionnaire, pretests and posttests, and parent surveys. Specific instruments were life skills achievement, literacy placement, civics inventory, parent understanding of schools, and a survey of parental involvement with their child's educational progress. Evaluation questions pertained to program process and to significant increases in literacy, parenting, civic involvement, and parent involvement. More than four hundred parents participated at eleven sites. All project activities were accomplished in a timely and satisfactory manner, and significant gain scores were reported for parents who completed the program. Staff recommendations addressed guidelines for managing replication of the project (Garcia, Hasson, and Younkin, 1992).

The 1992–1996 project was similar and built on the previous one. Placement and assessment instruments were developed and field-tested, incorporating criterion-referenced testing and portfolio assessment. More than three hundred parents participated at seven sites. The evaluation report described the participants' backgrounds and reported significant improvement on all indicators of parental involvement and language development. About two hundred adults did not complete the program, about a 40 percent attrition rate. Project staff contacted most of those people; the main reasons for discontinuance were work conflict, personal problems, getting a job, illness or accident, and moving away. The lower-than-anticipated attrition rate was attributed to participant recruitment and retention activities by staff (telephone calls, weekly letters, child care services, incentives for attendance, staff development for instructors, program quality). Project materials are available for use elsewhere. The evaluation part of the project guided program decisions, increased program responsiveness, and contributed to the applicability of the program and materials elsewhere.

In practice, participants, instructors, coordinators, and other stakeholders vary in their level of interest in personal and situational influences on initial and continued participation. When you plan an assessment related to participation, use your estimates of likely stakeholder interest to decide the extent and type of effort to devote to obtaining satisfactory cooperation. Attention to the continuum of participation before, during, and after an educational activity may increase interest in evaluation and the benefits of findings for the purpose of program planning and improvement as well as self-directed learning.

Workplace Literacy Education for Union Members

With funding from the U.S. Department of Education National Workplace Literacy Program, a collaborative worker literacy program for health care paraprofessionals was conducted by City University of New York and the NYC Central Labor Council (Perin, 1992). Previously, it was frequent for a paraprofessional with a high school diploma or equivalent who was interested in career advancement to be rejected from a college program because of low literacy.

Evaluation was related to several aspects of participation. Program applicants were screened for entry using a writing assessment for assigning college students to remedial classes. The program was similar to college remedial courses but contextualized regarding content pertinent to health care. The retention rate (60 percent for twenty-one weeks, 47 percent for the full twenty-eight weeks) was similar to retention in adult basic education generally. Completers and noncompleters did not differ significantly regarding educational background, age, family responsibilities, family support for participation, first language, current job, job objectives, or entry literacy level. However, completers had significantly higher reading and math scores twenty-one weeks into the program than participants who subsequently dropped out. Noncompleters reported that the pace of instruction was too fast; reasons for dropping were mostly family and personal.

Literacy level was assessed in two ways: by simulated college placement tests in reading, writing, and math; and by teacher ratings. Both methods showed gains for writing, the tests showed gains for math but not reading, and teacher ratings showed gains for reading but not math. These anomalies were not explained.

The follow-up survey in the third and fourth month after the program reported that 65 percent of a sample of ninety-six participants had been accepted to a college, mostly to study in a health field. Many passed college placement tests in reading, writing, and math. The labor unions were active partners in the program and continued their use of instructional materials beyond the funded project. The evaluation report included recommendations to select teachers committed to the program's dual emphasis on health and literacy, increase teacher involvement in curriculum revision, and increase staff development with dual emphasis on health and literacy.

Data Collection and Analysis

Planning and implementation of data collection and analysis for evaluation related to participation reflect a focus on the developmental process by which adult learners progress through the program. Such planning decisions involve project design, source and type of data collection, and program aspects addressed in data analysis and use of findings.

An early fundamental decision is the general evaluation design that best addresses the evaluation issue related to learner participation. The objectives and scope of the evaluation should be desirable and feasible. When the focus is on participation, limited time and money typically restrict the extent of the assessment. However, the findings should be useful to participants, instructors, and program coordinators. Attention to timing and sampling can produce a useful assessment in spite of limited resources. This is especially so because evaluation related to participation can be part of encouraging enrollment, reflecting and thinking critically, and applying new learnings. Evaluation findings related to the developmental process can enable learners, instructors, and other stakeholders to make sound program decisions and enrich their insights (Blackburn, 1994).

The most important source of data regarding participation is the learner. He or she can share perceptions regarding influences, expectations, progress, satisfaction, and benefits; the learner's understanding of such conclusions can contribute to using the evaluation findings. Instructors, counselors, coordinators, and members of the family or an organization with which the participant interacts are other useful sources of data. Their perception of influence, achievement, and benefit can cross-validate the data from participants. Additional procedures for data collection and analysis are reviewed in the middle portion of Chapter Four.

Clientele Analysis

Over the years, many providers of adult educational programs have done a participant survey to analyze their background, expectations, experience, and preferences so that the conclusions can be used by program staff to identify important subpopulations and increase program responsiveness for them.

For example, a public community college obtained external funding for a study of part-time students; it yielded information about demographics (age, previous education, occupation, tuition reimbursement, community participation, and interests), self-concept (for counseling and advisement use), and satisfaction with the program. Other features of the study were a test of verbal ability, comparison with findings from a similar study of university continuing education participants, comparison of new and continuing participants, and follow-up of dropouts. The evaluation report offered some comparison useful to administrators, instructors, and counselors, on first-time and continuing participants, and successful and unsuccessful students. Level of satisfaction; comparison of community college findings with several other continuing higher education survey results; analysis by five age categories, income level, level of verbal ability, and dropout status were all part of the analysis.

Another study of part-time students at the continuing education center of a large urban private university obtained several types of information, on demographics, volunteer and community participation, information-seeking practice, leisure activity, aspirations, continuing education activity, satisfaction, interests, and plans.

Usually, the findings of such an evaluation are in the form of a summary used by program staff to increase program responsiveness. Various data collection procedures support evaluation related to participation; they can be grouped and labeled as questioning, observation, documents, and comprehensive.

Questioning pertains to participant expectation and preference before an educational activity, satisfaction and progress during a program, and application and benefit afterward. It makes use of questionnaires, checklists, tests, interviews, focus groups, and nominal group technique. Observation and document analyses are especially desirable and feasible while learners are participating in a program, but they have value both before and afterward. For instance, workplace education efforts sometimes use personnel and performance records, along with self-assessment and supervisory performance reviews. To guide staff development activity, observation of performance in work, recreational, and musical settings can be a useful starting point for educational activity, a way of monitoring progress, and an indication of success. Three comprehensive ways of evaluating participation are simulation, portfolio assessment, and a pilot effort. Each permits focusing on participation in an educational activity, while also assessing personal and situational influences (Blackburn, 1994; Brinkerhoff, 1987). The examples given here illustrate several types of data collection related to participation.

HRD programs in a number of enterprises (business, industry, government, military, education, health) seek to enhance the proficiency of members who work there in the interest of career development and organizational quality and productivity (Brinkerhoff, 1987). In some programs, early assessment of educational program plans serves several purposes, notably increasing program responsiveness to the actual learners in the program. The evaluation conclusions are used to increase compatibility with participant interests, needs, abilities, preferences, values, and culture.

In addition to program participants, the evaluation project collects data from and reports conclusions to people in related roles who are also prone to change if the program is successful. Including potential participants and people in related roles in the evaluation process recognizes that they are the ones most affected by the educational program and that their understanding and commitment is essential for success. Their involvement in the evaluation can increase program fit with the total organization, stakeholder commitment to the program and its improvement, and assistance instead of resistance to participant application on the part of people in related roles.

An evaluation project assessing a program plan may include assessment of planning documents using a worksheet on participant or outcomes evaluation. The worksheet specifies plans about characteristics of the intended participants, the proficiencies to be enhanced, objectives regarding improved performance, and intended organizational benefits. The process and results of this worksheet assessment are similar to those of needs assessment, but in addition desired organizational benefits are identified early. This guides change in performance required and proficiency, and also selection of potential participants in HRD activities. Including stakeholders in evaluation of the draft program plan helps communicate and modify the plan and increase compatibility with the actual learners.

In most provider agencies, practitioners recognize that a concerted effort is required to attract and retain the type and number of participants who are central to their mission but tend to be underrepresented. The rationale for this strategy draws from marketing concepts and procedures. Evaluation and assessment are integral to the process and are referred to as market research; this is evident in ten steps to ensure marketing success (Simerly and Associates, 1989):

1. Establish a marketing-related research base (evaluation).

2. Write advertising copy that emphasizes how the participant benefits from enrollment (evaluation to increase effectiveness).

3. Integrate marketing concepts into daily routine (assessment of audience response).

4. Promote a comprehensive service orientation (assessment of client satisfaction, ongoing evaluation, and identification of market niches).

5. Design marketing activities to enhance the image of the provider organization (evaluating the fit between marketing activities and provider mission and goals).

6. Price programs and services competitively (assessing client expectations and desirable fees in relation to alternative programs and cost-recovery goals).

7. Develop an effective marketing mix of ways to communicate with potential participants (ongoing assessment).

8. Obtain professional assistance with graphic design (use past evaluation to guide design and ongoing evaluation to assess its impact).

9. Track results (ongoing evaluation through the communication model of sending information and receiving a response that underlies marketing practice).

10. Continuously analyze common marketing mistakes, to minimize them (a special aspect of evaluation focused on improvement).

Most of the ideas about marketing emphasize attracting participants, but many apply also to retention. Program quality and responsiveness are especially important for retention, and evaluation conclusions can be useful for this purpose (Cookson, 1989). Three reports on evaluation for marketing of cooperative extension programs show approaches that can be taken.

A decade ago, cooperative extensions in some states (including Louisiana) increased their attention to marketing (Coreil and Verma, 1992). The Louisiana marketing audit evaluated extension faculty perception of the importance of marketing procedures used in extension. In this example, the extension faculty members were the adult learners whose improved performance affirms use of evaluation to improve participation. The results indicated that most marketing procedures were perceived as very important. The evaluation conclusions emphasized the importance of a more comprehensive marketing strategy with both long-term and short-term plans embracing organizational and client objectives, resources needed, plan of action, and faculty orientation (based on evaluation results and designed to foster implementation).

A study at the University of Florida Cooperative Extension explored the extent to which evaluation data were used by 162 county extension faculty in Florida to market their program and organization. In summer 1992, a thirteen-item questionnaire assessed the extent to which evaluation data were used to guide mass media communication, indicate program impact, obtain public support, and create a positive image. Relatively few county faculty members used evaluation data to a great extent for marketing, but about half did so to some extent. Less use of evaluation data to attract participants occurred than for reports to funding agencies, where evidence of impact was emphasized. This may reflect extension reliance on external funding and not participant fees. One use of evaluation is to enhance participation of extension faculty members in staff development.

A report from Ohio State University Extension focused on use of evaluation results for planning marketing for three specific programs. The program on balancing work and family used focus group interviews with employers, case study interviews with employees, and preassessment and postassessment with participants (which included semantic differential, attitudinal, and Likert scales; ranking of preferred methods; and demographics). Application of the evaluation conclusions to marketing included use of statements from enterprises to promote programs to other enterprises, and a targeted brochure sent to enterprises (which reflected ideas from the evaluation). A specific application of evaluation findings was for staff development of extension faculty members to improve their use of marketing concepts.

Evaluation methods for an assessment center for public officials included preassessment and postassessment of participants, focus group interviews with participants and program developers, and participant testimonials. Application of the evaluation conclusions to marketing included targeted marketing to people aspiring to be county commissioners, preparing a brochure with testimonials from former participants, asking former participants to help recruit new participants, and issuing news releases. These instances illustrate how evaluation can help attract and retain staff development participants.

Tests and questionnaires are familiar ways of assessing achievement in educational programs for adults provided by educational institutions and enterprises. For instance, various forms of assessment are used in adult basic education programs for screening, diagnosis, and accountability. The next example illustrates such types of evaluation procedure, including a rationale for their coordinated use in guiding learner progress. Because participants typically enter an adult basic education program with a major gap in their preparation, ongoing assessment is important for screening, diagnosis, and accountability (Rose and Leahy, 1997). Among the various types of assessment that are available are norm-referenced standardized tests, other formal assessments that are referenced to criteria or performance, and informal assessments (observation, self-assessment, reading inventory, retell exercise, writing sample, checklist, portfolio). It is desirable for evaluation purposes to guide data collection and analysis.

The Educational Testing Services National Adult Literacy Survey eliminated grade equivalents and instead reported scores on five levels of proficiency. Their resulting tests of applied literacy skills, and American College Testing's work keys test, use standard scores and are contextual with versions that assess the level of workplace literacy. The advantage of a standardized test is that it yields comparable results regardless of location or program type; the disadvantage is that it may be irrelevant to actual program content. This distinction is important in using testing to assess the progress of an individual participant.

Criterion-referenced assessment does not compare the learner's performance with a norming group but rather with the participant's earlier performance. Performance-referenced assessment evaluates achievement through paper-and-pencil tests, computer simulation, or real-life demonstration, using activities such as renting an apartment.

With participant and instructor interest in individual progress, informal assessment may be desirable. The instructor can observe participant achievement and progress using an observation guide or comments in a journal or student folder. Self-assessment encourages participants to reflect on their progress and assume responsibility for their learning activities. Among informal reading inventories are word lists and a series of graded reading passages to assess both silent and oral reading. A retell exercise requires the participant to tell what he or she has read. Writing samples collected over time help document the participant's growth as a writer. Checklists enable learners to record their extent and type of reading, writing, and math outside the educational program.

In general, there are three recommendations for assessing participation and progress: establish guidelines based on the purpose of the assessment, involve participants in the assessment process, and review evaluation procedures regarding their appropriateness and effectiveness.

In a detailed research report by the Center for the Study of Liberal Education for Adults, Miller and McGuire (1961) document the rationale, procedures, and instruments from a project of several years to evaluate liberal or general education programs for adults. The emphasis was on continuing higher education; a major purpose was to develop evaluation instruments (tests, questionnaires, simulations) that participants and instructors could use to assess achievement. The next example focuses on this purpose, which enables participants to monitor their progress in mastering quite general content and enables the instructor to assess learner achievement and use conclusions to increase program responsiveness. The example is fairly detailed because it is one of a few on evaluation of general education for adults.

The authors worked with almost one hundred continuing higher education practitioners (engaged in liberal adult education) and evaluation experts in developing a rationale and drafting evaluation instruments (many of which were included in the report). In an initial stage, they selected widespread liberal adult education objectives to guide evaluation procedures, among them developing new interests, increasing knowledge of pertinent concepts, analyzing personal and social attitudes, appreciating intellectual and aesthetic values, thinking critically, making informed judgments, understanding relationships, and empathizing with divergent viewpoints.

The project rationale acknowledged the lofty goals of liberal education but stated that program objectives can be worded more specifically than is usually the case, to specify the type of intellectual behavior that indicates the program is achieving its purpose. For example, learners who understand relationships should be able to classify phenomena into appropriate categories, recognize that some categories are more important than others for a specific purpose, understand the relationship between an instance and a principle, formulate a hypothesis to account for connection among phenomena, and apply a concept to other pertinent domains. Subgroups of project participants worked on four content areas (political and social problems, community participation, ethical and moral values, and appreciation of the arts). To develop evaluation instruments, three criteria were used: realism, interest, and flexibility. It was assumed that a liberal adult education program likely to help participants achieve the intended objectives would have five features. The participant should:

1. Become aware of the inadequacy of current proficiency
2. Understand a model of desired proficiency
3. Have the opportunity to practice activities likely to enhance proficiency
4. Receive feedback and reinforcement related to the desired proficiency
5. Have an appropriately graded sequence of materials

In each of the four content areas, this was the progress reported by the subgroups:

1. Defined the area regarding concepts, issues, information, and materials of special importance to adults
2. Identified important objectives for actual programs in the area
3. Drafted evaluation instruments and suggesting additional types of instrument and procedure for future development (emphasis was given to case analysis)
4. Initiated small-scale field testing of some of the instruments

To illustrate development of evaluation instruments to collect data and their pertinence to assessing participation, let us look at highlights drawn from part four of the report on the process of making moral decisions. Great books discussion groups are examples of an adult education program that focuses on values as an object of study. If participants complete an evaluation instrument part way through an educational program, receive feedback regarding their responses and those of other participants, discuss the conclusions in relation to their current understanding, and do so several times during the program, they can use the resulting feedback themselves (and it can be used by the instructor in summary form). The conclusions can then guide the developmental process of learning to make moral decisions. As with all four content areas, case situations were developed as the basis for evaluation questions.

Here is a case example used to evaluate liberal education achievement. Similar cases can be used in evaluating other types of adult educational program. A promising young middle manager named Held was in a yearlong reorganization project that entailed long hours and much travel. His wife consoled herself with plans for a two-week vacation, which coincided with her parents' fortieth anniversary celebration. Three weeks before the vacation, his immediate supervisor, Collins, asked him to reschedule his vacation to attend an important meeting that others were unable to attend because of illness or commitments. Collins asked the branch manager to persuade Held to reschedule his vacation, which Held said he was unwilling to do.

Learners are asked to suppose that they are the branch manager who must make the decision; learners also are given a series of questions the answers to which reflect what they value when making moral decisions. For instance, on a list of twelve statements the learner checks the four that are most important, and the two least important, for the branch manager in making such a decision. Some statements reflect these considerations:

- Managerial sacrifices like this greatly benefit a business.

- Senior executives gain satisfaction from such extra efforts.

- Marital problems for managers reflect conflict between job and family loyalties.

- Managers have important responsibilities for their businesses.

- A manager's family should not be damaged by job responsibilities.

- Lines of executive authority should be adhered to.

Additional items requested participants to select, from a list of options, those that supported a decision, belief, or conclusion. For instance, regarding the branch manager's decision about asking Held to postpone his vacation, the participant was to select one question as most important (such as disobeying his superior, deserving a vacation, or a serious problem arising from postponing the vacation). Another item contained a list of ten statements related to the case situation, from which the participant was to select the two most important in favor of postponing the vacation and the two most in favor of taking the vacation as scheduled.

The purpose of such evaluation items is not to assess the correctness of a learner's values and beliefs. Instead, the evaluation intent is to encourage participants to reflect on the fit between a specific instance and general principles, and to reflect on the assumptions and implications of a course of action that addresses material and ethical issues. Such feedback can be of educational value at various stages of a program. Evaluation conclusions can offer useful feedback to the individual participant, a basis for group discussion of evaluation summaries, and helpful indications to the instructor regarding learner progress and program effectiveness. All three types of feedback can contribute to program responsiveness and participant persistence.

Another way of assessing participation is with a portfolio. It usually assesses achievement related to a course, although it sometimes deals with prior learning. Although the instructor typically helps

the participant assemble a portfolio, it is important to orient learners to its purpose, contents, structure, and intended outcomes. As
participants add material to a portfolio, they should include their
rationale and reflections about their studies; the instructor should
review the portfolio with them to discuss progress toward important
goals.

Portfolio assessment as an evaluation procedure pertains to various aspects of participation. One use is for prior learning assessment
for an adult learner returning to formal education. The portfolio
may have extended essays about learning activities along with documentation and a rationale to justify award of credit for proficiency
gained in various ways outside the provider organization (Rose and
Leahy, 1997).

Miller and Associates (1993) recount an example of using program portfolios to evaluate participation and empowerment. One
part of a large educational project that used a community development approach to the issue of at-risk youth focused on parent education. Portfolio assessment was used as a supplementary way of
presenting the evaluation plan results. Local program portfolios and
panel reviews of the portfolios were central to the assessment. Staff
development was a major outcome. Portfolios contained descriptions, documents, data, and statements arranged to best represent a
project. They differed greatly but fit their projects by explaining the
project and giving perspective to the evaluation results.

Preparation was only half the evaluation review process; the
other half was getting people to read and use the information. This
was accomplished by organizing review panels of knowledgeable
people diverse in background, viewpoint, specialty, ethnicity, and
region. Panelists received two hours of orientation and devoted four
days to the task. Orientation covered review tasks and timing, ideas
about value and worth, statement of goals, and the general content
of the portfolio. The review process was structured by each panel
with members working alone and together. A panelist completed a
one-page summary report on each portfolio, which included open

questions on especially valuable features and on suggestions for the project. Although no interrater reliability was reported, similar projects had reported better than 90 percent agreement among panel members. A major conclusion from the portfolio review process was that an important outcome of the project was staff development, which is relevant to assessment related to participation and progress by staff members.

At its best, evaluation related to participation entails interactive assessment of the developmental process of initiating and persisting in educational activity. Such evaluation can be informal self-assessment related to self-directed learning, or it can be more formal assessment by participants and other stakeholders regarding learner progress in various kinds of educational activity for adults. Rose and Leahy (1997) suggest five principles for assessment. Assessment

1. Recognizes various ways of knowing and learning about resources.

2. Recognizes and reinforces cognitive, conative, and affective domains of learning.

3. Focuses on active engagement in learning and self-assessment.

4. Embraces learner involvement and impact on roles in work, family, and community.

5. Accommodates the learners' increasing differentiation from one another, given varied life experiences.

Portfolios to assess prior learning have been used in higher education for about thirty years (Rose and Leahy, 1997). They typically contain statements that describe learning experiences, identify resulting proficiency pertinent to college courses, and present documentation. They serve as vehicles for communication among students, faculty, and institutions, especially for the returning student. By assessing knowledge gained outside college to meet requirements for college credits, the adult student was seen as a coproducer of academically credible knowledge and not just a recipient. However, a potential disadvantage is the emphasis on objective and organized knowledge at the expense of experiential and personal knowledge. This can be especially difficult for an adult from a minority subculture. Portfolio assessment helps connect nonformal and formal education and enables adult learners to guide the continuum of their lifelong learning.

These concepts regarding evaluation related to participation are applicable to many aspects of the learner's initial and continued engagement. In practice, a specific evaluation project focuses on one or a few aspects:

- The learner's motivation and perceived expectancy regarding educational activity

- Information-seeking patterns

- Triggers that activate educational activity

- Type and extent of critical reflection on performance

- Action or inquiry

- Solving ill-defined problems in context

- Past experience in educational activity and experiential learning

- Influences on participation in educational activity

- Preferred learning style

- Satisfaction with educational activity

- Initiation of educational activity, along with persistence and withdrawal

- Educational achievement

- Application of new learning and practice adoption

Another evaluation ingredient is seen in action research. Action research uses evaluation as part of a cycle of problem posing and problem solving to achieve program improvement. Practitioners guide the action research and use the conclusions (Quigley and Kuhne, 1997). The rationale is based on early writings by John Dewey on reflexive thinking and by Kurt Lewin on action research. As adult education practitioners use action research, they become more proficient in solving the ill-defined problems they confront. In this sense, they are the participant using evaluation to guide their learning as an instructor, counselor, and administrator.

Developing an action research project can be conceptualized in three phases: planning, action, and reflection (each of which includes evaluation). The planning phase encompasses the first three steps. Step one is understanding the problem (state it briefly, why it exists, prior students, why it is worth working on, evident causes, initial ideas). Step two is defining the project (proposed project, when to begin, managing process and results, needed materials, needed approvals, gaining cooperation, who will help assess it). Step three is selecting the measures (specify baseline and criteria for success, time line for evaluation, methods for data collection, potential deterrents).

The action phase constitutes step four, implementing an action and observing the results (following plan, data collection that closely monitors progress, continued cooperation, data summary).

The reflection phase includes steps five and six. Step five is evaluating the results (conclusions about the problem and intervention, relation to criteria for success, opinions about the project). Step six is reflecting on the project (replication, a second or third cycle of the project).

The action research approach illustrates the many connections between evaluation and participation in staff development and program improvement, which extends from initial engagement through learning activities to application.

Evaluation (assessment, research) is an important part of the broad type of adult educational activity referred to as action inquiry (action inquiry technologies). Six variations on this theme are action research, action-reflection learning, action science, popular education, participatory action research, and collaborative inquiry. In each variation, adult and continuing educators involve the participants as active collaborators in an effort to change individuals, a group, an organization, or a society with evaluation, reflection, and action as essential ingredients (Brooks and Watkins, 1994).

Action research is an iterative, cyclical process that includes forming a group from the people who have a problem, reflecting about problems in the group, collecting data about the problem, conducting group analysis and feedback, and having the group design an intervention to solve the problem.

Action-reflection learning participants typically come from diverse contexts in which they address and evaluate solutions to their different work problems, and then meet for group reflection regarding their insights and progress in solving real organizational problems.

Action science participants evaluate their interaction experience from a systems perspective to recognize patterns of learning (metalearning) and thus change their behavior.

Popular education proceeds from the premise that social change is essential in solving (or reducing) problems of oppressed peoples; it emphasizes praxis in which action occurs concurrently with emerging consciousness of systemic social, class, gender, and ethnic influences on problem solving.

Participatory action research emphasizes egalitarian participation by members of a community of people who belong to a social system experiencing a problem, use critical reflection and data to understand and reformulate the problem, and develop and implement solutions.

Collaborative inquiry integrates the participation and knowledge of both practitioners and scholars to construct informal knowledge to guide action in participants' everyday lives and experiences.

A common theme is a search for valid evaluation in the action inquiry process. Four types of validity criteria are suggested: on proficiency, relevance, system, and norms. *Proficiency* refers to ways to develop capability regarding both action and evaluation among participants and scholars to ensure that the solution works in context. Participants are empowered and transform their beliefs. *Relevance* refers to ways of assessing the usefulness of evaluation conclusions in relation to needs in the problem context (problems are solved, there are cost savings). *System* refers to assessment of the extent to which problems are solved in ways that encourage ongoing system learning (future problem solving is enhanced). *Norms* refers to consistency of procedures and outcomes with the normative theory guiding the approach (participants learn and situations are transformed in ways predicted by the action inquiry model).

In general, evaluation is an essential part of action inquiry in which participants collaborate in empowering participation and cogenerative dialogue. Truth is in the process of inquiry characterized as reflexive and dialectical, ethical and collaborative. Among the questions to guide evaluation: Did participants solve problems? Did they attain self-understanding? Did they learn forms of inquiry and assessment? Did they achieve greater self-determination?

Persistence is an important part of participation, especially in a program such as adult basic education where it is difficult to attract and retain participants (Comings, Parrella, and Soricone, 1999). Useful findings for encouraging persistence should address the combination of influences that help and hinder persistence. Understanding such influences can enable participants, instructors, coordinators, and policy makers to reinforce positive influences and perhaps deflect negative ones. For example, for adult basic education participants evaluation findings can be used to enhance support from other people, self-efficacy, goal setting, and supportive arrangements such as program quality.

In adult basic education staff development, the instructors, counselors, tutors, and coordinators are adult learners. As an alternative to traditional in-service education, in which an expert conducts a session on a topic, inquiry-based professional development uses evaluation as a way to help a staff member become an active and reflective generator as well as user of knowledge and a constructor of his or her professional practice (Sissel, 1996). This action research approach builds on the richness and diversity of staff member experience and knowledge. It entails organized collection, analysis, and interpretation of data gathered in program sites. Staff members generate the inquiry questions that guide the evaluation and use of conclusions. The inquiry may analyze current practice or assess the process and outcomes of an innovation. Staff learning is thus embedded in their work setting; they need time and support to invent local solutions for their concerns. The inquiry approach blurs the distinction between teaching and inquiry, between evaluation and practice.

When this approach was used for adult basic education staff in Philadelphia, practitioners from various provider agencies constituted a learning community in which they met for six years in seminars to construct and implement inquiry approaches to their professional development. Midway through each year, participants shared materials and assessments from their portfolios and discussed common themes. In the seminars, which university faculty members and graduate students also attended, participants shared inquiry questions of interest and discussed evaluation procedures and conclusions. Doing so within a learning community contributed to critical reflection. As a result, participants recognized their practice as a rich site for learning, positioned themselves as a generator of knowledge, viewed research as a way to generate local knowledge, and recognized inquiry as a way to enrich theories of practice. Thus, evaluation was central to their ongoing professional development.

Selection of one or more aspects of participation on which to focus assessment (expectations, satisfaction, persistence, achievement, application, influences) should lead to evaluation questions to guide the data analysis, selection of data collection method, and identification of likely sources. Leadership on behalf of evaluation related to participation consists of coordinating the total effort, especially stakeholder contribution to selecting evaluation questions, interpreting data, and encouraging use of findings.

Leadership

Usually, when evaluation related to participation occurs, someone coordinates the effort. This leadership is somewhat distinctive because findings are used mainly to attract and retain participants and provide feedback and self-assessment materials to adult learners to guide their progress. As a result, leadership for such evaluation is usually the job of a program coordinator. However, an interested instructor or outside consultant could also coordinate the evaluation.

Leadership of evaluation related to participation entails many considerations: who does the coordinating, how to obtain cooperation, criteria for planning regarding focus and scale, considering feasibility and obtaining necessary resources, arranging for reporting and use of conclusions, the contribution of meta-evaluation, and addressing ethical issues.

Regardless of who coordinates the evaluation, several ingredients are important for success. As with any administrative or management role, an essential ingredient is winning and maintaining cooperation. Understanding evaluation concepts and procedures is also important. If the evaluation coordinator does not possess all the expertise required, the remainder can be obtained from experts and materials. It is desirable for the coordinator to be quite familiar with the program related to the evaluation, to understand the context, the people to involve, and how to encourage use of conclusions. If the focus of evaluation is on self-assessment and self-directed learning, each participant may assume major responsibility for managing the evaluation process and using conclusions.

Obtaining cooperation to help plan and conduct an evaluation project regarding participation can be the most important and difficult part of coordination. With the focus on participation, it is essential that adult learners understand the process and use the conclusions. In the previous examples reflecting use of action inquiry approaches, participants were major partners in the process. The instructor is also a major stakeholder, especially in relation to valuing the purpose of the evaluation, helping to collect data, and understanding and using conclusions to modify teaching to enhance persistence and achievement. Other stakeholders whose cooperation may be important in a specific instance are funders supporting a large educational project and enterprises assisting with needs assessment and application of new learnings (Patton, 1997).

The criteria regarding focus and scale vary greatly, depending on the circumstances that prompt the evaluation project and in which it is conducted. For instance, a program coordinator and several instructors may decide to evaluate participation by underserved learners whose attrition rate is unusually high. Without special funding for this purpose, but with a strong commitment to doing so, they may initiate a modest project in which they identify, interview, track, and follow up the underserved participants to better understand personal and situational influences on their persistence. By contrast, a state director of adult basic education might recommend a federal project to evaluate the experience of new participants, so that the resulting conclusions from a national study can guide local policies and procedures to better attract and retain various categories of underserved adults. An example from Quigley and Kuhne (1997) illustrates such a project. There are, however, some general criteria that help decide on focus and scale and assess the results (Knox and Associates, 1980). The evaluation should:

- Be cost-effective

- Focus on issues important to key stakeholders

- Occur with minimal program disruption

- Be based on valid and balanced information

- Consider both quantitative and qualitative data

- Encourage the stakeholder to use conclusions

Assessment of the cost-effectiveness of an evaluation project entails considering desirability and feasibility. To consider feasibility and obtain necessary resources, cooperation is central; for all but the smallest evaluation projects, so are time and money. For most local evaluations related to participation, time tends to be more important than money. However, planning, conducting, and completing such an evaluation project can be enhanced by a budget estimate and timeline, even though they are only used by the project coordinator (and perhaps someone else who allocates modest resources for the purpose). An unfortunate result of underfunding an evaluation project (regarding time as well as money) is that it damages cooperation and can terminate an evaluation project with little benefit.

Poor reporting and disuse of conclusions can nullify the benefits of even a completed evaluation project. Regarding use of conclusions, the essential contribution of an evaluation coordinator is to clarify early on the stakeholders most likely to care about the evaluation and to involve them appropriately in the process to increase their contribution, understanding, and ultimate commitment to use of conclusions. Partnership is visible in the earlier example on workplace literary education for union members.

The form of reporting typically varies among stakeholders. It may be a self-assessment inventory for self-directed learners, suggestions regarding increasing persistence and reducing attrition for instructors, an executive summary for policy makers, or a full technical report for a program coordinator (and perhaps the funder).

Meta-evaluation can take various forms. For assessment related to participation, evaluation of the process and report can occur in one of several ways. Some participants and some instructors may constitute a small focus group to discuss the project and make recommendations regarding a draft report and improved procedures for future evaluation projects. The counterpart of the evaluation coordinator at a similar provider agency would welcome receiving a copy of the report and in return might critique it. An evaluation expert could review the evaluation plan, preliminary findings, draft report, and a follow-up so as to strengthen the process (formative evaluation) and prepare for future evaluation (accountability and planning).

As with any evaluation, there are ethical issues: resolving conflicting expectations among various stakeholders, clarifying who has access to the data and related confidentiality concerns, ensuring a valid and balanced report, making assumptions and value judgments explicit, allowing cross-validation related to key conclusions, and so on.

As you reflect on this overview of evaluation related to learner participation, consider these questions:

- Which aspects of participation (expectations, satisfaction, persistence, achievement, application) should receive special attention regarding assessment?

- How can you best strengthen evaluation related to participation?

- How should you involve pertinent stakeholders in evaluation regarding participation?

Summary Guidelines

Here is a checklist to review the basic guidelines for evaluation related to learner participation. You can use it to improve your rationale and procedures for evaluating learner participation and progress.

Concepts, Stakeholders, and Purposes

1. Evaluation related to participation includes formative evaluation to help stakeholders enhance program responsiveness and feedback to encourage learner persistence and achievement.

2. Participation assessment addresses a developmental process that includes expectations and preparation before an educational activity; learning style, achievement, and satisfaction during the activity; and application and benefits that result from the activity.

3. Conclusions from other aspects of program evaluation (needs assessment, teaching-learning transaction, outcomes) can contribute to evaluation related to participation.

4. Participation assessment reflects program characteristics; it can contribute to responsiveness of a formal program, learner influence on a nonformal program, and self-assessment to enable participants to guide self-directed learning.

5. Evaluation related to participation pertains to five levels: satisfaction, achievement, performance, benefit, and return on investment.

6. Attention to the developmental process of participation before, during, and after a program can contribute to stakeholder interest in evaluation related to influences on participation.

Data Collection and Analysis

7. An early decision about assessment objectives and scope can help produce an evaluation that is both desirable and feasible.

8. Usefulness to key stakeholders helps ensure adequate resources for the purpose of evaluation related to participation.

9. Such evaluation conclusions can help encourage enrollment, reflection, and application.

10. Participants, instructors, counselors, coordinators, and group members are all sources of information related to participation that allow cross-validation.

11. Questions regarding participant expectations, achievement, and application can be answered from information derived from a questionnaire, test, interview, focus group, documents, observation, or portfolio.

12. Such means of data collection pertain to informal self-assessment and to more formal assessment of learner progress.

Leadership, Coordination, and Utilization

13. A program coordinator (or sometimes an instructor or consultant) should lead the evaluation effort in ways that include relevant stakeholders.

14. Among leadership considerations are who contributes, the project size, resources, and use of conclusions.

15. Effective coordinators obtain cooperation, have (or arrange for) evaluation expertise, and understand the context.

16. Cooperation is especially important from participants, instructors, and funders.

17. Criteria to guide the evaluation project relate to cost-effectiveness, a focus on issues important to stakeholders, minimized disruption, valid information, and encouragement of use of conclusions.

18. Project success can be aided by planning and allocating time and resources.

19. Use of conclusions is related to stakeholder involvement, commitment to the evaluation, and attention to issues they value.

20. Evaluation plans and reports can be critiqued by participants, instructors, colleagues, and consultants.

21. Evaluation coordinators should address such issues as conflicting expectations, confidentiality, use of human subjects, and valid conclusions.

9

Program

The educational program itself is a major influence on participant achievement and a usual focus of program evaluation. The scope of program evaluation can be as specific as a single brief course or workshop or as broad as a provider agency's entire range of course offerings for a year. Program evaluation is done for reasons of periodic accreditation review, improvement of an individual course, modification of the mix of course offerings, and so on. This scope can include attention to the type and number of learners served, course objectives and content, method of teaching and learning, and supportive resources. The heart of a marketing audit includes such program characteristics. Additional reasons for evaluating a program are accreditation, accountability, increasing program quality, monitoring program operation, providing feedback to help the participant learn, reporting on learner progress, improving a course, recognizing and correcting a source of failure, making public the criteria for judging program quality, and enhancing critical and reflective thinking (Ramsden, 1992; Curry, Wergin, and Associates, 1993; Brinkerhoff, 1987; Caffarella, 1994; Rothwell and Cookson, 1997; Posavac and Carey, 1992). For programs that strive for broad societal impact beyond individual learner achievement and satisfaction, program evaluation can address the capability of achieving the intended outcome. As illustrated by accreditation review, program evaluation often takes the form of self-study by people closely associated with the program, or external review by an outside expert.

This chapter has three sections: concepts, planning, and coordination. It concludes with a listing of summary guidelines.

The great breadth, large scale, and infrequency of overall program evaluation create a special challenge. Before reading this chapter, consider the issues you are likely to confront in doing so. Reflect on examples and guidelines, and note implications that fit your context. Here are questions suggesting probable issues:

- What is likely to prompt a decision to conduct an overall program evaluation?

- What is distinctive about an overall program evaluation?

- How might you identify program difficulties or opportunities that warrant a program evaluation?

- How can you focus on the issues that are most important to stakeholders?

- When conducting a program evaluation, how can you include attention to participation, instruction, activities, influences, and benefits?

- What are some ways to understand the relationship between expectations and performance?

- Which types of data are especially important for program evaluation?

- What are major challenges to coordinating a program evaluation?

Concepts

The usual focus in evaluating adult and continuing education is on the educational program and its interaction among content, learners, and instructor. The program is the context for assessment of such aspects as needs, staff, materials, and outcomes. This section reviews concepts and procedures for evaluating the teaching-learning transaction, along with planning and implementing the program offerings. The section covers consideration of program characteristics, evaluation purpose and design, use of conclusions for decision making, and who contributes to conducting the evaluation.

Program characteristics related to evaluation are goals, scope, content, learners, instructors, methods, and resources for decision making. Regarding these characteristics, formative evaluation for program planning and improvement is especially pertinent (Deshler, 1984; Kiernan and Brown, 1992). Evaluation of an educational program for adults reflects efforts to ensure that the program characteristics fit together (Worthen and Sanders, 1987). For example, evaluation conclusions can be used to be sure that training and education for enterprise members is well designed and evaluated. This might entail selecting program objectives, content, instructors, and materials that fit enterprise and learner expectations, within resource limitations (Curry, Wergin, and Associates, 1993).

A preliminary review of program characteristics can indicate in a specific instance how much and what type of information to include in a program evaluation. Some characteristics (such as goals, instructors, and resources) may be given and subject to only minor adjustment, while others (learners, content, methods) may be central to an upcoming decision for which evaluation conclusions would be quite useful. For example, evaluation findings regarding learner background and preferred learning style combined with specific content and methods that are responsive to objectives and

learner expectations could be a high priority for a program evaluation (Ramsden, 1992).

It is especially important to assess certain characteristics of adult
learners in relation to a program on a technological topic (such as
computer software instruction). For instance, many adults prefer
concrete, hands-on experience to learn such skills (Ference and
Vockell, 1994). Ference and Vockell report that nine events of
instruction (as posited by Gagne, Briggs, and Wager, 1988) create
a useful framework for diagnosing instructional difficulties:

1. Gaining the learner's attention by using multiple senses, and
   encouraging early application

2. Encouraging learner motivation by assessing the benefits of
   learning and consequences of not learning, and by declaring
   clear objectives and an optimal challenge

3. Stimulating recall of prerequisite content by valuing the
   learner's previous experience and encouraging the learner to
   examine it to find solutions to new problems

4. Presenting content using a teaching style characterized by
   clarity and relevance, organization that does not overwhelm,
   and allowance for self-pacing

5. Guiding learning by asking questions and giving suggestions

6. Encouraging performance, if the participant has not achieved
   mastery, by promoting retention and transfer, and especially practice accompanied by frequent feedback and reinforcement

7. Providing feedback (which is particularly important for adult
   learners) from instructors, peers, and learners themselves
   through self-assessment (as errors occur, it may be useful to
   minimize concern and repeat a learning performance or feedback loop repeatedly until mastery is achieved)

8. Assessing performance more formally than with feedback (after a skill has been at least tentatively mastered, the ultimate test typically being in the adult life situation)

9. Promoting retention and transfer by encouraging the participant to use new skills outside the educational program

Evaluation conclusions related to each of these nine events can guide decision making by instructors and participants.

Such information about program and learner characteristics can guide specification of the issues on which to focus an evaluation project. Sometimes evaluation addresses program perspectives to review, such as design or implementation. Each of these requires attention to such program elements as the participant, instructor, topic, and context. The example given here indicates the type of evaluation question that might be included in such an assessment, along with ways to collect pertinent data (Knox and Associates, 1980.

There are various ways in which to assess how a subcategory of participants view program aspects. For instance, a brief questionnaire might request ratings on a four-point scale, from highly satisfied to not satisfied, using a list of statements on the learning atmosphere of the program. The statements might include type of participant, social interaction, level of communication, and commitment to learning. An anonymous questionnaire might also have items on age, gender, experience, and interests. By tabulating responses according to participant subcategory and for the total returns, the evaluation can indicate whether the program atmosphere is an issue for any or all participants. Similar impressions obtained from staff or dropouts can prompt further evaluation to decide what the problem is and what to do about it. Participants can complete a similar rating form at any point in a program, indicating their reactions and satisfaction, which instructors and coordinators can then consider as they make decisions related to program relevance and responsiveness. They can respond to a five-point scale (from strongly agree to strongly disagree) and note comments for statements regarding:

- Importance of content

- Flexibility of plans

- Applicability of content

- Instructor enthusiasm

- Content coverage

- Instructor clarity

- Organization of content

- Availability of materials

- Sequencing of topics

- Usefulness of materials

- Pacing of progress

- Provision of evaluative feedback

Green and Associates (1984) offer other criteria for evaluating the educational process. In a listing of more than one hundred criteria for planning and evaluating the quality of continuing education for the health professions, these pertained directly to program design and implementation (the number in parentheses after each criterion refers to the original quality element number):

Instructional Strategies

1. Sequence content to help learners meet learning objectives (84).

2. Ensure that instruction includes enough examples of concepts to be learned (85).

3. Allow active involvement, especially if changing attitudes is an objective (86).

4. Create opportunity for practice, especially if development or maintenance of skills is an objective (87).

5. Give participants feedback on their progress (88).

Implementing Programs

6. Implement educational activities as designed (89).

7. Ensure that instruction occurs in a manner, time, and place convenient to participants (90).

8. Help participants obtain resources to meet educational objectives (91).

Such criteria can guide evaluation of program planning and implementation, including the teaching-learning transaction and the stakeholders most directly involved in the process.

The concepts discussed here pertain to evaluation design and implementation related to the educational program. Because the program is connected with all other aspects (goals, context, participants, needs, staff, materials, outcomes), it is essential that evaluation of the program focus on the issues that are most important to stakeholders and have an effective and manageable design that will be implemented and will attract necessary resources and cooperation. This is most likely to occur if the scope is restricted to major variables related to the selected issues, the design is well fitted to the evaluation purpose and scope, there are sufficient resources, and requisite evaluation expertise is available.

An example from Brinkerhoff (1987) centers on monitoring program implementation. The extent and type of evaluation should reflect program characteristics and assessment purposes in various enterprise HRD programs. Monitoring a three-hour workshop for supervisors on a new performance appraisal system might include these evaluation activities:

- Comparison of actual participants with those intended

- Instructor notes during the session on suggestions for improvement next time

- Participant completion of a brief opinionnaire about the session

This minimal assessment seems warranted for a brief, well-developed, frequently repeated workshop because it encourages accountability and responsiveness, notes whether it was implemented as planned, and captures ideas for revision.

By contrast, when a new intensive three-day workshop for sales personnel on a new product line was carefully planned for delivery at branch locations throughout the world, an elaborate evaluation system was put in place:

- Records of preparation and attendees at each location

- Participant reaction forms completed at the end of each day

- A knowledge inventory completed at the end of the second day, with both a group summary and scores given participants as feedback to guide their study during the final day

- A feedback form of several pages, completed by the coordinator of each session or location, covering documentation and suggestions for revision

This elaborate assessment system focused on quality control of a major program at decentralized locations. Conclusions allowed central office educators to monitor implementation, give assistance where needed, and revise subsequent programs.

If the need for a program arises suddenly, the evaluation may be more extensive and detailed to identify discrepancies between plan and implementation of an experimental program. For instance, in response to an upsurge in accidents, an experimental safety education program was launched for supervisors. New safety procedures and materials to explain them were used and assessed in a number of ways:

- Participants completed a detailed end-of-session form, from which indications of quality were summarized for use in a postsession meeting of participants.

- Participants met after each session to discuss reactions to the program, which were noted for later analysis.

- Two observers attended sessions and noted departures from the plan and participant interaction and reaction.

Because of the experimental program, detailed information helped to identify discrepancies, which served as an opportunity for the educators to improve the program.

Sometimes a classification of evaluation purposes (plan, improve, justify), perspectives (design, implement), and elements (participant, instructor, topic, context) can help identify some basic considerations in deciding on the evaluation design. An equally important early consideration is encouraging involvement and support from the main stakeholders in evaluation planning, implementation, and above all using conclusions (Patton, 1997).

A valuable concept regarding evaluation design is discrepancy analysis (Knox and others, 1974). This typically entails comparing desired with actual characteristics. For example, many instructors and participants seek deep processing of ideas, leading to sound understanding, proficiency, and application. The opposite is superficial processing of ideas, misunderstanding, mere memorization, and inability to use content in practice. Evaluation is not only a form of assessment; it affords reinforcement and operationalizes expectations.

Assessment can clarify the relationship between participant progress and overall program evaluation. If assessment of participant progress and achievement focuses on basic ideas and procedures (such as recall of facts) and largely ignores high-level educational objectives (understanding relationships, analysis, evaluation), learners may be discouraged from seeking understanding and commitment. An evaluation design can specify such a discrepancy between desired and actual testing practices, which can lead to conclusions about how to modify program expectations, participant intentions, instructional methods, and assessment procedures (Ramsden, 1992). In some instances, evaluation of intended and actual outcomes is essential (Abrahamson, 1985). Green and Associates (1984) offer useful evaluation questions regarding program design and implementation.

An example from Ramsden (1992) illustrates assessment to clarify expectations and encourage autonomy. The conclusions can contribute to overall program evaluation. There are various ways to use assessment to deepen understanding, diagnose misunderstanding, and judge achievement. To take an example, an anatomy instructor used evaluation procedures that encourage participants to demonstrate their understanding and discourage a superficial approach. He does not use multiple-choice questions that might reinforce remembering unconnected facts. Instead, he uses brief essay questions and oral dialogue to encourage the learner to explain important principles and summarize descriptive information. In this way, the teaching function of assessment takes first priority. Conclusions can be used to decide on program objectives, instructor selection and development, and which educational methods to emphasize.

In another instance, an interior design instructor used personal consultation and other forms of assessment first to help participants identify important concepts and, by understanding the problems they were experiencing from their perspectives, do their best; and second, to suggest directions they had not thought of pursuing. Assessment procedures are asking participants to identify information necessary to translate design into reality, establish an accessible format, evaluate the information, and present a plan concisely and as a coherent argument. The instructor also evaluates participant ability to provide peers with high-quality and constructive feedback on a cooperative case study. In this instance, the instructor also employs a model answer to a sample question similar to one that the participants have already attempted, to encourage their self-assessment. Conclusions can also guide any decision about program content and methods.

An engineering instructor used varied assessment techniques designed to develop deep understanding of such matters as principles, increased professional responsibility, problem-solving ability, and constructive criticism of colleagues' work. Assessment techniques use a critique of the consultant report, instructor assessment of basic technical ideas, and a worked example on a difficult topic. Presentations based on these materials offered many opportunities for discussion and feedback. Assessment was both formative and summative, with increased weight toward the end of the course so participants can use early feedback to improve their performance. Conclusions can also enable the instructor or coordinator to improve program quality and impact.

Anyone who has (or should have) a stake in the educational program is the intended recipient of evaluation conclusions. This is especially so for program evaluation, where the stakeholders are participants, instructors, coordinators, policy makers, and funders. When planning and implementing program evaluation, consider the decisions that such stakeholders are likely to make; they should be informed by evaluation conclusions. An essential feature of many program decisions is that they reflect the relationship among characteristics of learners, instructors, goals, content, and methods. This was illustrated in all three examples given here. As a result, program evaluation should obtain information from and about such sources, as well as analyze relationships (not just tabulate frequencies). This can result in a somewhat complex evaluation design (Knox and Associates, 1980; Ramsden, 1992).

The Minnesota Extension Service decided to address quality improvement by use of an instrument called SERVQUAL, to assess quality through comparing expectations of participants and staff with perceptions of performance (Chen, Krueger, and Leske, 1993). The instrument includes twenty-two pairs of items with a seven-point rating scale regarding expectation of excellent service and perception of delivered service. Subsets of items pertained to tangibles (personnel, materials, facilities), reliability (accurate and dependable service), responsiveness (willingness to respond with prompt service), assurance (staff trust, knowledge, courtesy), and empathy (caring and individualized attention). The evaluation focused on two gaps: between the participant's expectations and staff perception of the participant's expectations; and between the participant's expectations and the perception of received service. The three evaluation objectives were to modify and validate the SERVQUAL instrument and to identify discrepancies first between participant expectations and staff perceptions of those expectations and second between participant expectations and perceptions of their received service.

The evaluation procedures were sampling, instrumentation, administration, and analysis. Questionnaires were sent to extension staff, and to participants on county extension mailing lists, by randomly selecting two participants from any county in each of the five extension districts. The SERVQUAL instrument was revised and validated using two panels of practitioners and of scholars; it was pilot-tested with one hundred participants in a county not included in the evaluation. The response rate was 66 percent; responses and written comments were used to clarify language in the final draft. Personalized cover letters from county extension directors accompanied questionnaires, and there was a two-week follow-up of nonrespondents. A test-retest procedure was used with the first one hundred respondents (staff and participants) to test consistency of responses. The return rate was 77 percent; Spearman Brown coefficient was .87.

Return rates were 92 percent of 261 county educators, 85 percent of 19 administrators, 86 percent of university department heads, and 66 percent of 500 participants. The modified instrument was well received in instrument development and field testing, indicating acceptable face validity. Although there were statistically significant discrepancies between staff perception and participant expectation of service quality on the one hand and the participant's actual expectation of service on the other, the differences were small and not of practical significance. The participants' expectation of excellent service was higher than their perception of received service for almost all questions, but the differences for only three items were of practical significance (responding quickly to community crisis, providing current and accurate research-based information, and informing participants about service).

A concept related to stakeholder expectation is the continuum of evaluation, which entails data collection at various program stages, analysis of time series data, and use of conclusions to guide program decision making (Curry, Wergin, and Associates, 1993). The interactive and ongoing nature of effective program evaluation suggests building ongoing assessment into everyday teaching and learning activities, as well as program planning. The likelihood of this is increased if the instructor and coordinator plan for such evaluation, cooperate with other stakeholders, and share conclusions with them (Angelo and Cross, 1993).

An instructor might decide to assess participants' perception of how small-group discussion influenced their writing (Angelo and Cross, 1993). To help inexperienced writers view their writing from the reader's viewpoint, the instructor can ask small groups to read and critique each other's drafts. At the end of a half-hour critique session, a workgroup evaluation form is distributed and in five minutes they answer two questions, using full sentences and giving specific examples:

1. What specific comments and suggestions did your group members offer to help you improve your draft?

2. What specific comments and suggestions did you offer other group members to help them improve their drafts?

Project assessment helps the instructor see the activity through the participant's eyes, thus gaining feedback on the learning value for the participant (Angelo and Cross, 1993). This kind of assessment is especially valuable when the adult learner brings experience with the content to the assessment. The procedure involves selecting a project that is repeated or ongoing, writing two or three structural and open-ended questions regarding the value of the project to the participant's learning, preparing a simple assessment form, reviewing the completed form for themes, and selecting a few exemplary comments for the individual to be shared with participants in the summary. Doing this assessment may motivate some participants to complete a project.

Although anyone with evaluation expertise and assistance can conduct a program evaluation, the complex relationships make a team effort likely; it is to be coordinated by someone who understands and can deal with the various components such as learners, instructor, content, and method. For example, coordination of program evaluation for accreditation purposes may include self-study (sometimes with a decentralized team using a common framework) in preparation for external review by a site visitation team. On a smaller scale appropriate to a single course or workshop, a coordinator or instructor coordinates the program evaluation, which may comprise self-assessment by participants and instructor, peer review (focused on content, methods, and materials), and discussion among stakeholders of preliminary conclusions so as to enrich the evaluation report and encourage use of conclusions.

Planning and Implementation

Evaluating an adult and continuing education program entails a variety of procedures to collect and analyze data regarding numerous aspects of the program: content, learners, methods, collaboration, and resources (including data). Guidelines have been suggested to ensure that these aspects are considered during planning, data collection, analysis, and use of conclusions (Angelo and Cross, 1993; Ramsden, 1992).

Content

In most adult educational programs, there is an effort to specify objectives and content in relation to both provider and instructor expectations and the participant's interest in and capability of achieving the objectives. Sometimes, the program goals are set early and participants are attracted who are sure to have the interest and ability required for achievement. This is especially so when the program purpose is to prepare specialists and when acquisition of content is a major aim. In such a case, specifying program objectives and content is an early evaluation decision (Worthen and Sanders, 1987; Miller and McGuire, 1961). Sometimes, though, the starting point is the participants themselves (as in organization development for quality improvement, or community development for community problem solving). In this instance, specifying educational program objectives and content occurs later in the process as participants recognize what they want to learn in order to solve a problem or pursue an opportunity.

Specifying program objectives and content in relation to participant interest and ability helps select an evaluation goal that fits (Angelo and Cross, 1993). For example, regarding the teaching-learning transaction, if the program goal is to emphasize understanding and application (and to deemphasize memorization and imitation), this should be stated and reflected in evaluation procedures that reinforce and reward understanding and application (Ramsden, 1992). Regarding broader program assessment, if the concern is greater responsiveness of educational program offerings to rapid developments in the field, the program evaluation might combine a review of current offerings with environmental scanning to identify emerging threats and opportunities.

Participant Characteristics

A second program aspect to consider in planning and implementing evaluation is participant characteristics and their relation to the program plan. This means the number and location of the learners to be served, as well as characteristics such as age, educational level, occupational specialization, leisure interests, and health. In addition to objectives and content, a program plan can reflect program format (individual coaching or distance education using instructional technology, temporary group interaction in a course or workshop, organization development, community development). Program evaluation procedures and use of findings can focus on how to achieve a desirable match between program and participant. For this purpose, information is collected from participants, the instructor, and the coordinator regarding their views of current and desirable program aspects. The information could include program objectives and content, participant interests and abilities, instructor background and methods, facilities and equipment, and assessment procedures.

The formative evaluation purpose and multiple role perspectives for program evaluation make discrepancy analysis a useful assessment approach (Knox and others, 1974). This typically entails separate data collection instruments for each stakeholder role while combining the data for analysis purposes. Most items obtain information about intended practice (desired, should) and current practice (actual, is), so that discrepancies can be recognized. For the many program characteristics assessed, information can be collected from various stakeholders (participants, instructor, observers, coordinator, director, and program records).

For instance, a participant questionnaire might include items on reason for attending, actual benefits, supportive climate, and level of difficulty. Instructor questionnaire items might ask about desired and actual features regarding responsibility for assessment and orientation of participants, topic emphasis, method of instruction, and program goals. An observer's rating form on course interaction might rate the teacher's responsiveness, formality, and encouragement; student attentiveness and active participation; and facilities and equipment. The program coordinator and director might respond to questions similar to those for the instructor, including how participant achievement is and should be evaluated. A program statistics form can be used to rate information from program records, such as number and characteristics of participants, instructor, facilities, courses, and finances. Such items yield quantitative and qualitative data. All stakeholders are asked for their suggestions for improvement. Displaying their responses in a matrix, for comparison related to roles, makes it easy to identify shared views and difference of opinion. Each of these conclusions might be useful for strengthening the program. Discrepancies readily lead to recommendations for improvement.

Methods and Activities

The foregoing example also applies to the third program aspect, the methods and activities that constitute the teaching-learning transaction. This is the heart of most programs, toward which program development and resource allocation decisions are aimed. Assessment should also focus first on learning, and second on encouraging participant effort and persistence. Other assessment functions can be supplementary and compatible, including effectiveness of materials and trends in persistence, achievement, and application.

Assessment criteria related to education for reflective thinking can vary greatly with the type of problem and content (Curry, Wergin, and Associates, 1993). To take an example, consider the desire to improve decision making related to reduction of accidents on icy bridges. Evaluation of improved reflective thinking might focus on assessing the results of efforts, in which evaluation of a solution is related to gains that justify the costs (so that when deciding on alternative ways to travel to an appointment when time is short, one may employ the evaluation criterion of arriving on time).

Another instance of reflective thinking is an architectural school design problem of fitting a school to an unusually contoured site, the criterion being to fit a slope to the school or to fit rooms into the slope. In a third instance, the problem is a phone call from a patient about sunburn and medication; the criterion may be patient feedback after advice and medication being given. As indicated in these examples, evaluation can encompass assessing the process of reflective thinking along with the results.

The ongoing formative evaluation emphasis on diagnosis, planning, and improvement can be preserved, while giving some attention to summative evaluation related to application and performance (Ramsden, 1992). Program evaluation can contribute to assessment of teaching and learning activities, progress toward achievement of program objectives, and feedback for program improvement (Knox, 1986). Evaluation conclusions can also contribute to making decisions regarding program goals, materials, facilities, resources, participant's prior experience and ability, instructional expertise, desirable participant involvement and self-direction, and the relationship between teaching and learning methods (Rothwell and Cookson, 1997).

The process of program planning and implementation can be thought of as a series of decisions over time related to components, each of which is evaluated. One model has been labeled ADDIE, as an acronym to reflect five components: analysis, design, development, implementation, and evaluation (Rothwell and Cookson, 1997). To focus on the first component (analysis), information about needs and context serves as input to the analysis, with performance requirements and program content as outcomes. Related evaluation questions pertain to data accuracy and completeness for the purpose, some data interpretation, feasibility of achieving performance requirements through education, and completeness of proposed course content.

In the design component, attention is given to course content, instructional methods, materials, and assessment criteria. Similar evaluation questions pertain to instructional objectives for performance requirements, assessment of objectives, how materials contribute to achievement of objectives, and instructional methods.

For the development component, specifications regarding instructional methods, materials, and assessment become input; outcomes are the actual methods, materials, and assessments. Related evaluation questions pertain to effective materials and assessment instruments.

For the implementation component, inputs pertain to instructor, course components, and facilities. The main outcome is the actual program that occurs.

Related evaluation questions pertain to instructor capability, satisfactory facilities, participant content, mastery and application, and suggested program improvement.

Setting

A fourth program aspect is the setting in which the program takes place, in particular any collaborative relationships. Sometimes one or a few learners engage in a small, independent educational activity that one person facilitates. In such an instance, evaluation planning and implementation can be similarly small, informal, and integral to the teaching-learning transaction. However, as the scale and form of cooperation increase, so does the complexity of the evaluation if it is to address program relationships fundamental to quality and success. Complexity covers diverse participants, multiple sites, various methods and materials, teams of instructional staff, interconnection with a large parent organization, and collaborative relationships with cosponsors and funders (Votruba, 1981). Most educational programs lie between these two extremes. The main suggestion for evaluation planning is to consider the specific setting and reflect the main features in the evaluation plan.

For example, during the 1990s an eastern state department of continuing education developed an effective process for peer review of local, publicly funded educational programs for adults.

They prepared an excellent guide for conducting such program peer reviews, which reflected their sound rationale and extensive experience. The rationale reflected use of program standards for quality improvement to benefit participants. The peer review process was focused on review team site visits of about three days' duration, which include orientation of the team, observation of program activities and especially teaching and learning activities, comparison of their conclusions with a self-study report prepared beforehand by the local staff, and preparing a report with recommendations.

The peer review guide included sections on:

• The role of the state department of continuing education (select the review team leader and members, provide review materials and guidelines, orient team members, advise during the site visit, and receive and disseminate reports)
• The role of the review team leader (make all arrangements; work with local staff and review team; coordinate a draft report; schedule team activity to include observation, discussion, and input to report; make an oral report to local staff to reflect contents of written report; arrange for all reporting and reimbursements)
• Contents of the review team report (self-study report, review team report, list of team members, list of local people contacted, schedule of activities, and a narrative section with description and recommendations)
• The role of the review team members
• Local program staff roles related to the site visit
• Suggested review team activities (observation, interviews in person and by phone, documentation, visits to sites)
• Edit interview procedures
• Form for assessment related to program standards, which includes statement of standards, rating of how well the program meets standards, space for comments and for methods of evaluation (sections for standards are learner progress, program development, instruction, staff development, recruitment, retention, support services, administration, facilities)

Following a similar review process for many years, local programs were reviewed on a four-year cycle, which allowed comparison across programs regarding the evaluation process and across four-year reviews for each local program regarding recommendations and improvements. Early reports commented on lack of consistency in site visits, which was addressed by using the peer review guide. In the annual reports, for each category of standards there was a brief summary reflecting comparison between self-study and review team reports as well as interpretation that presented conclusions (relative ratings), commendations, and recommendations.

The annual reports cautioned that although the review reports encouraged exchange of ideas during the program, comparison across programs was not warranted owing to differences in review teams and local context. Some annual reports noted striking improvements from year to year, which could be documented because of the time series data using similar review procedures. Commendations and recommendations each contained specific narrative examples reflecting process and outcomes. Each year, the review process itself was also evaluated; this meta-evaluation contributed to ongoing improvement in the review process. The review reports across the categories of program standards allowed analysis of program functioning and potential improvement that took into account multiple influences (outcomes, participants, instructor, content, coordinator, materials, and facilities).

In another example, a peer review process included more than a dozen educational programs for inmates, related to the department of corrections. The peer review findings were quite similar to the conclusions that corrections staff had already reached, so they afforded confirmation. The ongoing peer review process can be cumulative. An earlier report noted major improvements that had occurred in recent years, and a more recent report noted policy and funding changes that adversely affected correctional education programs. As a result, improvements included increased cooperation with outside educational programs for adults, procedures for recognizing learner progress, and ways to have records of an inmate's educational achievement move from one facility to another. Correctional education staff continued to express confidence in inmates' ability to learn and benefit from educational programs. The peer review process recommended (and was itself a way of) strengthening staff development for correctional educators.

Resources and Data

The fifth program aspect pertains to resources and attention to data. In addition to funding, there are various resources on which educational programs depend (volunteer effort, use of facilities, and mailing lists among them). Program evaluation can assess the extent and type of resources that are used and that are desirable, and connection to program quality and effectiveness. Evaluation can also enable various stakeholders to share their views regarding current and desired resources.

Data collection decisions deal with the type of information to collect regarding the program (such as the foregoing five aspects) and the procedures for doing so. Many procedures are available for data collection from participants, instructor, coordinator, and other stakeholders: questionnaires, tests, performance reviews, interviews, observations, external reviewers, self-assessments, and simulations (Caffarella, 1994; Curry, Wergin, and Associates, 1993; Ramsden, 1992; Worthen and Sanders, 1987). Program evaluation should not neglect assessment of participant learning (Kirkpatrick, 1994). In addition to evaluating achievement through a test or simulation, a participant questionnaire can obtain much information about content, process, instruction, arrangements, and the overall program (Caffarella, 1994). The conclusions can reflect participant perspectives on many program aspects.

For example, sometimes detailed information from participants is helpful. This is especially so if there are indications that a program could be improved but it is unclear how participants in various categories view it. An anonymous questionnaire can present items that allow cross-tabulation of responses by category of participant, such as extent of prior experience, level of educational preparation, preferred learning style, role, or level of financial assistance. Statements grouped by broad features of a program can be rated on a scale of desirability followed by a space for comments and suggestions (Caffarella, 1994). Some representative statements:

- Session content and process (clear and realistic objectives, learn what is expected, relevant content, appropriate presentation of content, adequate time for each topic, instructional methods, opportunities for active participation, relevant content, effective instructional materials, program organization)
- Instructor performance (preparation, enthusiasm, knowledge, supportiveness, assistance, response to diversity, interest, timing of coverage)
- Logistical arrangements (prior information, registration, time schedule, facilities, meals, housing)
- Overall program (applicability, challenge, quality, strengths, improvement, other comments)

When selecting data collection procedures, consider some questions that increase the likelihood of success (Angelo and Cross, 1993). As you choose an assessment technique, consider whether it fits the assessment goal and the educational activity, and whether it is reasonably simple and likely to contribute to learning on the part of one or more stakeholders. In applying an assessment technique, consider trying it beforehand, explaining the purpose and process to respondents, and estimating whether there is sufficient time.

The specific data analysis and interpretation procedures that should be used for a program evaluation project depend on the purposes of the project, the type of data collected, the intended recipient(s) of the evaluation report, and desirable form of the report. The complexity of relationships among selected program aspects should be reflected in the complexity of relationships included in the evaluation. For example, the main issue for an evaluation might

be impact (on participant satisfaction, persistence, and achievement) from a change of instructional methods to encourage more
active learning. In this instance, data analysis might compare these
relationships for some participants using the less active methods
with comparable participants using more active methods. A more
complex multivariate analysis might be warranted if evaluation of
active learning also includes instructor characteristics and application of new learning by participants. A simpler analysis might occur
if an instructor just wants peer review of current instructional methods and suggestions for improvement.

As you plan an evaluation project, it is wise to consider some
feasibility questions regarding data analysis (Angelo and Cross,
1993). Is there a specific plan for data analysis? Is the amount and
type of data about right for the intended analysis? Is the analysis
plan relatively simple? Is sufficient expertise available to carry it out?
Is enough time allowed for the analysis? The most cost-effective
evaluation projects tend to be modest in scale and viewed as one of
a series of efforts to understand and improve a program.

An example from Kiernan and Brown (1992) highlights some
benefits of formative program evaluation. The purpose of this formative evaluation was, by identifying barriers, to increase the capacity of an educational program to enable participants and staff to
evaluate impact. The program consisted of four home study lessons
on osteoporosis risk reduction for working women, provided at
worksites and childcare sites. Formative evaluation findings were
used to modify the program (sites, marketing, program methods, and
evaluation instruments). The staff concluded that formative evaluation was desirable for program implementation. Here are the evaluation objectives (for each, I include the evaluation designs and
data collection methods that were used):

• To decide on sites for reaching working women, ages twenty-
one to forty-five, who were raising children (comparison group
design and data collection methods, among them demographic

information from enrollment forms and feedback from participants and onsite program managers)

• To assess the appeal of written materials and of two methods of learning—one just reading the materials and the other a brief motivational meeting (comparison group design of the two methods, using response sheets for each lesson for participants to record their reactions, four focus groups with a sample of participants following the series of lessons, and a meeting with the group of program managers who presented the lessons)

• To assess program impact on participants (participants completed a pretest and a posttest of knowledge, attitudes, and behavior changes)

• To refine evaluation procedures (analyzed demographic variables, completion rates, errors in pretest and posttest scores, and comments from focus groups)

The purpose of data analysis is to produce conclusions and recommendations based on both data analysis and interpretation, which usually includes value judgment. Most evaluations combine quantitative data (numerical) and qualitative data (natural language), each of which has its own analysis procedures. The evaluation goals and criteria should guide the data collection, analysis, and interpretation. Worthen and Sanders (1987) give an overview of data analysis and interpretation, including suggested readings for more detailed guidelines (regarding quantitative data analysis, see Gall, Borg, and Gall, 1996; Hopkins, Glass, and Hopkins, 1987; and Krathwohl, 1993; on qualitative data analysis, see Miles and Huberman, 1984; Strauss and Corbin, 1990; Bogden and Biklen, 1992; and Guba and Lincoln, 1981).

When planning the combination of data to collect and analyze, consider the evaluation issues, questions, and goals. This understanding can guide selection of methods of data analysis and interpretation likely to be most understandable for the people who receive the evaluation report.

Typical quantitative data analysis procedures are a frequency distribution to discover variation among responses, cross-tabulation to discover associations between two variables displayed in a matrix, test of significance to indicate the probability that an association between two or more variables will occur by chance, and multivariable analysis to reflect more complex relationships. Quantitative data is usually collected with a scale, test, or instrument that results in numerical scores. An early stage of analysis attends to the reliability of the instrument (consistency or stability of scores) and its validity (the extent to which it measures what it purports to measure). Quantitative analysis usually entails data reduction to obtain valid scores or indicators, and identification of patterns of relationships in the data that fit explanations and interpretations. Sound sampling allows generalization to a larger population from which a representative sample was selected.

Typical qualitative data analysis procedures tend to occur at stages during data collection. Qualitative data can be from a questionnaire, interview, observation, or self-report and narrative. Analytic induction is a search for patterns in the qualitative data that results in explanatory categories and patterns. This typically begins with forming impressions from the initial detailed data, identifying and recording themes, using working hypotheses and testing them with subsequent data, verifying them by subject of the evaluation, and triangulating (cross-validating from multiple sources). Tentative conclusions should then be related to what is known about the object of the evaluation.

Encouraging use of evaluation conclusions and recommendations should be a concern throughout planning and implementing an evaluation (Patton, 1997). However, it becomes even more central during the interpretation and dissemination stages. Successful utilization can be enhanced by early consideration of such questions as, Who are the main recipients of the evaluation report? What forms of reporting are likely to be effective with them? Are the recommendations feasible regarding timing and extent of change entailed? Will the proposed changes fit other important plans and activities (Angelo and Cross, 1993)? Such considerations are especially important for a complex program evaluation that can affect multiple stakeholders who are likely to require differing involvement in the evaluation process and forms of reporting.

The next example illustrates formative evaluation to address multiple issues and recipients (Walsh and Craft, 1990). Beginning in 1987–88, the Veterans Administration (VA) Regional Medical Education Centers (RMEC) prepared people at workshops as AIDS/HIV trainers to conduct train-the-trainer programs at VA facilities throughout the country. A subsequent program evaluation was based on separate questionnaires sent to every director and liaison and to RMEC trained trainers. The purpose of the evaluation report was to understand program functioning and to draw conclusions relating to these issues:

- Training implementation. Much staff training was taking place, and the trainers were providing much of it. Lack of time was the biggest obstacle to implementation. Creative methods should be explored to allow time for such training.

- Participation. Both directors and trainers cited physicians as the staff category most underrepresented in training.

- Goal achievement. Directors reported that trainers were mostly or completely responsible for such training, that the program was mostly finished or was completing its goals, and the most important contribution was reducing staff anxiety from misinformation and unreasonable fears.

- Additional trainers. VA facilities with trainers do not need more of them, and those without such trainers want some; but other RMEC trained AIDS/HIV educational resources may be needed for related purposes.

Various resources support evaluation. Money and in-kind contributions are self-evident. Less evident are materials and experts on the process of data collection and analysis. Such resources are also valuable for dissemination and utilization. If the people who are conducting an evaluation do not have such expertise, an important part of evaluation planning is to obtain them. In the middle portion of Chapter Four, I review additional examples of data collection and analysis.

Coordination

Coordinating more complex program evaluations can be a management challenge. Published program evaluation standards present many useful guidelines (Sanders, 1994). However, the main influence on the success of a longer evaluation project is interpersonal relations (Patton, 1997). This section explores three vital topics: self-study, external review, and meta-evaluation.

In most evaluations focused on an educational program, there are a few stakeholders who are central to teaching and learning and whose involvement in the evaluation process is important for validity and utilization of conclusions. A usual way to win and maintain their cooperation is through self-study. This is a regular part of an accreditation review that occurs every five or ten years for educational institutions. Someone typically coordinates a self-study during the several years of planning, data collection, analysis, and reporting. National or regional guidelines allow adaptation to local circumstances. During planning, stakeholders review the general plan, obtain clarification, and suggest modifications (suggesting distinctive questions and issues to be added). Equally important is their commitment to the process. For a larger self-study, sampling of program areas, courses, instructors, and participants can serve the evaluation purposes and reduce the financial and time demands. Coordination at this planning stage entails arranging for dissemination of background materials, explaining and planning meetings, making suggestions, and continuing cooperation.

At the data collection and analysis stages, coordination includes monitoring and assistance for a largely decentralized process. Backup arrangements are useful if data collection does not occur as planned; they might include replacement respondents and multiple data sources. A pilot study and periodic progress reports are well worth the effort, as are ongoing incentives and recognition for cooperation. The most valuable incentive is receipt of authentic findings having direct implications for program planning and improvement. This becomes even more valuable toward the end of the self-study, when interest and commitment can lag. Coordination of a self-study also includes validating reports and disseminating them to stakeholders and external reviewers.

Sometimes another person coordinates an external review; this requires some liaison to ensure compatibility. When an accreditation agency carries out oversight, the guidelines can contribute to such cooperation. Coordination of the external review can be greatly aided by a sound self-study or similar report on program characteristics (inputs, process, and outcomes) that include stakeholder perspectives. External review coordination also includes selection, orientation, and supervision of mutually satisfactory members of an external review team, who read the self-study reports and external review guidelines, spend time onsite to understand the program and interpret the self-study reports, and prepare their report and recommendations. There are many opportunities for misunderstanding; it can be minimized by effective coordination. The examples given here are of strategies for coordinating program evaluation of varying complexity.

When adult and continuing education practitioners have a clear need to know how their program is progressing, they sometimes shift from ubiquitous informal means of doing so to a more formal and routine evaluation system to monitor their program. Formal monitoring is a form of evaluation aimed at auditing program coverage and implementation, and as a precondition to assessing effectiveness. Here are three instances of monitoring that were grounded in the realities of the situation.

Monitoring was used to evaluate early implementation of lay health advocates, trained in medical school, in a rural area with scarce local health care providers. Because there were no predetermined standards for the health education and referrals that the health advocates were to provide, monitoring was designed to discover how this experimental program was functioning. It was assumed that local residents would discuss their health-related concerns with a health advocate. The advocate would offer accurate and appropriate health information, including suggested referrals. The advice and referrals would then be recorded on contact records reviewed quarterly by medical staff, who would note any problems on the contact record forms. Project staff held continuous training for the health advocates regarding record keeping, thus monitoring their performance and giving attention to the weekly contact records and quarterly analyses. One problem related to evaluation and monitoring was the accuracy of the contact records.

A second example entailed an ongoing two-year certificate program for experienced state government supervisors (called a "public management institute"). Monitoring was instituted to enable the director to keep track of program functions. The director recognized the importance of knowing how well the institute was functioning so that adjustments could be made if needed to help ensure continued financial support for the institute from state agencies that send supervisors to attend. The monitoring included information about the representativeness of participants, the elective topics they chose, participant satisfaction, and the completion rate. Most of the data were obtained from standard operating procedures such as application and enrollment forms and course evaluation. Informal interviews were also used. A separate data processing system enabled the director to obtain early warning of potential problems, to allow adjustment so as to avoid criticism and maintain the support of state agencies whose representatives were on the institute's advisory committee.

In a sunbelt state in which turf grass for golf courses and residents was a major economic consideration, a county cooperative extension adviser having this specialty developed a monitoring system that served several purposes. It obtained information from the professional turf managers and homeowners who participated in the turf grass education program regarding the extent to which they were following recommendations. Information was also available from copies of soil test reports (in particular level of potassium), which were sent routinely. A check on such practices came from gardening stores and fertilizer dealers regarding sale of fertilizers with a high level of potassium. Additional monitoring information came from phone inquiries to the extension regarding pertinent problems and phone interviews, conducted by the adviser and members of a turf grass committee, with a sample of people who had had soil tested recently. The evaluation report also mentioned land development trends based on information from real estate brokers, which indicated future need for such a program. In this instance, most of the monitoring information was from outside the extension and included program impact and environmental influences.

Considerations related to use of monitoring systems are adaptability, burden, and resources. The utility of monitoring is related to routine data collection and use of conclusions. The process can be of special benefit to practitioners who learn about program functioning.

Meta-evaluation is assessment of the evaluation process and product (Knox and Associates, 1980; Sanders, 1994). For a large evaluation project, there are additional useful guidelines:

- Conduct meta-evaluation in parallel with a large program evaluation

- Allocate sufficient resources for the purposes

- Assign responsibility for documenting the evaluation process and products throughout

- Select a respected person or team to conduct the meta-evaluation

- Have guidelines for the meta-evaluation, including responsibilities, reporting, and agreement

- Include all stages of data collection and analyses in the critique

The basic ideas regarding self-study, external review, and meta-evaluation apply to most small-scale program evaluations. For example, a knowledgeable program coordinator helping one instructor plan and conduct an evaluation of a course or workshop could in a few hours extend sufficient assistance with the basics:

- Enumerating a few guidelines and excerpts related to the proposed focus of a program evaluation

- Identifying people and materials that might be useful at various stages of evaluation planning and implementation

- Sharing an example of a small self-study for a comparable situation

- Suggesting arrangements for plan review, which might include observation and informal interview

- Discussing plans and progress as the evaluation proceeds

- Responding to requests for suggestions regarding modification of the process for future evaluation

In the course of interaction between the coordinator and instructor, it may be useful to discuss interpretation of the data analysis (Worthen and Sanders, 1987). Here are possible questions:

- Were the evaluation objectives achieved?

- Did any ethical issues occur?

- How valuable were the conclusions?

- Did any stakeholders review the conclusions and offer their comments?

- How did the findings compare with those from similar evaluations?

Effective management of program evaluation reflects understanding of basic concepts regarding program goals, evaluation purpose and design, who conducts the evaluation, and connecting conclusions with program decision making. It also addresses the program aspects on which the evaluation focuses. Such potential aspects for inclusion are objectives, learners, instruction, setting, and resources. Data collection, analyses, and reporting of conclusions should address the selected aspects, but on a manageable scale. Self-study can contribute to stakeholder understanding and commitment, in addition to validity of conclusions, especially when combined with external review. Meta-evaluation can help a coordinator monitor and improve the evaluation process and product, and learn from the process.

As you reflect on this overview of comprehensive program evaluation, consider these questions:

- What is the desirable scope and timing for future comprehensive program evaluation?

- Which program aspects should be emphasized in such an evaluation?

- Which resources are likely to support the next program evaluation?

- What are desirable arrangements for leadership and coordination of the program evaluation?

Summary Guidelines

This checklist reviews the basic guidelines for planning and conducting evaluations of the educational program. The guidelines can help you enhance your rationale and procedures as you plan or strengthen your evaluation of the overall program.

Concepts

1. Evaluation conclusions can be used to improve the fit among such program characteristics as goals, scope, content, learners, instructor, method, and resources.

2. A preliminary review of such characteristics can guide specification of the issues on which to focus the evaluation project.

3. When evaluating a program, consider goals, accreditation, quality, feedback to participants, learner achievement, and teaching and course improvement.

4. Evaluation design should reflect program issues, evaluation purpose, available expertise, discrepancy analysis, and encouragement of stakeholder involvement.

5. Involving stakeholders (participants, instructor, coordinator, policy makers, funders) in program evaluation can contribute to useful viewpoints on program relationships and encourage use of conclusions.

6. Ongoing program evaluation can guide decision making on the part of the main stakeholders.

7. Coordination of internal and external evaluation is especially important for a complex project.

Planning and Implementation

8. Specification of program objectives is important for evaluation purposes; it may occur early for a program that attracts participants and late for a program in which participants help decide on objectives and content relevant to inquiry or problem solving.

9. A second program aspect to evaluate is participant characteristics in relation to the program plan, to help ensure a good fit.

10. A third program aspect to evaluate is the teaching-learning transaction.

11. A fourth program aspect to evaluate is the setting, especially collaboration.

12. A fifth program aspect to evaluate is the connection between resources (funding, unpaid contributions) and program quality and effectiveness.

13. Program evaluation data can be collected from a number of sources and stakeholders, by use of various procedures (a questionnaire, test, review, interview, observation, focus group, case study, program records, external review, self-assessment, simulation).

14. Assessment of participant learning can include relations among achievement, content, process, instruction, arrangements, and the overall program.

15. Selection of an assessment technique should consider evaluation goal, educational activity, simplicity, and value to stakeholders.

16. Selection of data analysis and interpretation procedures should consider evaluation goal, data types, and the reporting form appropriate for recipients.

17. Feasibility concerns for program evaluation are planning, scale, simplicity, expertise, and timing.

18. Most program evaluations employ quantitative and qualitative data; there are detailed references on specific procedures that can be consulted, along with evaluation goals and criteria.

19. Specific evaluation project issues can guide selection of data analysis procedures likely to be most understandable to the people who receive the evaluation report.

20. Quantitative data analysis reflects sampling, valid instruments, tabulations, data reduction, associations, multivariate analysis, and significance.

21. Qualitative data analysis entails analytic induction from natural language narrative to identify themes; suggest explanations; and test them with additional information, cross-validation, and verification by subjects.

22. Throughout a complex program evaluation in particular, utilization can be encouraged by attention to appropriate reporting methods for the recipients, and feasible recommendations that fit other plans and activities.

Coordination

23. Interpersonal relations can be the main influence on a successful program evaluation.

24. Someone should coordinate a self-study (as for accreditation) that contributes to cooperation from stakeholders closest to the teaching-learning transactions.

25. During self-study planning, coordination can include obtaining stakeholder understanding, suggestions, and commitment.

26. During self-study data collection and analysis, coordination can involve monitoring, assisting, pilot testing, encouraging, validating, and disseminating.

27. Coordination of external reviews of a program can entail liaison with a self-study, selection of external reviewers, and monitoring of reviews and reporting.

28. Guidelines for meta-evaluation of the program evaluation process and products pertain to current conduct, sufficient resources, documentation responsibility, expertise, guidelines, and critique of data collection and analysis.

29. Even a small-scale program evaluation can be assisted by making guidelines available, identifying people, sharing examples, suggesting peer review, discussing progress, and responding to requests.

30. Discussion of interpretation of the data analysis can encompass questions about achievement of evaluation objectives, ethical issues, value of conclusions, stakeholder review, and comparison with similar evaluation reports.

10

Materials

Educational materials sometimes receive separate and detailed evaluation from the rest of an educational program. Some of this appraisal of materials is summarized and reported by those who produce them, as with a teacher's guide. Sometimes the evaluation is external, as with a book review. In addition, an instructor can readily obtain feedback from learners regarding satisfaction and achievement so as to guide selection of materials for the specific situation.

Instructional technology for distance education and classroom use may receive special evaluation attention for several reasons. One is that the investment of time and money may be great enough to warrant such evaluation. Computers and electronic media facilitate collecting, storing, and summarizing information useful for evaluation purposes.

Among the stakeholders who can contribute to materials evaluation are learners, the instructor, the materials developer, and an external reviewer. Because most adult and continuing education materials can be used in many settings, it seems desirable to widely disseminate sound evaluation of such materials to guide choices. Materials evaluation findings can also be used to guide development and refinement of educational materials as well as to demonstrate their effectiveness and benefits. (*Consumer Reports* is a good example of such dissemination regarding commercial products.) Criteria for evaluation of educational materials address topics such as content, ease of use, intended audience, recommended procedures, and evidence of effectiveness.

The chapter has three sections, on concepts, planning, and coordination. Each section includes an overview of concepts and procedures, references to specialized reading on the topic, and brief examples showing how to assess print and electronic educational materials. Use of educational materials, especially for distance education, entails teamwork among specialists on content, technology, and instructional design. For each type of media and material, typical evaluation procedures feature checklists and rubrics that indicate standards and criteria for judging quality. Therefore, the first third and last third of this chapter make use of checklists. The chapter concludes with a listing of summary guidelines.

Evaluation of materials has some distinctive features that contribute to the issues and decisions likely to be important. As you read this chapter, consider implications for your evaluation activity. Issues to consider are suggested by these questions:

- What is the main reason or purpose for a specific instance of materials assessment?

- How should the evaluation be relevant to distinctive characteristics of specific materials (print, electronic, simulation)?

- Which stakeholders should help critique materials, and how: using learner reactions, peer review, external reviewers?

- What criteria and standards should be used to evaluate materials?

- How can ongoing evaluation funding contribute to strengthening materials at various stages (selection, development, revision, sequencing)?

- What resources are likely to be necessary and available in evaluating materials?

Concepts

Evaluation of educational materials can benefit from general application of assessment concepts and procedures. However, there are some concepts that are especially pertinent for evaluation related to a specific assessment regarding type of material and stage of development. These pertinent concepts are grouped into sections on purpose, decisions, characteristics, guidelines, and effectiveness. Assessment of materials typically uses checklists, which are characteristic of this chapter.

Evaluation Purpose

Each instance of materials assessment is selective regarding the type of decision to be made on the basis of evaluation, the characteristics of the materials to be evaluated, the guidelines to be applied, and the use of conclusions to increase the effectiveness of the materials. This selective focus for a specific instance of materials assessment is essential because the range of potential aspects for evaluation is enormous. Clarifying the main purpose of an evaluation at the planning stage of an assessment can help ensure that the time and money invested in doing so is justified by the benefits reflected in the effectiveness of the materials.

Decisions

Evaluating current and potential materials can remind you of the choices you make that pertain to effective communication by way of the educational materials you use (Anderson, 1983; Vaille, 1998). Assessment can help identify potential materials, select materials that are appropriate for the content and learners, develop materials if satisfactory ones are not available, revise materials that should be improved, sequence materials, and review their use in practice.

These decisions can be made by participants, the instructor, coordinator, materials developer, or publisher. Evaluation of materials can occur at various stages of materials development: an approximation test before preparing the actual materials, formative evaluation throughout materials development and refinement, selection from available materials, or assessment of materials effectiveness and impact (Anderson, 1983; Flagg, 1990; Grotelueschen, Gooler, and Knox, 1976; Vaille, 1998).

An example from Lerche (1985) illustrates the contribution of evaluation to decisions when selecting appropriate materials for an adult literacy program. The International Reading Association's checklist for evaluating adult basic education reading material is proposed to help practitioners select and classify materials, make objective judgments on the basis of a clear evaluation process, select materials that fit learner backgrounds and interests, allow individualized instruction, and assist with staff development. The material that is assessed can be used for purposes of introduction, reinforcement, practice, review, and application of content. The checklist for review and selection of materials groups criteria in four categories: readability, relevance, manageability, and responsiveness to special needs.

For review of commercial print materials, classification occurs regarding type of material and intended learner characteristics. A publication is rated on appeal, relevance, purpose, process (word analysis, comprehension, vocabulary), human relations (avoid stereotypes), evaluation function (encouraging reading, promoting reasoning), format, teacher directions, and content (progression, interest). There are procedures for use in assessing readability of a hundred-word passage; a well-known example is Gunning's Fog Index. A form for evaluation of computer software includes sections on specifications, purpose, procedures, content, technical issues, and a summary on quality and recommendations. The specifications section includes source, cost, and equipment requirements. The purposes section covers clientele and program type. The procedures section includes clear objectives, adult style, and useful feedback. The content section encompasses sound content, adjustable level of difficulty, and relevant concepts. The technical section deals with user-friendliness, flexible rate and sequence, and independent use by learners. The summary section has ratings of procedures, content, and technical characteristics along with recommendations and comments on use.

Characteristics

The decisions to be made regarding evaluation of materials, and the specific assessment guidelines, depend in part on the characteristics of the potential or actual materials. Examples are print text, graphics, slides, simulation, audiotape, videotape, and various computer-based materials and programs (self-contained or interactive online). Material of any such type can be used separately or as part of an educational program that includes interpersonal participation (Anderson, 1983; Gredler, 1994; Knox, 1986; Vaille, 1998).

Guidelines

Evaluation of materials typically uses criteria, guidelines, and rubrics to assess various features that are important for assessing the quality of specific materials. Some criteria pertain to appropriateness for the intended participants (Ference and Vockell, 1994). The criteria reflect concern for relevance, appeal, and comprehensibility given the learner's background, interest, goals, learning style, special needs, strengths, and weaknesses. Other criteria pertain to instructional considerations such as content, goals, instructional design, authority, bias, organization, searchability, supplementary materials, costs, utilization, and encouragement of innovative use and creative learning activities. A rubric usually specifies about three levels of quality for a criterion to be used in judging the excellence of specific materials (Flagg, 1990; Gredler, 1994; Grotelueschen, Gooler, and Knox, 1976; Lerche, 1985; Vaille, 1998).

An example from Vaille (1998) illustrates guidelines for evaluation of instructional technology. The main guidelines are in five sections: content, responsiveness to learners, program design, assessment, and instructional support, plus a supplemental applications appendix that includes distance and online learning experiences. For each section, there are subparts that can be rated on three rubrics (excellent, good, minimal). There are also screening criteria for video and interactive technology.

The learner responsiveness guideline includes criteria and features that are characteristic of an excellent rubric:

Criterion	Features
Creative	Constructivist experiences
	Cooperative learning
	Independent investigation
Critical thinking	Conclusions drawn
	Varied approaches
	Multiple solutions

Similarly with the program design guideline:

Criterion	Features
Effectiveness	Depth of content
	Multiple units
Interactivity	Easily used presentation branches prompted
Customizing levels of difficulty	Allow selection of concepts

The supplemental application rubrics for distance learning include criteria for delivery (ease of use, accessibility) and for interaction (among learners online and offline, available support staff).

Effectiveness

The usual reason for assessing materials is to contribute to a judgment or decision about their quality, effectiveness, and impact. Such
judgments typically are made by a number of stakeholders. They
should be involved in the evaluation process to an extent and in
ways that contribute to their understanding, acceptance, and use of
conclusions. This is especially important if the educational materials are central to the program, as in most distance education programs and with materials integral to a program that includes other
types of learning activity (Flagg, 1990; Knox, 1986; Nowak and others, 1997).

Communication with mass media (print or electronic) is sometimes used in combination with interpersonal reinforcement
(demonstration, group session) to help adults learn. This was the
case for a communication and adoption evaluation of USDA (federal Department of Agriculture) Water Quality Demonstration Projects (Nowak and others, 1997). In the context of this chapter on
evaluation of educational materials, the focus is on assessment of
media, but attention is also given to evaluation of interpersonal
intervention, which is often used in conjunction with media.

The USDA and cooperating organizations launched a national
Water Quality Program in 1989, one component of which was
demonstration projects designed to accelerate voluntary adoption
on the part of farmers and ranchers of agricultural best management practices (BMPs) that protect water quality while maintaining productivity and profitability. Ongoing assessment of this
effort included initial assessment of implementation, economic
assessment, and impact on water quality, as well as the current
University of Wisconsin evaluation of project influence on producer adoption of BMPs, during the initial two years of full implementation.

Evaluations were also reported for other aspects of the effort
to improve water quality, such as initial assessment of projects

(Rockwell, Hay, Ziebarth, and Niemeyer, 1991), a five-year update of residents' perception of water quality (Furgason, Hay, and Rockwell, 1996), and the output of public issues education programs on water quality (Marshall and Bennett, 1998).

The approach of the national evaluation of producer adoption (Nowak and others, 1997) was to focus on how quickly agricultural producers modified project-promoted BMPs. The purpose was to assess the impact of materials and related activities. The evaluation assessed changes between 1992 and 1994. As with the demonstration projects themselves, the evaluation used a comprehensive model to help select objectives, procedures, and data. Adoption rate and processes in the areas where producers had been exposed to demonstration projects were compared with nearly matched geographic areas where producers had not been exposed to the project. This allowed identification of specific impact of the projects, in contrast to broader societal influences. It was also important to take into account variations among the separate demonstration projects regarding context, goals, procedures, and resources.

The evaluation design allowed tracking of progress related to priority BMPs over two years, and identifying changes attributable to the project. Each of the eight state projects varied in context; prior effort; and producer background, knowledge, and preferred communication channels related to BMPs. Surveys and focus groups were used to decide on the emphasis, procedures, and appropriate practices in each project. Of the several BMPs promoted by each demonstration project, three or four given the highest priority were selected for tracking across the eight projects in the national evaluation, for a total of thirteen BMPs.

In each of the eight state projects, a watershed-level demonstration area was selected for intervention, along with a nearby comparison area that did not receive the demonstration project's mass media campaign (materials) and interpersonal reinforcement. In a baseline survey at the outset of the intervention, almost all producers had recently been exposed to information about protection of water quality. About half viewed water pollution as a serious problem in their state, but they believed that farm practices had no impact on local water quality; they were unconvinced that a majority of the BMPs were practical and profitable, and fewer than 10 percent saw water pollution as a serious problem close to their own farms. About one-quarter of the producers were already using the designated BMPs. Another survey occurred at the end of the intervention to identify progress. These features show why it is desirable to consider the context when evaluating materials.

This quasi-experimental evaluation design entailed three rounds of survey data from large representative samples of producers in demonstration and comparison areas. Comparison of adoption rate over time between demonstration and comparison areas was used to assess project impact on adoption and related variables. Additional information was collected from project staff about demonstration emphasis, procedures, location, and timing. Summaries and transcripts of this additional information for each state were reviewed by project staff for accuracy. Because of the differences among the eight projects, they were not compared.

At the start, most of the state projects explored the local applicability of the BMPs. They did so by recruiting local producers to help develop and test costs and benefits of recommended practices. This delayed the intervention stage of some projects. Although the eight interventions varied, all included multiple forms of intervention. Project staff and producers each preferred individualized coaching, which is labor-intensive and thus expensive. Each project also included demonstration farms and several group events each year.

All projects included extensive media campaigns (newspapers, radio, newsletters). These were the materials pertinent to this example. Contributions to effective projects were involving communication personnel, planning with clear objectives, relying on interagency communication, knowing about activities by respected producers, and using media to build awareness. The projects' use of media was contingent on both external and internal influences.

Among the external influences were receptivity of urban-oriented media outlets to agricultural stories and staff turnover at rural newspapers (which inhibited long-term relationship). Internal influences were having communication staff available to produce stories and contact media, and increasing staff priority on media. Some staff members believe that mass media outlets are ineffective because they are more interested in controversy than in useful dissemination of information.

From the detailed evaluation findings, a number of highlights emphasize the impact over the two years related to media and materials:

- On average, across the eight demonstration areas nearly half the producers gained awareness and positive recognition of the projects.

- Regarding BMPs showing significant gains, demonstration area producers' awareness, familiarity, or usage increased by 5–25 percentage points, with a median increase of 15 percentage points.

- Producers did not change their views about the seriousness of water quality, increase exposure to information about protection of water quality, or become more favorably inclined toward BMPs.

- Net gains in adoption process were similar in demonstration and comparison areas, probably because there were extensive agricultural communication systems in the eight sites.

The evaluation report discussion includes comments that have implications for interpreting these findings and planning similar evaluation of media and related activities in the future.

In contrast to adoption of production and marketing practices that are economically advantageous to producers, adoption of environmental protection practices takes more time as well as local evidence of profitability and practicality to convince producers. Information from project staff and area producers indicated that such local validation of some BMPs was insufficient, and that the time it took to conduct test demonstrations to ensure local applicability of BMPs also delayed other dissemination efforts.

Interpersonal communication channels (tours, field days, workshops, farm visits) emerged as the backbone of the information campaign. Use of nearby demonstration and comparison sites resulted in major media reaching both sites; this limited project mass media use to smaller-scale community-level media channels. Extensive use of media depended on more professional communication staffing. Extent of media use was less important than quality of media presentation and interplay with interpersonal communication. One-on-one education for producers was the predominant method and the one preferred by project staff.

Some of the pertinent recommendations for conducting such an evaluation are:

- Conduct site-specific test demonstrations to increase local applicability (profitability, feasibility) of recommended practices.

- Strengthen program development by using basic evaluation and marketing concepts.

- Segment audiences according to their stage of adoption (some have an outlook resistant to adoption).

- Develop clear and realistic adoption objectives to guide project planning, implementation, and evaluation.

Concepts from the detailed report of a comprehensive evaluation project can contribute to the rationale for conducting a specific evaluation of materials. Stakeholders can use evaluation conclusions to guide decisions about selection, development, and use of various types of material. Guidelines address types and features of material, such as appropriateness for participants, content, design, evaluation, and effectiveness. Evaluation can address context and related activities to place in perspective the contribution of media and materials.

Planning

The previous concepts about evaluation of educational materials give an overview of available ideas. In practice, a few such concepts are used to plan a specific instance of materials assessment. The next examples emphasize three aspects of planning. The first section shows several ways to design an evaluation study. The second section presents ways to use criteria and checklists to assess appropriateness, quality, improvement, and effectiveness of various types of educational material. The third section emphasizes the contribution of materials to teaching and learning activity.

Design

The purpose and scale of evaluation of educational materials vary greatly. Many are modest and short-term assessment efforts by instructors and teachers of adults to guide their decisions about selection and development of materials. Sometimes an evaluation is conducted by specialists as part of a design team that guides creation of materials (and sometimes development of the entire educational program). A few evaluations are large-scale, quasi-experimental studies designed to assess materials use and impact. The design suggestions that follow range from modest to extensive.

When a teacher of adults initiates an assessment of materials, it is helpful if it is part of ongoing evaluation (Knox, 1986). Although an instructor who decides to evaluate materials is probably somewhat prepared to do so, it is also helpful to have the assistance of a program coordinator familiar with at least basic evaluation concepts and procedures. The coordinator can assist directly and identify people and resources to contribute to evaluation planning and imple-mentation. The adult learners are the prime beneficiary of effective materials; they have a stake in evaluation and can contribute to it. At a minimum, they can provide feedback on how satisfactory the materials are from their perspective.

One advantage of brief local assessment is that the motivations that typically prompt the instructor to help evaluate also encour-age use of conclusions. Involving the program coordinator and at least some of the adult participants can strengthen planning, imple-mentation, and utilization. The increasing availability of criteria and rubrics for assessing educational materials generally, and of spe-cific types of media, constitutes a valuable resource if the instructor knows about them. The plan for data collection can include infor-mation about materials use and preferences from participants, the instructor, and other instructors in similar programs whose experi-ence with comparable materials can yield valuable perspectives. Information about learner background, progress, and achievement is usually valuable. Sampling concepts and procedures can keep an assessment manageable by enabling the instructor to select repre-sentative items, participants, and resources.

An early stage in evaluating materials is reviewing what the instructor already knows and has available from program records and ongoing assessment (Knox and others, 1974). The instructor and perhaps the coordinator might compare the sources and types of educational material currently used with what seems desirable and use the resulting discrepancy to guide a search for more appro-priate materials.

Another example of designing evaluation of materials is employ-ing a readability index to assess the difficulty level of print materials for possible use by adult learners with limited reading ability (Harvey, 1987). For high-interest materials that are too difficult for partici-pants, the teacher can use criteria for undercutting or simplifying the text so that it is at a satisfactory readability level. A coordinator can assist an interested teacher to assess readability with such revision.

In contrast to evaluation plans that can be made and implemented by a teacher, some assessment designs require specialized assistance. This was illustrated by the earlier example of a national evaluation of mass media materials on water quality (Nowak and others, 1997). For this major evaluation, the external evaluation team used a quasi-experimental design that compared preassessment and postassessment in eight geographic areas that received a media campaign (with interpersonal reinforcement) with nearby comparison areas that did not. It takes a great deal of time, money, and expertise to conduct such a multiyear external evaluation, with its overall assessment plan, sampling, instrument development, data collection and analysis, and reporting. Usually, such a large investment in external evaluation is justified by the much greater investment in the demonstration project and stakeholder interest in evidence of extent and type of impact and major influences. Conclusions of this kind can guide future decisions regarding the problem addressed by the demonstration project.

An example from Flagg (1990) of formative evaluation of interactive training materials reveals how and why assessment is an integral part of developing an interactive DVD that combines three media: computer, audio, and video. The evaluation assessed the program's appeal and comprehensibility at various stages in the development process. The quality of the completed videodisk program depended on orchestrating program development, project evaluations, and project staff.

The flowchart has thirteen phases:

Planning

1. Conduct project launch, including the project proposal and initial meetings to promote teamwork.

2. Conduct analysis of audience needs and profiles, along with situational influences and stakeholder expectations (evaluation).

3. Set project evaluation criteria, including goals, benchmarks, cost, training effectiveness, and learner acceptance (evaluation).

4. Prepare implementation plan, taking into account audience, strategies, and instructional procedures.

Design

5. Design the application, including specific objectives, content specifications, and scripting for each media element; a final storyboard; and a formative evaluation of storyboards to guide revision (evaluation).

Production

6. Link computer-based video and audio elements, and track information about program usage and learner progress (use for evaluation).

7. Produce video and audio sequences.

8. Merge and test, including integrative computer and videodisk components, and verify sequencing and branching (evaluation).

Implementation

9. Validation and final revisions, on the basis of independent assessment against standards by a quality assurance analyst, and a field test of the program with representative potential participants (evaluation).

10. Manufacture and replicate.

11. Implement and deliver.

12. Conduct summative program evaluation against program goals, on the basis of project records, surveys, interviews, and focus group sessions (evaluation).

13. Conduct ongoing project maintenance.

Formative evaluation mainly occurs at three phases: needs assessment during planning, preproduction assessment during the design phase, and formative evaluation during the production phase. Needs assessment helps identify content that is extraneous or missing, along with satisfactory sequences and the interactivity and control preferred by potential participants. Focus group members can indicate their preferred sequence of content, which can guide program decisions about interactivity and individual paths.

The preproduction evaluation of the first-generation storyboard addressed issues such as comprehension, interactivity, and appeal with a one-on-one walk-through by the evaluator and representative potential participants. Such walk-through evaluations of first and then final storyboards led to improvement at a stage when revision was feasible.

The production formative evaluation was done with a check disk (low-cost videodisk taken through preliminary debugging). This occurs both at the development facility with sample participants brought in and at a typical site under more representative conditions. Attention is given to participant attitude toward the mode of learning and role in dealing with this technology.

Evaluation data were collected by way of computer, questionnaires, interviews, and observations. Early evaluation feedback allowed improvement, which would be very expensive to make late in the production process. This example confirms the close connection between formative evaluation and program development decisions in producing electronic media.

Quality

An important part of planning an evaluation is deciding on criteria to judge the quality of materials, to guide selection and development of checklists to assess proposed or actual materials. The process of formulating and using these criteria should encourage use of conclusions to improve educational materials Knox (1986).

The instructor's use of criteria and guidelines for selecting, developing, and sequencing materials is fundamental to evaluation of any type of educational material. Coordinators and specialists can help. Criteria vary somewhat with the type of educational material (print, audio, visual, audiovisual, simulation, and examples).

The main criterion for selection of materials is the educational purposes they should serve. Additional criteria are materials assessment, specific features, and user satisfaction. When screening potential materials to identify those that seem most promising, consider pertinent content, appropriateness given the learner's background, organization to facilitate learner interaction, and maintenance of learner interest. To select from potential materials those for actual use, consider these evaluation criteria: the main program beneficiaries, the fit with prerequisite learner proficiency, encouragement of active questioning and problem solving, promotion of learner identification with materials, help participants internalize concepts and achieve mastery, and fit with the total instructional plan.

If you are developing educational materials, consider guidelines that can also be used for ongoing evaluation:

- Use of a clear rationale regarding educational purpose and learning process

- Content that is relevant to the learner

- Challenge and responsiveness to the learner's background and preferred learning style

- Early focus on the most important aspects

- Attracting and retaining the learner's attention

- Use of multiple communication channels

- Varied repetition

- Use of existing resources

- Applicability to various learners and circumstances

- Encouragement of active interaction

- Feedback to enable the learner to compare proficiency with standards

- Modification and refinement

More specific criteria can be used for ongoing evaluation of specific types of educational material; as examples think of slide sets or computer graphics. Evaluation criteria pertain to serving the educational purpose; beginning with the message and using materials to help visualize it; sequencing materials to engage the learner's attention, memorably present the main ideas, and encourage reflection and action; and taking logistics into account. Somewhat different criteria apply to printed materials, discussion cases, videotapes, and study guides.

These criteria can be used to evaluate the sequence of materials:

- Start with objectives.

- Consider learner preferences.

- Offer choice.

- Present relevant content.

- Focus on basics.

- Give opportunities for review.

- Include questions.

- Encourage application.

These guidelines and criteria can foster evaluation regarding selection, development, and sequencing of educational materials. Such ongoing evaluation can occur as part of planning, preparation, and use of educational materials.

A rating scale can be completed by the instructor, the coordinator, or other staff or volunteers to assess the quality of materials (Grotelueschen, Gooler, and Knox, 1976). An example of a rating scale used with a series of sentences is strongly agree, agree, disagree, strongly disagree. The sentences can be grouped by aspect of the materials to be rated. Each sentence can describe a part of that aspect—for instance, goals of material (clear objectives, importance to learner, comprehensiveness), content (relevance to learner, appropriate prerequisites, being representative), methods (match with learning styles, individualization, feedback) and utilization (versatility, teacher interest in use).

The instructor or coordinator can also use quality criteria and rubrics to assess online materials (Vaille, 1998). Excellent online materials (documents, simulations, reports, collaborative projects) can yield learning activities not readily available from other media. There are other desirable features of online materials:

- Access to current, broad, in-depth information

- Two-way communication with distant peers, mentors, and experts

- A means of sharing ideas with others

- Additional resources for instructors

Sample criteria and characteristics that make an excellent case for a recommendation to use online materials are:

- Collaboration (online resource facilitates many unique interactions: e-mail, joint projects, assistance from experts)

- Navigation (easy user control, nonlinear access, visual locator)

- Content (depth and richness of information, links to sources, graphics)

- Sharing (support for development, templates to create projects, accessibility of learner's work)

- Stability (reliability of online resource, citation of authorities, permitting of multiple viewpoints)

- Support (offline extension, access to other online resources, links to sites for individualization, assessment criteria)

Evaluation checklists are available for selecting and developing specific types of instructional media (Anderson, 1983):

Print

- Rough draft (simple words, short sentences, good fit with learner's background and comprehension)

- Layout (uncluttered, illustrated, good margins)

- Final copy (typeface, use of boldface, headings)

Filmstrip

- Suitable for content and objectives (content mainly visual, learners familiar with objects, representation of objects satisfactory)

- Sequence of visuals (simple, to avoid confusion; avoidance of excessive use of numbers; provision for cutaway or enlarged views; progressive buildup of visualized ideas)

Audiotape to Support Visuals

- Rough draft of script (active voice, conversational style, minimal jargon and technical terms, sound effects for realism)

- Playing of recorded script with storyboard visuals (narration that supports visuals only, conversational language)

- Notes on script while playing tape (final expert check on content, synchronization of visuals and narration, underlining of words to be stressed, pacing instructions)

- Final draft for narrator (wide left margin to describe visuals, note on pacing and sound effects at beginning of script)

Computer-Assisted Instruction (CAI)

- Review decision to use CAI (sufficient development time, sufficient resources to support, assistance for complex branching, available course materials)

- Computer-managed (guiding learners through materials, routing to remedial materials, course security, data storage, reference tools)

- Delivery system (necessary updates, student assessment and reporting, security of information, communication among participants and staff)

With increasing use of Websites for distance education, there are now evaluation criteria for critically analyzing information sources, similar to those librarians have used for print sources (Engle, 2000). The criteria suggested are content, authority, organization, searchability, graphic design, and innovative use. Also suggested are criteria for inclusion, authority of the author, compatibility with related sources, stability of information, appropriateness of format, and requirements regarding software, hardware, and multimedia.

Guidelines for evaluation of Internet resources are available (Descy, 1996), with criteria related to author credibility, character of producer, characteristics of site, extent and type of publication, purpose of document, date of publication, clear arrangement of information, intended audience, coverage, writing style and reasoning, and documentation by references.

Another rationale for evaluating Web resources embraces as criteria audience, purpose, accuracy, relative value (comprehensiveness, data, other resources), intrinsic value, credentials of author, authority, bias, reliability of links, graphic design, functional graphics, clear icons, creativity, interactivity, secure coding, and usability of site (Grassian, 1999).

According to Verduin and Clark (1991), distance education depends heavily on print and electronic materials that can be assessed for quality and effectiveness. They suggest for criteria learner achievement gain, reduced instructional time, attrition, access, quality of materials, suitability for content, cost-effectiveness, and response to expectations. The resource section contains abstracts of research and evaluation studies on learner achievement in distance education. Reviewing their conclusions can strengthen planning of distance education, materials, evaluation of this process and outcomes, and interpretation of specific evaluation conclusions.

Activities

Planning for evaluation of educational materials should consider what kind of learning activity the materials encourage. Here are suggested questions:

- Is the learner helped to reflect and build on current proficiencies related to the new content?

- Does the learner appreciate the importance and relevance of the objectives for use of materials?

- Is the difficulty level of the materials appropriate for the learner's background?

- Is there a satisfactory combination of support and challenge?

- Are the materials responsive to varied learning styles?

- Do the materials encourage active engagement?

- Is interaction among learners facilitated?

- Is the learner helped to pursue the content in greater depth if desired?

- Do the materials leave opportunity for practice that is interesting?

- Do the materials include provision for formative evaluation and feedback?

- Is the learner encouraged to apply what he or she learns?

Coordination

Coordination of assessment varies with the focus and scale of the specific evaluation project. However, in every instance decisions are made regarding who contributes to the evaluation, the resources that contribute to the evaluation, and the evaluation standards that guide planning, implementation, utilization, and assessment of the process and report.

Contribution

Anyone who helps make many of the decisions about an evaluation project can be considered the evaluation coordinator. For a small evaluation of materials for a course, the instructor typically does the coordinating. Course participants may contribute information about their opinions and progress, and a program administrator with some evaluation expertise may help plan the evaluation project. For a larger or broader evaluation of materials (say, for multiple courses or workshops), the program administrator typically coordinates the evaluation project, perhaps with assistance from media and evaluation specialists.

Resources

Evaluation of materials for use in a variety of adult education programs is becoming increasingly feasible. In recent decades, the quantity and quality of print and electronic educational materials suitable for adults have risen dramatically. This allows assessment and selection of materials based in part on evidence of successful use, as opposed to estimates of probable effectiveness. Because instructors and participants use materials, they are in a good position to assess them and then apply their conclusions to guide subsequent use of the materials. There are an increasing number of general overviews of evaluation concepts and procedures that can be adapted and applied to assessment of materials (Knox, 1998a; Boulmetis and Dutwin, 2000). A computer search of pertinent databases, such as ERIC, facilitates locating reports on evaluation of adult education materials that can help design an evaluation project and interpret the findings. As illustrated in the section on planning in Chapter Nine, there are checklists and guides available for assessing the quality and features of various types of educational media and material.

Simulations are increasingly available, used, and useful. Typically encompassing materials, simulation is the subject of numerous publications on its design and evaluation (Gredler, 1994). Effective use of simulation is enhanced by an understanding of the various types, the rationale for its use, and the basic characteristics (problem-based, uncertain solutions, active participant roles, natural consequences, virtual reality). Overall evaluation of simulation includes orientation and postsimulation discussion of process, results, and relation to actual experience. Assessment of simulation materials can include these aspects, but it normally focuses on the print and electronic materials that guide the simulation itself. For a variety of simulations, here are evaluation guidelines to use in coordinating assessment of materials and related activities.

Diagnostic

- Type and format (client management or mystery resolution, closed or open structure)

- Nature and scope (important problem, appropriate complexity, context indicated)

- For closed structure, is a booklet or a computer used?

- Opening scene (concrete and neutral description of situation, description of learner's role and conditions, type of media used)

- General sequence (branching, learner choice, provision for exiting)

- Options and responses (type of credible choice, causal relation, descriptive response, appropriate format and style)

Crisis Management

- Analysis of situation (background provided, scope of crisis, threat to decision makers)

- Decision roles (decision makers empowered to resolve, high threat for decision makers, active roles)

- Dynamics (participants, effects of experience, events evolving from crisis, increased time pressure as events accelerate)

Social System (Multiagenda)

- Precipitating event and context (positive and negative features, clear relation of task to event, credible precipitating event and complications, simple rules)

- Participant roles (active and essential, role card giving specifications, range of perspectives, simulation taking various directions)

These are guidelines that address distinctive features of several types of simulation. Coordinators can use such specific resources to help other stakeholders in the evaluation to adapt and use them.

The next example, related to computer conferencing, discusses coordination in evaluating electronic materials. Computer conferencing and similar forms of distance education are expanding thanks to such features as access and anticipated cost efficiency from economy of scale. Aside from assessment of the entire program, evaluation can focus on the supporting materials, on the software that enables interaction, and on print manuscripts of actual typed messages from the instructor and participants that occur during asynchronous interaction.

All of these messages (or a representative sample) that are sent and received by people engaged in computer conferencing can be printed and coded regarding the type of interaction (Henri and Rigault, 1996). By deciding on the dimensions of participation that are pertinent to the evaluation, the coding and content analysis of written message segments allows qualitative assessment of knowledge creation and search for meaning that is at the heart of teaching and learning. The dimension that is coded and analyzed can be the number of messages transmitted by an individual or subgroup, a statement unrelated to the content, a chain of connected messages, a statement that reflects the learning process, or a statement that reflects self-regulation of learning. Such a resource for evaluation of materials that are central to teaching and learning generally requires substantial evaluation expertise, which a coordinator can provide or arrange for. The computer can also be used to store and analyze evaluation data collected as the program proceeds. Additional examples of data collection and analysis are included in the middle portion of Chapter Four.

Standards

Coordination of materials evaluation can be strengthened by using media evaluation standards to guide planning and interpretation of conclusions. Here are topics regarding materials that such standards can address:

- Importance and relevance of the objectives implicit in the materials

- Prerequisite proficiencies for learners to deal with the materials

- Level of difficulty and challenge inherent in the materials for the participants

- Responsiveness of the materials in accommodating varied learning styles

- Stages of the program when the materials are likely to be most effective

- Extent to which the materials encourage active engagement

- How materials encourage interaction among participants

- Opportunities for practice that encourage persistence and progress

- Provision for evaluation feedback

- Materials that encourage and facilitate application and improved performance

As you reflect on this overview of materials assessment, consider these questions:

- Who should contribute to evaluation of educational materials?

- What are desirable criteria and guidelines for materials evaluation?

- What should be done to encourage utilization of conclusions from evaluation of materials?

Summary Guidelines

This checklist reviews basic guidelines for evaluation of materials. You can use it to improve your rationale and procedures for evaluation of materials.

Concepts

1. Clarify the evaluation purpose regarding type of material, evaluation guidelines, and use of conclusion.

2. Assessment of materials can guide decisions about potential materials, selection, development, sequencing, and review of materials in use.

3. Evaluation conclusions can be used by participants, the instructor, coordinator, materials developer, and publisher.

4. Considerations for selection of materials are audience, purpose, appeal, function, content, responsiveness, manageability, evaluation, and flexibility.

5. Characteristics of materials are print, graphics, slides, simulations, audiotape, videotape, and computer.

6. Guidelines and rubrics help assess such features of materials as appropriateness, usefulness, content, design, process, assessment, support, and effectiveness.

7. Assessment conclusions can help stakeholders make decisions about the quality, effectiveness, and impact of materials.

Planning

8. Evaluations of this kind vary greatly in purpose and scale; there are implications for evaluation design.

9. Assessment of materials is enhanced if it is part of ongoing evaluation.

10. Modest assessment of materials by the instructor, coordinator, and participants can encourage use of conclusions.

11. Evaluation specialists may be required for a large external evaluation.

12. Evaluation is useful at successive stages in developing and using educational materials (planning, design, use).

13. Materials quality selection criteria are purpose, features, content, satisfaction, and effectiveness.

14. Among the guidelines for development of materials: rationale, sound and relevant content, being challenging and supportive, active learning, and addressing diversity.

15. Guidelines for evaluating sequencing of materials recommend starting with objectives and preferences, presenting relevant content, offering choice, including questions and opportunities for review, and encouraging application.

16. Rating scales can be used to assess materials regarding goals, content, methods, and utilization.

17. Criteria for evaluation of online computer materials are collaboration, navigation, content, sharing, stability, and support.

18. Detailed checklists are available for specific types of media (print, filmstrip, audiotape, CAI).

19. Suggested criteria for evaluation of Websites are content, purpose, authority, organization, comparability, stability, design, creativity, and technical arrangements.

20. Criteria for assessing quality and effectiveness of distance education materials are learner achievement, reduced time, attrition, access, quality of materials, suitability for content, cost-effectiveness, and response to expectations.

21. Effective materials encourage learner activity related to such criteria as enhanced proficiency, appreciation of relevance, appropriate difficulty, active engagement, interesting practice, and encouragement of application.

Coordination

22. Evaluation of materials typically entails coordination by an instructor or, depending on the focus and scale of the evaluation, an administrator, with cooperation from other stakeholders.

23. Overviews of evaluation concepts and procedures are readily available to help design an assessment of materials.

24. Guidelines are available for evaluation of various types of simulation.

25. Printed transcripts of messages from computer conferencing can be used to evaluate types of interaction (connected messages, learning process, self-regulation of learning).

26. Evaluation standards for assessment of materials can address topics such as importance of implicit objectives, attention to prerequisite proficiencies, level of difficulty, responsiveness to learning styles, stage of program, encouragement of engagement and interaction, opportunities for practice, evaluation feedback, and application.

11

Outcomes and Impact

Summative evaluation of program outcomes and impact contrasts and complements the largely formative evaluation for program improvement of the aspects addressed in the preceding chapters. Summative evaluation emphasizes results and accountability, which is of special interest to external stakeholders such as policy makers and funders, who tend to be more interested in results than process. Program administrators make evaluative judgments about needs, context, resources, staff performance, learner progress, materials effectiveness, and program improvement. However, such decisions are strengthened when information about inputs and process is combined with information about outcomes, benefits, and impact.

As a result, evaluation of outcomes is typically more comprehensive than process-oriented evaluation of aspects such as staff performance, learner progress, and materials effectiveness. Sound impact studies include multiple indicators of outcomes, benefits, and other key variables. They also address unintended consequences and do not restrict the evaluation to achievement of stated objectives. Follow-up studies are a valuable source of information on application and benefits during an elapsed time that allows such results to occur.

Comprehensive program evaluation typically entails synthesis of information about outcomes in relation to other aspects of the program. This may take the form of attention to inputs (participants, instructors, resources), process (learner progress, teaching effectiveness, materials development, program improvement), and context (agency functioning, relation to parent organization, other providers in service area, societal influences). At the same time, summative evaluation of outcomes should focus on the issues of highest priority for the stakeholders who are the main recipients of the evaluation report. External stakeholders mainly value impact and benefits.

The chapter contains three sections: concepts, planning, and coordination. Each section includes an overview of concepts and procedures, references to specialized reading on the topic, and brief examples of how to assess the outcomes, impact, and benefits of a variety of adult educational program types. The chapter concludes with a listing of summary guidelines.

Evaluation of outcomes and impact tends to be complex and infrequent. Consider the issues and decisions in each section of this chapter that have implications for your evaluation activity. Issues to consider are suggested by these questions:

- In what ways are evaluation conclusions likely to be used for planning, improvement, and accountability?

- What are distinctive features of impact evaluation, such as a follow-up study or a combination of internal self-assessment and external review?

- What are likely sources and reasons for resistance to outcome evaluation?

- What are some alternative assessment approaches to consider—such as those focused on achievement of objectives, case study, expert review, and quasi-experiment?

- Why should evaluation conclusions include the relationship between process and outcomes?

- How do you decide on the scale (detail, level of effort) of an impact evaluation?

- What are typical sources of information for outcome evaluation?

- Which categories of stakeholder are likely recipients of impact evaluation reports?

- Who should be considered for coordination of outcome evaluation?

Concepts

Some basic ideas constitute the rationale for evaluating impact and results. Outcomes assessment emphasizes summative evaluation of impact and benefits, but it includes more comprehensive and systemic information about context, inputs, and process to place outcomes in perspective in aiding understanding of influences on the extent and type of impact that occurs. Use of multiple indicators of program outcomes is important, both to allow valid conclusions regarding impact and to recognize unintended consequences (Delaney, 1997). It is especially desirable that outcome evaluation reports emphasize issues that are important to stakeholders.

Assessment of program outcomes can be for purposes of accountability, improvement, or planning; it can focus on participants, instructors, topics, or contexts (Knox and Associates, 1980).

Accountability assessment of outcomes pertains to participants (to what extent were their educational achievements valued by the provider agency?), to instructors (were the unintended outcomes of instruction desirable?) to topics (how useful were the topics to the participant?) and to context (how valuable were the outcomes to a group, organization, or community with which the participant was associated?)

Outcomes evaluation for improvement purposes also pertains to each of these four elements, but the questions apply to strengthening an ongoing program instead of justifying one that was completed. Questions concern attention to the participant (how might learner achievement be enhanced?), the instructor (what instructional modifications are likely to enhance learner achievement?), the topic (would it be beneficial to have a different scope and depth to the topic?), and to the context (based on what they are learning, how might participants' contributions to family, work or community be enhanced?).

Again, outcomes evaluation for planning purposes pertains to each of these four elements, but the questions apply to vision and future direction. Questions deal with attention to the participant (how realistic and desirable are the intended outcomes for similar participants in a future program?), to the instructor (to what extent is an instructor likely to help attain the desired outcomes in future programs?), to the topic (what are the relative benefits of this and alternative topics for a future program?), and to the context (how might the fit be improved between program outcomes and organizational expectations?).

Assessing results and benefits for other people who are associated with the participant in his or her role in family, work, and community can be challenging to all concerned. Advice from evaluators with experience conducting summative evaluation research has been forthcoming for decades (Weiss, 1977; Posavac and Carey, 1992; Shadish, Cook, and Leviton, 1995).

Kirkpatrick (1994) offers these guidelines for evaluating results and outcomes, beyond participant learning and performance change:

- Use a comparison group if practical.

- Allow time for results to be achieved.

- Measure before and after the program, if practical.

᥍ Repeat the measurement at appropriate times.

• Consider cost versus benefit.

• Be satisfied with evidence if proof is not possible.

Fortunately, summative evaluation of outcomes can be especially desirable and feasible in an enterprise workplace learning program. Information can be obtained from participants, peers, supervisors, and organizational records to indicate whether the cost of education was justified in relation to increased productivity (Knox, 1979a).

Although the main purpose of summative evaluation is to assess outcomes and impact, it is important to include some information about context, inputs, and process. Without such information it is difficult to interpret information on outcomes and to explain likely influences that helped or hindered the results (Knox, 1979a; Shapiro, 1995). In practice, results and outcomes are toward the end of a chain of effects that occur early as participants, the instructor, and other people associated with a program are attracted and begin interacting with content (reflected in objectives, materials, and activities). The results of these decisions and interactions greatly influence subsequent links in the chain of effects, especially the teaching-learning transaction. The results of these middle program developments and instructional links in the chain can greatly affect program impact on group, organization, and community. They do so through enhanced proficiency and improved performance on the part of participants who complete an educational program. They also do so through persistence among participants and the instructor, and through cooperation from various stakeholders.

For some educational programs, systemic changes are central (Brinkerhoff, 1987; Bennett and Rockwell, 1995). For instance, when extension programs target outcomes, evaluation can help track the extent to which intended outcomes are achieved, to identify changes in planning and implementation that are likely to improve results. Progress reports from impact or product evaluation can serve several purposes, notably encouraging continued stakeholder cooperation, clarifying outcomes, validating evidence of impact, and recognizing influences on results (Madaus, Scriven, and Stufflebeam, 1983).

Fortunately, there are many ways to assess the aspects of program functioning that allow evaluation at various levels of detail. This enables evaluators to use multiple valid indicators regarding major intended outcomes, and to use brief summary information regarding other program characteristics. Two examples here recount systemic evaluation related to the impact of continuing medical education and cooperative extension programs (Knox, 1979a).

The level of educational effort that it takes to produce a desired impact is one conclusion that can result from evaluating outcomes. A four-year study of educational interventions with one thousand primary care physicians at multiple sites in Michigan explored the impact of voluntary, action-oriented continuing medical education on improvement of ambulatory medical care delivery (Knox, 1979a; Payne and others, 1978, 1984). The essence of the educational intervention was that physicians must perceive recommended changes as useful, there must be sufficient encouragement of change to sustain initial commitment to it, and there must be sufficient time for change to be made and stabilized.

The first level of intervention was minimal, almost a control group, amounting to dissemination of information about performance to the physicians. The second level consisted of several day-and-a-half workshops, which included discussion of problem-solving procedures and implications for planned change. The third level added consultation with hospital administrators to help plan how to increase staff involvement in making clinical changes and managing ambulatory services. First-level reporting intervention produced minimal change in performance. Second-level seminar intervention produced significant improvement. The addition of the third-level intervention greatly increased the improvement.

A representative Wisconsin county was selected for an impact study in which local efforts were supplemented by state staff and contracted telephone interviews (Knox, 1979a; Forest and Marshall, 1978). Local stakeholders were involved to increase understanding, cooperation, and use of conclusions. The impact assessment covered all aspects of cooperative extension programs in the county. Many sources of data were used: reports, documents, and records covering several years. Several hundred leaders and one thousand residents were interviewed, with the conviction that perceived value on the basis of multiple contact is understandable and relevant to extension decisions, and phone interviews are much less expensive than observation and personal interviews. Interviews covered levels three through seven of the Bennett and Rockwell hierarchy (1995): participation, reactions, achievement, practice, and end results.

Improvements to which extension was reported to have contributed pertained to the local economy, government, health, abilities, environment, and educational opportunities. Before reporting, groups of stakeholders were asked to establish standards that should be attained by extension programs. This increased their interest in interpretation of findings and allowed comparison of actual impact with desired impact. Extension staff and leaders in Wisconsin and other states were asked to evaluate the evaluation and indicate how they used the reports.

There are several reasons for including multiple indicators in an impact evaluation. One is that conclusive proof of causal relationships is seldom feasible, so analysis of several types and sources of evidence allows cross-validation. A second is that evidence related to several links in the probable chain of effects enables evaluators to offer a plausible explanation of program functioning to accompany the main focus on outcomes. This allows greater use of findings than just saying that a program did or did not have an impact. A third is that multiple indicators allow portrayal of multiple benefits and consequences of a program, some of which may be unintended (Brinkerhoff, 1987; Delaney, 1997; Worthen and Sanders, 1987). For example, a longitudinal study of adult basic education revealed multiple outcomes: achievement, employment, self-esteem, and community participation (Bingman, 2000).

Usually, a strong interest in results and benefits prompted evaluation of outcomes and impact. However, most programs have multiple stakeholders who typically vary in their interest and involvement in the evaluation process. Program staff members may appreciate the importance of sharing evaluation conclusions with major stakeholders, who may not have the same degree of interest in receiving them. It is thus desirable in the reporting process to emphasize issues important to stakeholders. Recognizing this early enables the evaluator to involve stakeholders appropriately in the ways and to the extent they prefer, especially to report the findings and interpretations in a way that reflects both the issues stakeholders value and how they prefer receiving the conclusions. The form of the reporting is thus likely to differ for participants, the instructor, policy makers, and funders (Worthen and Sanders, 1987).

Planning and Designs

Planning and implementing an impact evaluation shares some similarities with assessment of other aspects of an educational program for adults. Most successful evaluations address issues of concern to stakeholders, are responsive to them, collect and analyze data related to valid conclusions, and encourage use of conclusions. However, there are some features of outcome assessments that are distinctive: accountability, outcomes, combination of internal and external data collection and analysis, use of follow-up studies, and relation to organizational and social change.

When assessing the impact of educational programs for adults for purposes of accountability, many types of research and evaluation design can contribute. Reviews of summative evaluation reports have concluded that excellent programs can have a substantial impact, and that various evaluation designs and models have been used (Knox, 1979a).

Educational programs for adults target a range of outcomes. Some are personal, in which enhanced proficiency for the individual participant is the main benefit and there are few other direct beneficiaries. Among nonoccupational programs are those for personal enhancement regarding cultural, recreational, health, spiritual, artistic, and social topics. Although family and friends may benefit indirectly, their involvement is seldom essential to participation or application, and their benefits tend to be incidental. Some outcomes and benefits occur for a group or team, who usually learn together to apply what they learn in concert (group learning activities related to music, recreation, self-help, and quality improvement). Some outcomes are focused on organization development and productivity. Many enterprise HRD programs are assessed in terms of enhanced work performance on the part of the learner and organizational results in terms of increased production or sales. Still other outcomes are aimed at social, economic, and environmental benefits that occur in the broad community. An example is a cooperative extension program for community resource development (Bennett and Rockwell, 1995).

For programs with each type of targeted outcome, somewhat different evaluation designs are warranted. For example, when the scope shifts from individual to group to organizational to community impact, the number of people and complexity of variables increase and the ease of depending on a few informants for a rich sense of impact and influence declines. If an expertise-oriented evaluation approach based on professional judgment is used, an ad hoc individual review might work well for personal benefits, as does an ad hoc panel review for group benefits, but for organizational and community benefits a review system is more promising (Worthen and Sanders, 1987).

The design of a specific outcome evaluation study can reflect one assessment approach or a combination (Caffarella, 1994). Each approach can be followed at various levels of investment in time and money, depending on resources available and the seriousness of the issues to be addressed. Although one approach is typically selected in a specific instance, sometimes a combination is preferable. For example, several case studies might complement an expert review by offering an in-depth portrayal of how some representative program areas actually function.

An objective-based review assesses the extent to which stated program objectives were met. Objectives focus on participant learning achievement as applied in individual, group, organizational, and community settings. Questions pertain to how the program contributes to enhanced participant proficiency, which may have an impact in group, organization, and community settings to achieve program objectives. Data collection procedures are observation, a test, questionnaire, interview, and review of performance or product.

A case study gives a rich and detailed description of a program as it is experienced and perceived by participants, staff, or other stakeholders. Questions in this regard pertain to program features, strengths, and weaknesses that the stakeholders value. Data collection procedures in this instance are interviews, observations, and documents.

A systems analysis assesses the functioning of the program as a social system: implicit goals, planning, implementation, and use of resources in relation to achieved outcomes. Questions concern program effectiveness and benefits related to resources. Data collection procedures are interview, questionnaire, document analysis, and cost-benefit analysis.

In an expert review, a panel of experts uses a set of standards to analyze program resources and processes in relation to outcomes, on which to base judgments and recommendations. Questions regard the discrepancy between the actual program and its internal goals as well as external standards. Appropriate data collection procedures are document analysis, self-study report, interview, and product review.

An experimental study seeks causal explanation by random assignment of participants and staff to experimental and control treatments; it uses pre- and postdata collection to assess program features that contribute to varying levels of impact. Questions examine the relative influence of alternative program features on selected outcome criteria. Data collection procedures emphasize quantitative measures such as test scores, rating scales, and documented indicators of impact (scales, production figures, and performance ratings; Blackburn, 1994; Abrahamson, 1985). There are few instances in which actual program conditions allow an experimental evaluation; experienced evaluators have noted cautions to consider when doing so (Madaus, Scriven, and Stufflebeam, 1983).

Sometimes the naturalistic setting allows an experimental or quasi-experimental design. An example is when there are many potential participants for a small educational program, and they can be randomly assigned to concurrent or consecutive sections varied by experimental treatments, while other potential participants who are waiting to start constitute a control or comparison group. Time series data before, during, and after the program in a cross-sequential design allows conclusions about program and other influences on change in participant performance. The water quality evaluation described in Chapter Ten illustrates a quasi-experimental design to assess impact (Nowak and others, 1997).

Impact evaluations have been reported for various types of adult educational program (Knox, 1979a; Condelli, 1997; King and others, 1995; Ziegler and Sussman, 1996). The examples given here reveal some of the designs and approaches.

A follow-up study of clients in a newly established educational and career counseling and referral service in the Reading, Pennsylvania, public library obtained information about impact in the form of outcomes reported by clients as a result of their contact with the service (Knox, 1979a; Toombs and Croyle, 1977; Toombs, 1978). Among the outcomes reported were further education, job change, and inactivity. Half of the former clients who were sent

questionnaires responded. Of those who responded, about 40 percent reported enrolling in an educational program, and about 20
percent reported a major job change, each aided by contact with
the service. A variety of other outcomes were also reported. It is
likely that most of the clients were moving toward adjustments in
their lives anyway, but the counseling service facilitated the process
and was much appreciated by the clients.

A company had been conducting various management seminars
on topics such as conflict resolution and performance appraisal, but
there was little indication of impact on management performance
(Brinkerhoff, 1987). Although past support for staff development
was strong, the prospect of future budget cuts prompted the director of staff development to do some impact evaluation. On the basis
of reports on learning and instruction, the director arranged for in-
depth interviews several months after the program with seven participants who performed especially well during the seminar, on the
assumption that they were among those most likely to apply what
they learned. Actually, many applications were discovered, some
unanticipated.

Benefits included forestalling a lawsuit through conflict resolution; and conducting better, shorter, and more satisfactory meetings
(the cost of salaried time saved was as much as the budget of the
entire staff development program). These success cases were used
for a follow-up survey of all management seminar participants (with
findings shared among all managers to encourage greater application of seminar content) and as examples in seminar sessions.

Various stakeholders of an adult basic education (ABE) program
wanted answers to questions about impact:

- What proportion of ABE participants obtain new or
  different jobs or greater responsibility as a result?

- Do work supervisors believe that ABE participation
  contributes to better performance? Are ABE partici-

pants better able to benefit from staff development than nonparticipants?

- Do participants become more active in the community?

- Does ABE participation contribute to effective parenting?

Data collection instruments and sources contribute to at least partially answering such questions. For instance, a questionnaire on general satisfaction with elements of an ABE program can be answered by participants, the instructor, coordinator, other staff members, work supervisors, educational administrators, and community organization leaders. One item may have the respondent indicate his or her relationship to the ABE program. Another item might allow the respondent to check a four-point scale (from highly satisfied to not satisfied) for a listing of program elements. Some elements pertain to the program (goals, participants, staff, materials, facilities); others have to do with benefits and outcomes (general results, self-esteem, work advancement, family literacy, further education, community participation).

Another questionnaire for work supervisors might request confidential assessment of the participant's work performance relevant to ABE program effectiveness. In addition to a brief description of the participant's work role, a listing of aspects of work performance (knowledge, activities, skills, habits, improvements, reading, math) might allow ratings of supervisor satisfaction with participant work performance along with suggestions of related contributions that the ABE program might make or has already made (Grotelueschen, Gooler, and Knox, 1976).

Most impact studies focus on improved performance, particularly outcomes that benefit an organization or society generally (Caffarella, 1994). Because an impact study tends to be complex and expensive, it is important to consider the level of effort that is warranted in a specific instance. Attention to improved performance paves the way to assessment of organizational and societal benefits, which depend on individual and team performance.

Assessment of improved performance can use such procedures as an interview, observation, documents, and follow-up survey with past participants and their peers. Some of the resulting data may yield proof of improvement, but much of it constitutes evidence to substantiate a rationale regarding probable improvement. Indicators are productivity, absenteeism, errors, and tangible and direct benefits to people served. Evaluation conclusions related to improved performance are used for documenting application from past programs, planning increased application for future programs, and planning assessment of organizational and societal benefits.

Here are guidelines that pertain to planning evaluation of improved performance:

- Use the results of needs assessment and contextual analysis when planning evaluation of improved performance attributable to an educational program.

- Involve participants and other stakeholders in the evaluation.

- Identify which participants are applying what they learn.

- Identify which parts of the program content are being applied.

- Analyze how (and how well) participants are using what they learn.

- Identify how, when, and where new learnings are being applied.

- Discover successful applications and nurture them.

- Help participants use self-assessment to guide their learning and application.

- Use existing data where possible.

- Avoid overcontrol in evaluation to reduce participant or instructor resistance.

- Be willing to attempt difficult but important evaluation.

Evaluation of results and benefits to an organization or society can build on evaluation of improved performance (Brinkerhoff, 1987). Here are questions to guide evaluation of the organizational and societal benefits of an educational program:

- What benefits resulted from the program?

- What is the value of each benefit (in monetary or other terms)?

- How do these benefits compare with the program costs?

- To what extent was the initial need or problem resolved?

Here are examples of the connection between improved performance and ultimate benefit:

- A program enables equipment operators to alter their maintenance practices so maintenance improves; there is less down time, which results in increased production.

- Research and development staff learn how to improve, so more new projects are begun and supported, which results in a more competitive organization with a larger product line.

- Citizens enhance community leadership proficiencies, so
  more people are more effective in community leadership
  and volunteer positions, which results in more effective
  leadership in community agencies and projects.

The level of effort that should be devoted to an outcome assessment varies greatly with specific contingencies in each instance.
Considerations include the urgency of the issues regarding benefits,
concern about such issues on the part of stakeholders, availability
of resources to support an evaluation project, and the cost-benefit
ratio for the program.

Three examples from Brinkerhoff (1987) illustrate types and
level of outcome assessment.

A company offers maintenance and repair training for licensed
dealers nationwide who sell and service the washing machines they
manufacture. As part of its customer service and quality assurance
program, the company collects information from every dealership
on the nature and frequency of repairs, which is centrally aggregated
in the company's computer. As a simple indicator of its maintenance and repair training, the training division obtains periodic
computer printouts of summary repair data by region in relation to
recent training. Printing out these summaries takes the training
division secretary about ten minutes per month, to indicate how
much and how well its training is being used.

A manufacturing firm recently hired many new drill press operators. A skill training program was begun for them, on the basis of
information from performance audits, customer rejects that were
traced back to high scrap rates, and faulty quality measurement procedures. Furthermore, selection procedures failed to identify the
operators' unfamiliarity with the procedures they were using. In
addition to the skill training, their supervisors received training on
accurate statistical quality control. Follow-up audits two, six, and
eighteen weeks afterward resulted in revised training, including brief
refresher sessions for operators and supervisors. A second round of

audits revealed great improvement in scrap, quality, and assessment. Training was terminated since no new hiring was projected, but ongoing audits continued to assure management of prospects for high performance.

An office furniture company had experienced declining sales and profits for some years, but prospects for an improved economy and new markets led to companywide productivity studies. As a result, a decision was made to capitalize on the coming strong market by instituting a team production approach. The HRD director agreed to offer team building and project management training, which an employee survey and literature review indicated were crucial for a product team approach.

A pilot program was begun with the first three product teams. After one year, a review of company profits and customer satisfaction was strongly positive, and a survey of team performance showed correct use of training content. A high-level review panel recommended extension of team training to all product teams, on the basis of the impact evaluation and data indicating that the cost of training was less than 3 percent of total production costs.

These are three examples of the value of assessing outcomes. Guidelines that can be used to evaluate ultimate benefits are to:

- Consider a broad range of impact variables.

- Explore specific ways in which improved performance can contribute to organizational or societal benefit.

- Obtain perspectives from multiple stakeholders when assessing program value and impact.

- Consider various categories when assessing program costs.

- Use data and conclusions from preceding evaluation stages related to participants (performance, achievement satisfaction), and from other aspects of program evaluation (needs, context, instructors).

Impact evaluation studies require some expertise for planning and implementing design, sampling, data collection and analysis, and reporting. The evaluation coordinator may have some of this expertise and should arrange for the remainder from staff or consultants. The ideas presented here are useful for planning various forms of impact evaluation (self-study, external review, follow-up study, cost-benefit analysis, and practice adoption).

Early planning regarding evaluation, and outcome assessment in particular, pertains to such capacity building. Some standards for provider agency planning and assessment serve the purpose of impact evaluation, as seen in the examples given here from continuing education in the health professions; the parenthetic numbers refer to the quality elements in the original publication (Green and Associates, 1984).

- Identifying agency staff and volunteers with evaluation interests and capabilities (92.1)

- Specifying needs for evaluation (92.2)

- Focusing the evaluation (92.3)

- Specifying the desired and actual resources for conducting evaluation (93.4)

- Deciding the scope of the evaluation (93.2)

- Selecting evaluation methods that fit the evaluation goals and resources (94)

- Developing an evaluation plan (95)

- Implementing the evaluation plan (96)

- Analyzing the evaluation data (97)

- Reporting the evaluation conclusions and recommendations (98)

- Using the evaluation results to make decisions about
  issues on which the evaluation was focused (99)

Much has been written about designing research and evaluation studies applicable to impact evaluation. The overview given here can help evaluation planners review their current expertise and decide on obtaining additional assistance.

Some approaches to outcome evaluation are nonexperimental; sometimes they are sufficient given a specific evaluation goal and circumstance. However, it is important to recognize their limitations (often referred to as threat to internal validity). For example, one set of observations at the end of a program may indicate participant achievement, but a pretest-posttest design produces convincing evidence about extent of actual improvement. However, nonprogram-related changes may affect interpretation of data for an impact study. Such influences as aging, events, participant selection or attrition, and the methods of collecting data may obscure improvement that the program did produce or suggest changes that cannot be attributed to the program. Because single-group design is less intrusive and expensive than experimental design, it can be useful for estimating likely impact, assessing the usefulness of more rigorous evaluation, identifying promising variables related to program benefits, and preparing stakeholders for more stringent evaluation (Posavac and Carey, 1992).

Quasi-experimental approaches to outcome evaluation are fairly widespread because they can be less disruptive and expensive than an experimental approach. One way to distinguish improvement from an unrelated trend is by using time series designs, in which pertinent quantitative indicators are identified and data collected over a number of time periods before, during, and after a program. Data collection from a comparison group helps identify improvement attributable to the program (Posavac and Carey, 1992).

Random assignment of participants or instructors to experimental and control groups helps to distinguish experimental design.

This approach is infrequent because of cost, disruption, resistance, and rigidity. However, when a new program is being initiated, or when continued support is in question, sometimes the cost of not evaluating a program rigorously may be greater than the cost of doing so (Posavac and Carey, 1992).

One of the most important planning decisions regarding impact evaluation is selection of social and economic indicators to identify program contributions toward achieving the outcome target. Multiple outcome indicators serve as criterion variables for evaluation design and allow tracking of impact for accountability and subsequent programming. These indicators can be used to assess program results through time series data that also include outcomes related to program participants, other people associated with them, and members of comparison groups who did not participate in the program. Multiple indicators are important to reflect at least some of the program impact that might occur and to allow cross-validation. Sometimes understanding the type of impact may be as important as the extent of impact (Bennett and Rockwell, 1995).

Various data collection and analysis procedures can be used for outcomes evaluation: observation, a behaviorally anchored rating scale of actual performance, interview, test, performance appraisal, participant follow-up after an opportunity for application, document analysis, unobtrusive measures, success case method, portfolio, consumer survey, performance record analysis, productivity measurement, performance audit, cost-benefit analysis, return-on-investment analysis, and external review (Brinkerhoff, 1987). The middle portion of Chapter Four has additional examples of data collection and analysis procedures.

Expertise to help plan and implement outcomes evaluation extends beyond study design for sampling, data collection and analysis, and reporting. It is equally important regarding interpersonal relations to gain and maintain cooperation from the many people typically connected with impact assessment (Knox, 1979a; Patton, 1997). There are distinctive features of cooperation associated with each type of outcome evaluation (self-study, external review, follow-up study, cost-benefit analysis, practice adoption).

For instance, arranging for self-study related to outcomes depends on a trusting relationship with the people involved. This is so whether there is one instructor and a group of participants, or people (participants, instructor, coordinator, policy makers) associated with a large provider agency. Among the ways to obtain their cooperation are:

- Providing a clear and convincing rationale for the importance of and procedure for self-study.

- Arranging for able and representative people associated with the program to help plan and conduct the self-study.

- Making available specific guidelines for procedures (such as advance understanding, sampling, data collection and analysis, reporting).

- Reassuring people of the confidentiality of information they offer, to be summarized in the self-study report.

- Clarifying the intent of the self-study to identify desirable improvements in program outcomes and procedures so as to achieve change.

- Encouraging ongoing cooperation and offering assistance to facilitate such cooperation.

As seen in earlier chapters, a self-study is the usual preliminary stage of an outcomes evaluation that also includes an external review. This combination is typical of accreditation reviews of educational institutions and hospitals. The self-study stage assembles basic historical, descriptive, and evaluative information about the program, which constitutes a basis for an external review and for encouraging use of recommendations. Expertise related to external reviews can contribute in a number of ways to planning and implementation:

- Offering an overview and rationale

- Arranging for able review team members who together can accomplish the external review

- Orienting review team members

- Timing provision of the self-study report to review team members, if there is a self-study

- Monitoring and assisting the review team as they move through the process

- Arranging for review of the external review report, in relation to other reports, as a way of validating conclusions and establishing priorities for recommendations

- Encouraging use of conclusions (Worthen and Sanders, 1987)

Follow-up studies seek to conclude what happened as a result of an educational program, long enough afterward that people have had a chance to use what they learned. Three distinctive areas of expertise related to follow-up evaluation of impact are preparing for the follow-up so that cooperation occurs, keeping track of past participants so they can be located, and noting situational influences that may interfere with conclusions about program impact on outcome indicators assessed in a follow-up. In a specific follow-up, the purposes and resources shape selection of a few ways of collecting data from the range of possibilities: observations, questionnaires, interviews, documents, product or performance review, and cost-benefit analysis (Caffarella, 1994).

Cost-benefit analysis (similar to return on investment) is a special, quantitative type of outcome assessment. It entails assessing relationships between educational program outcomes and the costs of producing them (Caffarella, 1994; Posavac and Carey, 1992). The soundness of resulting cost-benefit rates and indexes depends on how satisfactorily both costs and benefits can be represented by numbers. Sometimes detailed monetary costs can be categorized (variable, fixed, incremental, sunk, recurring, one-time, hidden, obvious, direct, indirect, opportunity). However, it is seldom easy to assign monetary value to indicators of benefit. In addition to multiple program benefits and stakeholders who benefit differently, assessing the extent and type of benefit entails value judgment.

For many educational programs for adults, the people who pay for costs are not those who receive benefits. Placing monetary value on typical outcomes and benefits requires many assumptions and estimates regarding noneconomic aspects of peoples' lives and use of cost-benefit ratio for program decision making. One way to assess the influence of adult and continuing education on organizational and social change is to analyze adoption of practices recommended by educational programs. This procedure has been particularly useful for cooperative extensions; rural sociologists have been especially prominent in studying practice adoption. Guidelines for doing so are to:

- Specify a desirable practice of high priority for the educational provider and some of its clientele—a practice that can be readily studied.

- Describe the indicators of the practice that can be used to monitor its adoption, as use spreads through the population to be studied.

- Select a representative sample of respondents from whom to collect data (usually by interview or questionnaire).

- Find out when they adopted the practice (if they did) and the information seeking in which they engaged as some of them progressed from apathy to awareness, interest, trial, and adoption (and in some cases disadoption).

- Compare the timing of adoption as it spreads through the population (innovators, early adopters, early majority, late majority, laggards) in relation to educational program efforts aimed at accelerating the adoption process, and from resoondent comments on perceived contributions of the program, draw conclusions about the extent and type of impact the program had on practice adoption (Havelock, 1969).

• Employ the linkage model of reciprocal relationships between resource and client systems, which is especially useful regarding dynamics of interaction to consider and feedback that occurs.

Coordination

In addition to arranging for the plans and their implementation, coordination of outcomes evaluation typically confronts some basic challenges pertaining to such matters as who conducts the evaluation, interpersonal relations, political pressures, ethics, and meta-evaluation.

Coordination of an impact assessment usually means working closely with only a few people to evaluate the outcomes and results of a single course or workshop, but perhaps hundreds of people to assess the results of a comprehensive program by a provider agency. Thus two basic questions regarding coordination of outcomes evaluation arise: Who should help conduct it? What are their roles?

In a large and complex impact assessment, for each category of stakeholders an appropriate sample may contribute data that are representative of the remainder. In selecting people to help plan and conduct an outcomes evaluation, two considerations to be balanced are representativeness and involvement. Representativeness is reflected in the involvement of people in the evaluation who are similar to other people in their stakeholder category, especially in a report that fairly and accurately reflects the actual program and its impact. Involvement in the evaluation is important to encourage stakeholder understanding and commitment to use evaluation findings, but without distortion and special pleading in the evaluation report. One effective outcome evaluation design feature that addresses this balance is to include multiple small studies, which allows broad participation and multiple perspectives (Madaus, Scriven, and Stufflebeam, 1983, thesis 54). Selection of program areas to include can be an important decision (Knox, 1979a).

As an example of some ways to involve people in an outcomes evaluation, suppose an instructor wants to evaluate the outcomes of a course or workshop to assess impact and guide improvements (Knox, 1986). Evaluation of the results and benefits of the program and its components might include these procedures:

- Review expected outcomes and satisfaction with methods, to clarify the rationale for both the evaluation and use of conclusions.

- Locate reports on pertinent studies of similar outcomes and methods, to note findings and evaluation procedures.

- Review the resultant overview. If it is sufficient for decision making, use it; if not, proceed with the total evaluation.

- Decide on summative evaluation goals, indicators of impact, and preliminary rationale for the relationship between methods and outcomes.

- Characterize alternative methods to be studied.

- Describe content, learners, and context related to methods.

- Design a basic and efficient impact study likely to answer the main questions about outcomes.

- Use the preliminary review of past experience and literature, and a pilot study, to conduct the outcomes assessment; then use findings to improve the program, with formative evaluation to guide ongoing improvement.

- Collect data, using existing instruments where satisfactory and developing valid instruments and procedures that do not disrupt the program.

- Analyze data by comparing method effectiveness against indices of impact.

- Draft implications for improvement.

A simpler assessment of impact is in participant use of a work-related learning plan to guide individualization. Participants might help plan a results evaluation related to some shared goals, to include a set of rating scales on the extent of implementation as viewed by participants, peers, and supervisors. Participants who use these rating scales in a parallel evaluation can compare their findings and then discuss variations in program success and related influences.

A follow-up study can be combined with participants' early written projections of their expected outcomes related to implementation after sufficient elapsed time following the program. A copy of their expected use of what they learn can be sent to participants along with a reply form on positive and negative results of the implementation efforts. Their willingness to respond might be enhanced by the prospect of receiving a summary of implementation experiences of all those who respond.

Interpersonal relations to achieve understanding and cooperation are equivalent in importance to the technical aspects of evaluation (Patton, 1997; Shadish, Cook, and Leviton, 1995; Abrahamson, 1985). Encouraging use of impact assessment recommendations can be aided by recognizing barriers (as well as facilitators) to utilization. Suggestions to encourage utilization of outcome evaluation recommendations: prepare a brief informal report in simple language, tailor the report to the interests and communication styles of the stakeholders, include clear action recommendations with supporting rationale, and publicize evaluation findings in various media to increase the number of stakeholders who know about the findings and the reinforcement necessary for them to take action (Shadish, Cook, and Leviton, 1995).

Outcome evaluation recommendations often generate resistance among people in powerful positions in an organization or community who sense a threat to something they value. Sometimes such perceptions reflect general apprehension about the unknown. Involving some of these people as stakeholders in the evaluation process can expose them to both current and desirable program features as a rationale for evaluation recommendations. Some resistance reflects unfamiliarity or misconception about the evaluation process, which is declining as various professional fields give increasing attention to program evaluation and accountability (Abrahamson, 1985). Most of the examples here reveal ways in which coordination of outcome evaluation have included attention to political pressures from people and groups who could influence the evaluation process (especially use of findings). This issue is particularly important because evaluation of results addresses value judgments by external stakeholders.

Because educational programs for adults and related evaluation of outcomes can entail both change and resistance for multiple stakeholders, the circumstances typically exist for ethical issues to occur. Evaluation can contribute to problem solving by attention to solutions, explanations, and assistance to stakeholders (Shadish, Cook, and Leviton, 1995). All of this can contribute to conflict as differing expectations confront program changes. Two general ways to reduce such conflict and related ethical issues are through agreement and through negotiation. Evaluation standards reflect the issues that evaluators have experienced and the type of explicit agreement and understanding that can clarify goals and working relationships at the planning stage to reduce conflict and issues as the evaluation proceeds (Sanders, 1994). Negotiation for reduction of conflict and other issues is a way of dealing ethically with differences among stakeholders that may arise (Cervero and Wilson, 1994, 1996, 1998).

These concerns about political pressures and ethical issues related to impact assessment make meta-evaluation especially pertinent. This evaluation of the evaluation process and conclusions is a way to strengthen reports and utilization, address criticism, and learn from evaluation experiences to improve planning of future assessment. The next example shows use of meta-evaluation and a follow-up study.

A fifteen-hour simulation workshop for administrators on evaluation procedures was assessed by verified personal follow-up interviews to find out the extent to which past participants actually used the evaluation techniques from the workshop simulation in their subsequent work (Knox, 1979a). An inventory of nine specific evaluation activities included in the workshop content was covered in personal interviews in their offices before the workshop and ten months afterward. When administrators referred to use of evaluation techniques, the interviewer asked about examples, which administrators often shared for verification. In the first thirty-minute interview, the emphasis was on needs assessment; in the second it was on workshop effectiveness, so rapport was established with respondents and they were not defensive. Scoring gave weight to verified activities. Prescores and postscores of workshop participants were compared with those of a group of administrators who expressed interest in the workshop but did not attend. There was no significant change in scores for the comparison group, but a significant improvement for the participants.

Impact evaluation focuses on outcomes, but it often includes some attention to input and process. Evaluation of outcomes warrants effective coordination because it is typically complex, including information from self-studies and external reviews, and seeks conclusions relevant to external stakeholders.

As you reflect on the ideas about evaluation of outcomes and results, consider these questions:

- What is the rationale for the balance between self-study and external review?

- Which evaluation approaches and designs seem most promising?

- What coordination arrangements are likely to result in sound conclusions and utilization of them?

Summary Guidelines

This checklist reviews basic guidelines for outcome evaluations. As you plan or strengthen an outcome evaluation, the guidelines can help you enhance your rationale and procedures.

Concepts

1. Outcome evaluations focus on impact issues important to stakeholders, but they also include some system information about context, inputs, and process.

2. Impact assessment can be for purposes of accountability, improvement, or planning; it can focus on participants, instructor, topic, or context.

3. Assessing benefits to other people associated with participants can be challenging but made more feasible by attention to comparison group, elapsed time, pre- and postprogram measures, time series, costs and benefits, and use of evidence.

4. Ultimate outcomes occur late in a chain of effects, so evaluation of earlier links helps encourage continued cooperation, clarifies intended outcomes, validates evidence, and recognizes influences.

5. Multiple indicators contribute to cross-validation, explanation, and portrayal of multiple benefits and consequences.

6. Involving multiple stakeholders early and appropriately in the outcome evaluation process can enhance their use of conclusions.

Planning

7. Excellent educational programs for adults can have an impact to be evaluated.

8. Outcome evaluation designs tend to vary with the type of benefit for the individual, a group, an organization, or society.

9. For a specific outcome evaluation, one approach or a combination can be used, at any of several levels of investment.

10. An objective-based approach assesses the extent to which stated objectives were met.

11. A case study is a rich description of a program as perceived by various stakeholders.

12. A systems analysis assesses program functioning as a social system, which helps to identify implicit goals.

13. An expert review uses standards to analyze program resources and processes in relation to outcomes.

14. An experimental study seeks causal explanations, usually using predata and postdata and a comparison group.

15. Most impact assessments focus on performance and results that benefit the individual, a group, an organization, or a community.

16. Assessment of improved individual performance uses such procedures as an interview, observation, documents, or follow-up survey to substantiate a rationale regarding probable improvement.

17. Evaluation of organizational and community benefits can build on assessment of improved performance but focus on organizational and societal indicators.

Coordination

18. The level of effort for an outcome evaluation varies with specific contingencies, to reflect urgency of issues, stakeholder concerns, availability of resources, and cost-benefit ratio for the evaluation.

19. Guidelines for impact assessment pertain to range of variables, relation between improved performance and ultimate benefits, multiple stakeholder perspectives, type of cost, and using conclusions from assessment of improved performance when evaluating organizational and societal benefits.

20. The evaluation coordinator has or arranges for pertinent expertise.

21. A nonexperimental approach to outcome evaluation may be sufficient in some circumstances, but many times it limits conclusions about program impact.

22. A quasi-experimental approach to outcomes evaluation tends to use time series design and a comparison group to distinguish improvement from unrelated trends.

23. An experimental approach with random assignment of participants to treatment is used infrequently because of cost, disruption, resistance, and rigidity.

24. Multiple outcome indicators serve as criterion variables to assess program results.

25. Among data collection and analysis procedures are observation, performance rating, test, performance appraisal, follow-up, document analysis, unobtrusive measures, case, portfolio, survey, performance records analysis, productivity measurement, performance audit, cost-benefit analysis, return on investment, and external review.

26. Planning expertise also includes interpersonal relations to obtain cooperation and encourage utilization of conclusions.

27. Self-study cooperation is aided by a convincing rationale, able team members, specific guidelines, confidentiality of information, and encouragement.

28. A self-study is sometimes accompanied by an external review, which is aided by orientation and assistance to review team, effective timing and coordination, validation, and encouragement of utilization.

29. Follow-up studies, after time has elapsed for application, can be aided by preparing, locating past participants, and noting situational influences.

30. Cost-benefit analysis is difficult to conduct because of the assumptions and value judgments related to multiple benefits and stakeholder expectations.

31. Analyses of practice adoption attributable to an educational program is aided by specifying indicators of a desirable innovative practice, selecting representative respondents to find out when and why they adopted a recommended innovative practice, and tracking adoption of the practice as it spreads through the population of respondents.

32. Coordination of an impact assessment is usually a team effort, enhanced by considerations of representativeness and involvement.

33. Use of evaluation recommendations can be aided by recognizing barriers to (and facilitators of) utilization.

34. Outcomes evaluation recommendations often generate resistance from people in powerful positions who are apprehensive about proposed changes.

35. Prior agreements and ongoing negotiations can reduce conflict and ethical issues related to differing expectations.

36. Evaluation of the evaluation process and conclusions can strengthen reports and utilization, address criticism, and aid planning for future programs and evaluation.

Part III

Guidelines for Improving Evaluation Practice

12

How and Why

The preceding chapters offer guidelines, examples, and rationale to help you conduct your own evaluation of educational programs for adults. You and other people with a stake in your program frequently make informal evaluative judgments. Formalizing the evaluation process can enable you to use sound conclusions to strengthen program decisions.

Sound evaluations are useful in various ways. Early on, they help select the program aspects on which to focus the main evaluation. Other early considerations for planning an evaluation are resources, design, procedures, contingencies, and utilization.

Evaluation guidelines are not recipes, and the evaluation process is not a series of linear steps. Therefore the guidelines, examples, and rationale are meant to help you create an evaluation focus, approach, and strategy that fits your purpose and situation.

This concluding chapter reviews evaluation of all aspects of adult educational programs. It does so by listing guidelines on planning and implementing evaluation generally. This consolidated set of guidelines is based on those at the conclusion of Chapters Four through Eleven on specific program aspects. Each guideline is in three parts. The first is a how-to suggestion regarding evaluation procedure. The second is a brief rationale as to why the suggestion is important. The third part proposes how to strengthen and improve these evaluation procedures in the future.

Describe the Program

How. Describe the main characteristics of the program aspects to be evaluated, to ensure that the evaluation is responsive.

Why. The typical evaluation purpose is to produce conclusions useful to stakeholders regarding planning, improvement, and accountability. Such usefulness can be enhanced if people associated with the evaluation share a fairly accurate idea of the characteristics of the aspects to be evaluated. This description can include explicit and implicit goals and activities, so that the people conducting an evaluation can ensure a satisfactory fit between the aspects being evaluated and the evaluation purposes, focus, scope, activities, and resources. (This is illustrated in Chapters Four, Five, Six, Eight, and Nine.)

Improve. Two ways to strengthen this in the future are to help stakeholders appreciate the potential contribution of a brief program description, and use pertinent standards from meta-evaluation and other sources in preparing and using a program description.

Estimate Likely Results Through Small Preliminary Evaluations

How. Use past experience to estimate likely results of program aspects to be evaluated, as one basis for deciding the evaluation focus and scale. Conducting a pilot evaluation permits an evaluability assessment, explores feasibility, and prepares the way for selection of sound technical procedures and effective inclusion of stakeholders in the process.

Why. Excellent program features can contribute to achieving benefits. To decide how much to invest in evaluation, one consideration is an estimate of pertinent program features on which to focus. This assessment can include the likely type and extent of results; probable quality and extent of program features intended to produce the results; estimated influence of features on results; extent and type of stakeholder involvement; and recommended extent, focus, and design of an evaluation project. (This is illustrated in Chapters Four, Seven, Ten, and Eleven.)

Improve. Evaluators can strengthen this by reviewing guidelines and examples for evaluability assessments, pertinent writing about evaluation, and reports on similar evaluations. These reports can contribute to planning and implementing an evaluability assessment, including interpreting findings. A major benefit from meta-evaluation is validated indicators of program quality and results that can be used in a modest evaluation project to assess and monitor worth and effectiveness.

Specify Evaluation Purpose

How. Use indicators that a specific evaluation project is warranted, to help specify issues of concern to major stakeholders and preliminary purpose of the evaluation.

Why. It is important to clarify the evaluation purpose early because there are many aspects that can be evaluated and limited resources for doing so. Thorough evaluation of all aspects is more costly than conducting the program, and it is seldom warranted. Analysis of the symptoms and an assumption that in general an evaluation is desirable, along with clarification of issues important to major stakeholders, can contribute to specifying an evaluation's purpose, focus, priority, and a scale that is both desirable and feasible. The resulting rationale can help acquire and justify necessary resources and assistance, and attract stakeholder commitment to the evaluation and use of conclusions. A clear and compelling evaluation purpose can also guide planning and implementation decisions about evaluation procedures and utilization of conclusions. (This is illustrated in Chapters Four through Seven, Nine, and Ten.)

Improve. Evaluation purposes may be implicit or externally imposed. Specifying the purposes of an evaluation project makes them explicit and helps strengthen stakeholder contribution and utilization. Such specification can be augmented by review of evaluation overviews and guidelines, inclusion of stakeholders in the process, and insights from reports and evaluations related to similar evaluation projects. Negotiation can promote praxis between practical realities and desirable features on the basis of expectations and guidelines.

Consider Five Levels

How. An evaluation project might focus on any of five levels of evaluation: satisfaction, achievement, performance, benefits, and return on investment in the program.

Why. Each level has advantages and disadvantages. Typical application of the concept of evaluation levels has been to participant acquisition and use of knowledge, and organizational as well as individual benefits. However, the concept can apply to each aspect (needs, context, goals, staffing, participation, materials, and outcomes as well as the total program). At the levels of satisfaction and achievement, assessment is relatively straightforward and inexpensive to conduct, but it does not allow conclusions about impact that are of interest to some stakeholders. At the levels of organizational benefit and return on investment, conclusions about outcomes can be very useful, but conducting such an assessment can be complex and expensive. The ascending levels are cumulative, incorporating all underlying levels as prerequisite to the next. (This is illustrated in Chapter Eight.)

Improve. Evaluators can use an understanding of these five levels to help specify desired evaluation purpose and scale, along with requisite design, procedures, and resources. The concept's usefulness can be increased by recognizing its applicability to all program aspects. Sharing of evaluation reports and guidelines pertinent to each of the five levels can also help the evaluator explain the advantages and disadvantages of each level to stakeholders, and to obtain the resources and support requisite to the level selected.

Address Value Judgments

How. Values are part of evaluation; they should be addressed explicitly.

Why. Even when an evaluation is descriptive and quantitative, the values of stakeholders and evaluators are reflected in their perspectives and data selection and interpretation. Values are reflected in assumptions, priorities, and interpretations, as well as stated objectives and preferences. Making stakeholder values explicit (whether stated or estimated) helps evaluators build cooperation on shared values and address value differences. Negotiation can sometimes help address such differences. (This is illustrated in Chapter Four.)

Improve. Attention to values can be strengthened in several ways. One is to recognize the extent and ways in which stakeholder values influence the entire evaluation process. Such influences affect the technical process and interpersonal relations. Review of evaluation reports and writing that discuss values can help stakeholders recognize and address implicit and explicit values in their own evaluation project. It helps to consider not only the espoused rationale regarding priority, procedure, and interpretation but also implicit preferences and values. Values clarification procedures can be useful. Most important for improvement is practice addressing values and negotiating differences. Addressing values explicitly can help the evaluator reduce stakeholder resistance, which often surfaces in the form of not using conclusions.

Using Ongoing Assessment

How. Consider continuous evaluation and feedback before, during, and after the educational program or related activity.

Why. Many uses of evaluation conclusions pertain to the program development process. The developmental process includes aspirations, diagnosis, goals, plans, implementation, benefits, and support. Assessment before the program contributes to a sound and responsive plan. Assessment during the program allows ongoing improvement and participation on the part of stakeholders. Follow-up assessment typically focuses on benefits and support for future activity. Selective evaluation within this developmental process allows use of assessment conclusions for decision making that combines attention to planning, implementation, and benefits. One-shot evaluation is typically insufficient for this purpose and lacks cross-validation. (This is illustrated in Chapters Four, Eight, Ten, and Eleven.)

Improve. Ongoing assessment can be strengthened if the evaluator has a developmental rationale tied to a chain of program decisions. It also helps if the evaluation process includes quality indicators that allow monitoring effectiveness and worth.

Assess System Functioning

How. When evaluating any aspect or component of a program or activity, use relevant conclusions from other aspects.

Why. Because an educational program and provider agency is an open system functioning in a broader context, various aspects are interconnected. Therefore part of efficient and effective evaluation planning and implementation is recognizing such connections and using data and conclusions from other components. This is efficient and contributes to sound conclusions. A systemic approach also contributes to assessing aspirations and benefits for the individual, an organization, and stakeholders. (This is illustrated in Chapters Five, Seven, Eight, and Eleven.)

Improve. An evaluator with a systemic perspective on program development and evaluation can recognize potentially useful data and conclusions from related aspects, and also use evaluation conclusions to enhance the systemic perspective, which can then guide efforts to explain and strengthen program functioning.

Include Contextual Influences

How. In addition to contextual analysis, an evaluator can assess influences from the provider organization, other providers, and the societal context generally. The conclusions can be used to understand how program functioning is affected by such contextual influences.

Why. Program functioning is affected by inputs (participants, staff, money, cooperation) and by stakeholder satisfaction with results and benefits. These inputs and outcomes are in turn affected by the societal context of the parent organization and service area, in particular competition and economic conditions. Evaluation of any program aspect is more accurate and useful if it includes attention to such societal influences. (This is illustrated in Chapters Five, Six, and Nine.)

Improve. One benefit of strategic planning is conclusions about contextual threats and opportunities that can be used for evaluation purposes. A specific evaluation project can also include information about contextual influences directly related to the purpose of the evaluation, if the evaluator recognizes the value of doing so.

Arrange for a Coordinator

How. Have one or more people provide leadership and coordination for the evaluation, so there is satisfactory cooperation and continuity.

Why. Having explicitly designated coordination of an evaluation brings many advantages. It helps ensure continuity between planning and implementation. Familiarity with evaluation concepts can increase attention to technical procedures and interpersonal cooperation, both of which are important for successful internal and external evaluation. Effective coordination can also contribute to involvement of stakeholders, acquisition of resources, and reporting of findings. Familiarity with evaluation guidelines and standards can enable coordinators to guide the contributions of various stakeholders to conducting evaluation and utilizing conclusions. (This is illustrated in Chapters Four, Six, Eight, Nine, and Eleven.)

Improve. An early way to strengthen arrangements for coordination of evaluation is to consider the nature of the intended evaluation and requirements for coordination, as a basis for deciding on the person or people likely to carry out satisfactory coordination. If they are not familiar with pertinent evaluation coordination concepts and procedures, alert them to available guidelines.

Involve Stakeholders and Obtain Their Cooperation

How. Include a range of stakeholders in planning and implementing the evaluation. Their involvement typically varies according to their interests, ability, resources, commitment, and constraints.

Why. Useful evaluation combines sound conclusions and utilization for program planning, improvement, and accountability. The extent and type of stakeholder involvement in the evaluation process can greatly influence usefulness. Stakeholder cooperation can lead to asking evaluation questions that address issues they care about, producing credible conclusions that pertain to program development and teaching and learning decisions, and especially use of conclusions. Thus, establishing effective interpersonal relations with stakeholders is a major challenge for the evaluator. (This is illustrated in Chapters Four through Eleven.)

Improve. Stakeholder cooperation can be strengthened by use of sound guidelines based on experience with similar evaluation, conclusions that address issues they value, meta-evaluation to refine specific concepts and procedures, and experience with negotiation and other ways to promote agreement and cooperation.

Address Differential Stakeholder Influence

How. Consider the differences that sometimes occur in the relative power of various stakeholders to influence the evaluation. Use the resulting conclusions to include the viewpoints of the less powerful, and minimize distortions that reflect the bias of more power-ful stakeholders.

Why. Evaluation plans and conclusions can pertain to impor-tant and controversial issues on which various stakeholders have differing viewpoints. Stakeholders diverge in their ability to influ-ence an evaluation. Credibility and use of findings can be greatly enhanced if stakeholders are reassured that the evaluation is even-handed and takes various viewpoints into account. Leadership is sometimes required to achieve a balanced evaluation that is not distorted. (This is illustrated in Chapters Four, Five, Six, and Eleven.)

Improve. Leadership regarding differential stakeholder influ-ence and balanced evaluation can be strengthened by recognizing this issue, using evaluation standards, and including explicit nego-tiation so that stakeholders understand the concern and continue to be supportive of the evaluation. For an especially divisive issue, this may entail a minority report or commentary on conclusions.

Obtain Necessary Resources and Support

How. A successful evaluation requires various resources: money, materials, and especially the time of people with interest and spe-cialized expertise necessary for planning, implementing, and using the evaluation. Obtaining such resources usually takes thought and effort, reflected in a convincing rationale and proposal that include attention to benefits that stakeholders value and in which they are willing to invest.

Why. Resources for evaluation are also sought for other activi-ties and priorities. It takes a convincing rationale to win and main-tain cooperation and necessary resources. The potential benefits of many evaluations are unrealized because the resources are inade-quate, especially toward the conclusion of the evaluation process. Leadership on behalf of evaluation entails acquiring required resources in the interest of program quality. For this to occur, some stakeholders may require a convincing rationale for why an

investment in the proposed evaluation is warranted. (This is illustrated in Chapters Four through Eleven.)

Improve. Acquisition of necessary resources for evaluation can
be strengthened by specification of necessary resources and assistance, convincing rationales for resources and support, and familiarity with effective approaches to proposals and other ways to
obtain assistance.

Use Various Sources and Procedures to Obtain Evaluation Data

How. Consider various sources and procedures to obtain data that
are desirable regarding the purpose of the evaluation and feasible
regarding evaluation resources.

Why. Inclusion of various sources and procedures in the evaluation design has several advantages, among them soundness of conclusions, credibility with stakeholders, and encouragement of
utilization. Complementarity of procedures can be useful, as with
quantitative and qualitative data or self-study and external review.
Use of formal evaluation procedures contributes to exploring unfamiliar issues and the pertinence of impending program decisions,
but it requires attention to standards and coordination. (This is
illustrated in Chapters Four, Five, Seven, Nine, Ten, and Eleven.)

Improve. Data collection procedures can be strengthened by
familiarity with the advantages and disadvantages of potential procedure, by an evaluation approach and design that facilitate selecting especially desirable and feasible procedures, by use of follow-up
studies, and by inclusion of time series evaluation in ongoing management and instructional information systems.

Use Standards to Ensure Quality of Evaluation

How. Review evaluation standards when planning an evaluation
and when monitoring and making adjustments as the evaluation progresses.

Why. Guidelines and checklists help ensure that a complex series of evaluation decisions lead to an efficient and beneficial evaluation project. Guidelines on interpersonal relations and use of conclusions are as important as guidelines on technical procedures. (This is illustrated in Chapters Five, Seven, and Ten.)

Improve. Use of evaluation standards can be strengthened if evaluators know about them, are reflective as they select and adapt them for planning and implementation of specific evaluations, and develop and report useful guidelines that are of particular use in their context.

Analyze Data to Produce Useful Conclusions

How. Data analysis typically results in evaluation conclusions that are useful for planning, improvement, and accountability. This entails interpretation of major themes that reflect both descriptive information and value judgments.

Why. The intent of most evaluations is to judge the value of one or more program aspects. Value is reflected in quality, effectiveness, and benefits. Part of evaluation is descriptive, and part is comparative and interpretive. An example of a resulting explanation is clarification of discrepancies between current and desired features. Most evaluations include recommendations, which are especially useful if they include attention to both barriers and facilitators of progress. (This is illustrated in Chapters Five, Six, Nine, and Eleven.)

Improve. Data analysis can be strengthened by familiarity with the variety of available procedures, by recognition of the distinctive characteristics of evaluation regarding data analysis and interpretation, and by emphasis on use of conclusions by stakeholders.

Include Meta-Evaluation

How. Meta-evaluation is assessment of the evaluation process and findings. Meta-evaluation standards constitute criteria to guide planning and assessment of the soundness of the conclusions.

Why. Explicit meta-evaluation is desirable for several reasons. Standards can contribute to sound evaluation. Because of subjectivity and differing stakeholder perspectives, meta-evaluation can contribute to the validity and acceptability of conclusions. Criteria help compare an evaluation report with reports from similar evaluations. Participation in meta-evaluations helps stakeholders develop satisfactory explanations for program functioning and effective future evaluation. (This is illustrated in Chapters Four, Seven, Eight, and Nine.)

Improve. Use of meta-evaluation can be strengthened by the evaluator's familiarity with meta-evaluation concepts and procedures, by experience using meta-evaluation, and by contributions to reports on evaluation that enhance the evaluator's understanding of the process generally.

Use Evaluation to Enhance Program Vitality

How. Evaluations can go beyond assessment of program worth and quality to help stakeholders better understand the functioning of interrelated program components and thus enhance program vitality.

Why. By thinking of an educational program for adults as a system with interrelated components, stakeholders can use evaluation to better understand and explain how they function and can be improved. For example, the teaching-learning transaction is central, but it is interrelated with attraction of participants, staff, and resources, in turn affected by stakeholder perceptions of outcomes and benefits. Evaluation conclusions can include commendations for positive features that contribute to program effectiveness, as well as recommendations for desired improvement. Evaluation conclusions can thus help encourage ongoing support from stakeholders and consequently enhance vitality. (This is illustrated in Chapters Seven through Ten.)

Improve. The contribution of evaluation to program vitality can be enhanced if the evaluator and stakeholders recognize and use the potential of evaluation for this purpose, and not limit it to finding shortcomings.

Conclusion

Each evaluation is a unique reflection of its context, stakeholder expectations, available resources, and specific focus. Much of the success of your evaluation depends on the leadership you and others provide. Leadership includes attention to focus, coordination, expertise, and resources. Your familiarity with the local situation and your vision for future program direction are major assets.

The intent of this book is to enhance your mastery of evaluation concepts and procedures. This involves both technical procedures and interpersonal effectiveness—especially with appropriate stakeholders. Their contributions and support are crucial for use of sound conclusions. The guidelines and examples can also contribute to your innovations.

These guidelines can alert the evaluator to important considerations at the planning stage; they also figure prominently in metaevaluation. The rationale for why the suggested procedures are emphasized can help the evaluator make the decisions and judgments that compose a specific strategy. An evaluator who is reflective about the purposes and procedures of the evaluation project, and who publishes evaluation reports and commentaries, helps all of us strengthen our evaluations so that they are more practical and useful. This can allow us to assist our stakeholders to explain and improve educational program functioning. Learners, organizations, and society generally are the ultimate beneficiaries.

References

Abrahamson, S. (ed.). *Evaluation of Continuing Education in the Health Professions.* Norwell, Mass.: Kluwer, 1985.

Anderson, R. H. *Selecting and Developing Media for Instruction.* (2nd ed.) New York: Van Nostrand Reinhold, 1983.

Angelo, T. A., and Cross, K. P. *Classroom Assessment Techniques.* San Francisco: Jossey-Bass, 1993.

Argyris, C., Putnam, R., and Smith, D. M. *Action Science: Concepts, Methods, and Skills for Research Intervention.* San Francisco: Jossey-Bass, 1985.

Banta, T. W. *Assessment in Practice: Putting Principles to Work on College Campuses.* San Francisco: Jossey-Bass, 1985.

Baskett, H. K., and Marsick, V. J. *Professionals' Way of Knowing: New Findings on How to Improve Professional Education.* New Directions for Adult and Continuing Education, no. 55. San Francisco: Jossey-Bass, 1992.

Bennett, C., and Rockwell, K. *Targeting Outcomes of Programs (TOP): An Integrated Approach to Planning and Evaluation.* Washington, D.C.: USDA (Federal Extension Service); and Lincoln: Cooperative Extension, University of Nebraska, 1995.

Bingman, M. B. *Outcomes of Participation in Adult Basic Education.* (Occasional paper.) Cambridge, Mass.: National Center for the Study of Adult Learning and Literacy, Howard Graduate School of Education, Jan. 2000.

Blackburn, D. J. (ed.). *Extension Handbook.* Toronto: Thompson Educational, 1994.

Bogden, R., and Biklen, S. *Qualitative Research for Education: An Introduction to Theory and Methods.* Boston: Allyn and Bacon, 1992.

Boice, R. *First Order Principles for College Teachers: Ten Ways to Improve the Teaching Process.* Bolton, Mass.: Anker, 1996.

Boulmetis, J., and Dutwin, P. *The ABCs of Evaluation*. San Francisco: Jossey-Bass, 2000.

Boyer, E. L. *Scholarship Reconsidered*. Princeton, N.J.: Carnegie Foundation for the Advancement of Teaching, 1990.

Braskamp, L., and Ory, J. C. *Assessing Faculty Work: Enhancing Individual and Institutional Performance*. San Francisco: Jossey-Bass, 1994.

Brinkerhoff, R. O. *Achieving Results from Training*. San Francisco: Jossey-Bass, 1987.

Brookfield, S. *Becoming a Critically Reflective Teacher*. San Francisco: Jossey-Bass, 1995.

Brooks, A., and Watkins, K. E. (eds.). *The Emerging Power of Action Learning Technologies*. New Directions for Adult and Continuing Education, no. 63. San Francisco: Jossey-Bass, 1994.

Burnham, B. R. *Evaluating Human Resources, Programs, and Organizations*. Malabar, Fla.: Krieger, 1995.

Buskey, J. H. (ed.). *Attracting External Funds for Continuing Education*. New Directions for Continuing Education, no. 12. San Francisco: Jossey-Bass, 1981.

Caffarella, R. S. *Planning Programs for Adult Learners: A Practical Guide for Educators, Trainers, and Staff Developers*. San Francisco: Jossey-Bass, 1994.

Calderhead, J., and Gates, P. (eds.). *Conceptualizing Reflection in Teacher Development*. Bristol, Pa.: Falmer Press, 1993.

Cassara, B. B. (ed.). *Adult Education in a Multicultural Society*. London: Routledge, 1990.

Cervero, R. M., and Wilson, A. W. *Planning Responsibly for Adult Education: A Guide to Negotiating Power and Interests*. San Francisco: Jossey-Bass, 1994.

Cervero, R. M., and Wilson, A. W. (eds.). *What Really Matters in Adult Education Program Planning: Lessons in Negotiating Power and Interests*. New Directions for Adult and Continuing Education, no. 69. San Francisco: Jossey-Bass, 1996.

Cervero, R. M., and Wilson, A. W. "Working the Planning Table: The Political Practice of Adult Education." *Studies in Continuing Education*, 1998, 20(1), 5–22.

Chen, C., Krueger, R., and Leske, G. *The Application of the SERVQUAL Assessment System in Measuring the Quality of Service Provided by Minnesota Extension Service*. Proceedings of American Evaluation Association, Dallas, Nov. 1993.

Cichon, D., Sperazi, L., and Jurmo, P. *Collaborative Learning for Continuous Improvement*. (Evaluation final report.) Albany: Office of Workplace

Preparation, New York Workplace Literacy Program, New York State Education Department, Nov. 1997.

Comings, J. P., Parrella, A., and Soricone, L. *Persistence Among Adult Basic Education Students in Pre-GED Classes.* (NCSALL report no. 12.) Cambridge, Mass.: National Center for the Study of Adult Learning and Literacy, Harvard Graduate School of Education, 1999.

Condelli, L., and Kutner, M. *Developing a National Outcome Reporting System for the Adult Education Program.* Washington, D.C.: Office of Vocational and Adult Education (ED), Division of Adult Education and Literacy, Pelavin Research Institute, 1997. (ED405463)

Cook, T. D., and Reichardt, C. S. (eds.). *Qualitative and Quantitative Methods in Evaluation Research.* Thousand Oaks, Calif.: Sage, 1979.

Cookson, P. S. (ed.). *Recruiting and Retaining Adult Students.* New Directions for Continuing Education, no. 41. San Francisco: Jossey-Bass, 1989.

Coreil, P. D., and Verma, S. *Utilizing Evaluation to Develop a Marketing Strategy in the Louisiana Cooperative Extension Service.* Presentation at Annual Conference of American Evaluation Association, Seattle, 1992.

Curry, L., Wergin, J. F., and Associates. *Educating Professionals.* San Francisco: Jossey-Bass, 1993.

Darkenwald, G. G., and Knox, A. B. (eds.). *Meeting Educational Needs of Young Adults.* New Directions for Continuing Education, no. 21. San Francisco: Jossey-Bass, 1984.

Darkenwald, G. G., and Larson, G. A. (eds.). *Reaching Hard-to-Reach Adults.* New Directions for Continuing Education, no. 8. San Francisco: Jossey-Bass, 1980.

Davis, D. A., and Fox, R. D. *The Physician as Learner.* Chicago: American Medical Association, 1994.

Delaney, A. *An Inter-Professional Program Evaluation Case Study: Utilizing Multiple Measures to Assess What Matters.* (Annual forum paper.) Presented at the thirty-seventh annual forum of the Association for Institutional Research, Orlando, May 18–21, 1997. (ED410892)

Descy, D. E. "Evaluating Internet Resources, 1996." (http://www.lme.mankato.MSUS.edu/dedlltt/19eval.html)

Deshler, D. (ed.). *Evaluation for Program Improvement.* New Directions for Continuing Education, no. 24. San Francisco: Jossey-Bass, 1984.

Diamond, R. M. (ed.). *A Guide to Evaluating Teaching for Promotion and Tenure.* Littleton, Mass.: Copley, 1987.

Duning, B., Van Kekerix, M. S., and Zaborowski, L. M. *Reaching Learners Through Telecommunications.* San Francisco: Jossey-Bass, 1993.

Engle, M. "Evaluating Web Sites: Criteria and Tools 2000."
(http://www.library.correll.edu/okuref/research/webeval.html)

Evans, C. "Support for Teachers Studying Their Own Work." *Educational Leadership*, 1991, 48(6), 11–16.

Ference, P. R., and Vockell, E. L. "Adult Learning Characteristics and Effective Software Instruction." *Educational Technology*, 1994, 34(6), 25–31.

Flagg, B. N. *Formative Evaluation for Educational Technologies*. Hillsdale, N.J.: Erlbaum, 1990.

Forest, L., and Marshall, M. *Impact of Extension in Shawano County*. Madison: University of Wisconsin, 1978.

Furgason, J., Hay, D. R., and Rockwell, S. K. *Nebraska Residents' Perceptions of the State's Water Quality: Five Year Update*. Lincoln: Cooperative Extension, University of Nebraska, 1996.

Gagne, R. M., Briggs, L. J., and Wager, W. W. *Principles of Instructional Design*. (3rd ed.) New York: Holt, Rinehart, Winston, 1988.

Gall, M. D., Borg, W. R., and Gall, J. P. *Educational Research*. (6th ed.) White Plains, N.Y.: Longman, 1996.

Garcia, D. C. *Family English Literacy Network Program: Evaluation Report*. Miami: Florida International University, 1990.

Garcia, D. C., Hasson, D. J., and LeBlanc, P. *Families Learning at School and Home Program*. (Final evaluation report.) Miami: College of Education, Florida International University, 1997.

Garcia, D. C., Hasson, D. J., and Younkin, W. F. *Family English Literacy: Adult Sheltered Instruction*. (Program evaluation, 1989–1992.) Miami: College of Education, Florida International University, 1992.

Glaser, B. G., and Strauss, A. L. *The Discovery of Grounded Theory*. Hawthorne, N.Y.: Aldine de Gruyter, 1967.

Glassick, C. E., Huber, M. T., and Maeroff, G. I. *Scholarship Assessed: Evaluation of the Professoriate*. San Francisco: Jossey-Bass, 1997.

Grassian, E. "Thinking Critically About World Wide Web Resources." 1999. (http://www.library.ucla.edu/libraries/college/instruct/web/critical.htm)

Gredler, M. *Designing and Evaluating Games and Simulations: A Process Approach*. Houston: Guff, 1994.

Green, J. S., and Associates (eds.). *Continuing Education for the Health Professions*. San Francisco: Jossey-Bass, 1984.

Grotelueschen, A. D., Gooler, D. D., and Knox, A. B. *Evaluation in Adult Basic Education: How and Why*. Danville, Ill.: Interstate Printers and Publishers, 1976.

Guba, E. G., and Lincoln, Y. S. *Effective Evaluation*. San Francisco: Jossey-Bass, 1981.

Guba, E. G., and Lincoln, Y. S. *Fourth Generation Evaluation*. Thousand Oaks, Calif.: Sage, 1989.

Hanna, D. E. "Strengthening Collegiate Faculty Rewards for Continuing Education." In J. D. Votruba (ed.), *Strengthening Internal Support for Continuing Education*. New Directions for Continuing Education, no. 9. San Francisco: Jossey-Bass, 1981.

Harvey, R. L. "Write, Rewrite, and Evaluate Adult Materials." In C. Klevius (ed.), *Materials and Methods in Adult and Continuing Education: International Illiteracy*. Los Angeles: Klevans, 1987.

Havelock, R. G. *Planning for Innovation*. Ann Arbor: Center for Research on Utilization of Scientific Knowledge, ISR, University of Michigan, 1969.

Hayes, E., and Colin, S. (eds.). *Confronting Racism and Sexism*. New Directions for Adult and Continuing Education, no. 61. San Francisco: Jossey-Bass, 1994.

Henri, F., and Rigault, C. R. "Collaborative Distance Learning and Computer Conferencing." In T. T. Lido (ed.), *Advanced Educational Technology: Research Current and Future Potential*. Berlin: Springer-Verlag, 1996.

Hopkins, K. D., Glass, G. V., and Hopkins, B. R. *Basic Statistics for the Behavioral Sciences*. (2nd ed.) Upper Saddle River, N.J.: Prentice Hall, 1987.

Houle, C. O. *The Literature of Adult Education*. San Francisco: Jossey-Bass, 1992.

Johnson, D. M. (ed.). *A Handbook for Professional Development in Continuing Higher Education*. Washington, D.C.: National University Continuing Education Association, 1990.

Jones, B. "The Community Artist as Community Development Catalyst: An Evaluation of a Pilot Project." *Journal of the Community Development Society*, 1988, *19*(1), 37–50. (EJ 371524)

Jurmo, P. *Rethinking How to Plan and Evaluate Workplace Education Programs: Innovations in New York State*. Brunswick, N.J.: Learning Partnerships, 1993. (ED 362-643)

Kasworm, G. E. (ed.). *Educational Outreach to Select Adult Populations*. New Directions for Continuing Education, no. 20. San Francisco: Jossey-Bass, 1983.

Kazemekas, L. *The Development of Instructional Strategies by Clinical Medical School Faculty*. Rockwell, Md.: AHCPR, n.d.

Kiernan, N. E., and Brown, J. L. *Formative Evaluation: How to Reshape Aspects of the Delivery Method, Instructional Materials, Marketing, and Evaluation Protocol for a Summative Evaluation of an Extension Worksite Education*

Program? Proceedings of Annual Conference of the American Evaluation Association, 1992.

King, C. T., and others. *JTPA Success Stories in Texas and Illinois: The Who, How and What of Successful Outcomes.* (J-9-M-3-0068.) Dekalb: Center for Governmental Studies, Northern Illinois University; Austin: Lyndon B. Johnson School of Public Affairs, University of Texas; Washington, D.C.: Employment and Training Administration and National Commission for Employment Policy, Department of Labor, 1995. (ED404512)

Kirkpatrick, D. L. *Evaluating Training Programs: The Four Levels.* San Francisco: Berrett-Koehler, 1994.

Knox, A. B. (ed.). *Assessing the Impact of Continuing Education.* New Directions for Continuing Education, no. 3. San Francisco: Jossey-Bass, 1979a.

Knox, A. B. (ed.). *Programming for Adults Facing Mid-Life Change.* New Directions for Continuing Education, no. 2. San Francisco: Jossey-Bass, 1979b.

Knox, A. B. "Evaluating Continuing Professional Education." In R. Cervero and C. L. Scanlan (eds.), *Problems and Prospects in Continuing Professional Education.* New Directions in Continuing Education, no. 27. San Francisco: Jossey-Bass, 1985.

Knox, A. B. *Helping Adults Learn.* San Francisco: Jossey-Bass, 1986.

Knox, A. B. "Influences on Continuing Education Participation." *Journal of Continuing Education in the Health Professions,* 1990a, *10*(3), 261–274.

Knox, A. B. "Leadership Challenges to Continuing Higher Education." In D. M. Johnson (ed.), *A Handbook for Professional Development in Continuing Higher Education.* Washington, D.C.: National University Continuing Education Association, 1990b.

Knox, A. B. *Strengthening Adult and Continuing Education: A Global Perspective on Synergistic Leadership.* San Francisco: Jossey-Bass, 1993.

Knox, A. B. *Evaluating Adult and Continuing Education.* (Information series no. 375.) Columbus: Ohio State University, ERIC Clearinghouse on Adult, Career, and Vocational Education, 1998a.

Knox, A. B. *Recognizing Excellent Outreach Performance.* (Technical report.) Madison: Continuing and Vocational Education, University of Wisconsin, Dec. 1998b.

Knox, A. B. "Assessing Excellent Faculty Outreach Performance." *College Teaching,* 2001, *49*(2), 71–74.

Knox, A. B., and Associates. *Developing, Administering, and Evaluating Adult Education.* San Francisco: Jossey-Bass, 1980.

Knox, A. B., and others. "An Evaluation Guide for Adult Basic Education Programs." New York: Teachers College, Columbia University, 1974. (ERIC Document Reproduction Service no. ED 091 537)

Krathwohl, D. R. *Methods of Educational and Social Science Research.* White Plains, N.Y.: Longman, 1993.

Lerche, R. S. *Effective Adult Literacy Programs: A Practitioner's Guide.* New York: Cambridge, 1985.

Lewis, L., and Dowling, L. "Meaning Making and Reflective Practice." *Adult Learning,* Jan. 7, 1992.

Lincoln, Y. S., and Guba, E. G. *Naturalistic Inquiry.* Thousand Oaks, Calif.: Sage, 1985.

Lund, D. A., and Mason, R. C. *Year-End Report. Illinois State Board of Education, Community and Family Partnerships, Adult Education Program Evaluation, Fiscal Year 1996.* Dekalb: RE/ACE Office, Northern Illinois University, June 1996.

MacKinnon, D. W. "How Assessment Centers Were Started in the United States." (Monograph no. 1.) Pittsburgh: Development Dimensions International, 1991.

Madaus, G. F., Scriven, M., and Stufflebeam, D. L. (eds.). *Evaluation Models.* Norwell, Mass.: Kluwer, 1983.

Marion, R., and Zeichner, K. *A Guide to Practitioner Research Resources in North America.* Madison: Department of Curriculum and Instruction, University of Wisconsin-Madison, Nov. 1999.

Marshall, M. G. "The Quality of County Plans of Work and Materials Used in Their Preparation: An Assessment by County and District Extension Faculty." College Station: Texas Agricultural Extension Service, Texas A & M University, Mar. 1990.

Marshall, M. G., and Bennett, C. F. *Outputs of Public Issues Education Programs.* Vol. 5: *National Extension Targeted Water Quality Program, 1992–1995.* Washington, D.C.: USDA, Cooperative State Research, Education, and Extension Service, 1998.

Merriam, S. B., and Caffarella, R. S. *Learning in Adulthood: A Comprehensive Guide.* (2nd ed.) San Francisco: Jossey-Bass, 1999.

Miles, M. B., and Huberman, A. M. *Qualitative Data Analysis: A Sourcebook of New Methods.* Thousand Oaks, Calif.: Sage, 1984.

Miller, H. L., and McGuire, C. H. *Evaluating Liberal Adult Education.* Chicago: Center for the Study of Liberal Education for Adults, 1961.

Miller, J. P., and Associates. *Program Portfolio Review as Participation and Empowerment Evaluation*. Dallas: Proceedings of American Evaluation Association, 1993.

Monette, M. L. "The Concept of Educational Need." *Adult Education*, 1977, 27(2), 116–127.

Monette, M. L. "Needs Assessment: A Critique of Philosophical Assumptions." *Adult Education*, 1979, 29(2), 83–95.

Moore, D., Bennett, N., Knox A., and Kristofco, R. "Participation in Formal CME: Factors Affecting Decision Making." In D. Davis and R. Fox (eds.), *The Physician as Learner: Linking Research to Practice*. Chicago: American Medical Association, 1994.

Moses, J. L., and Byham, W. C. (eds.). *Applying the Assessment Center Method*. New York: Pergamon Press, 1977.

Mulcrone, P. *Harper College Faculty Evaluation System*. Palatine, Ill.: Harper College, 1997.

Naisbitt, J. *Megatrends*. New York: Warner, 1982.

Naisbitt, J., and Aburdene, P. *Megatrends 2000: 10 New Directions for the 1990s*. New York: Morrow, 1990.

Nowak, P., O'Keefe, G., Bennett, C., Anderson, S., and Trumbo, C. *Evaluation Report: Communication and Adoption Evaluation of USDA Water Quality Demonstration Projects*. Washington, D.C.: USDA, CSREES, Plant and Animal Science Production, Protection, and Processing, 1997.

Okun, M. (ed.). *Programs for Older Adults*. New Directions for Continuing Education, no. 14. San Francisco: Jossey-Bass, 1982.

Patton, M. Q. *Utilization-Focused Evaluation*. Thousand Oaks, Calif.: Sage, 1980.

Patton, M. Q. *Qualitative Evaluation and Research Methods*. (2nd ed.) Thousand Oaks, Calif.: Sage, 1990.

Patton, M. Q. (ed.). *Utilization-Focused Evaluation*. (3rd ed.) Thousand Oaks, Calif.: Sage, 1997.

Payne, B. C., and others. *Method of Evaluating and Improving Ambulatory Medical Care*. Ann Arbor: Office of Health Services Research, Department of Post-Graduate Medicine, College of Medicine, University of Michigan, 1978.

Payne, B. C., and others. "Method of Evaluating and Improving Ambulatory Medical Care." *Health Services Research*, 1984, 19(2), 219–245.

Pennington, F. (ed.). *Assessing Educational Needs of Adults*. New Directions for Continuing Education, no. 7. San Francisco: Jossey-Bass, 1980.

Perin, D. *Workplace Literacy Instruction for College Preparation of Health Care Workers*. (Final evaluation report.) New York: Center for Advanced Study in Education, City University of New York, 1992.

Phillips, J. *Handbook of Training Evaluation and Measurement Methods*. Houston: Gulf, 1991.

Posavac, E. J., and Carey, R. G. *Program Evaluation: Methods and Case Studies*. (4th ed.) Upper Saddle River, N.J.: Prentice Hall, 1992.

Pratt, D. D. "Andragogy as a Relational Construct." *Adult Education Quarterly*, 1988, 38(3), 160–181.

Pratt, D. D., and Associates. *Five Perspectives on Teaching in Adult and Higher Education*. Malabar, Fla.: Krieger, 1998.

Queeney, D. S. (ed.). *The Practice Audit Model*. University Park: Continuing Professional Education Development Project, Pennsylvania State University, Mar. 1981.

Queeney, D. S. (ed.). *An Agenda for Action: Continuing Professional Education Focus Group Reports*. University Park, Pa.: Office of Continuing Professional Education, Division of Planning Studies, Pennsylvania State University, 1990.

Queeney, D. S. *Assessing Needs in Continuing Education*. San Francisco: Jossey-Bass, 1995.

Quigley, B. A., and Kuhne, G. W. (eds.). *Creating Practical Knowledge Through Action Research: Posing Problems, Solving Problems, and Improving Daily Practice*. New Directions for Adult and Continuing Education, no. 73. San Francisco: Jossey-Bass, Spring 1997.

Ramsden, P. *Learning to Teach in Higher Education*. New York: Routledge, 1992.

Robinson, D. G., and Robinson, J. C. *Performance Consulting: Moving Beyond Training*. San Francisco: Jossey-Bass, 1995.

Rockwell, S. K., Hay, D. R., Ziebarth, A., and Niemeyer, S. M. *Nebraska Residents' Perceptions of the State's Water Quality*. Lincoln: Cooperative Extension, University of Nebraska, 1991.

Rose, A. D., and Leahy, M. A. (eds.). *Assessing Adult Learning in Diverse Settings: Current Issues and Approaches*. New Directions for Adult and Continuing Education, no. 75. San Francisco: Jossey-Bass, 1997.

Ross-Gordon, J. M., Martin, L. G., and Briscoe, D. B. (eds.). *Serving Culturally Diverse Populations*. New Directions for Adult and Continuing Education, no. 48. San Francisco: Jossey-Bass, 1990.

Rothwell, W. J., and Cookson, P. S. *Lifelong Education Program Planning: A Contingency-Based Approach for Business and Education*. San Francisco: Jossey-Bass, 1997.

Rothwell, W. J., and Kazanas, H. C. *The Complete AMA Guide to Management Development*. New York: American Management Association, 1993.

Salant, P., and Dillman, D. A. *How to Conduct Your Own Survey*. New York: Wiley, 1994.

Sanders, J. *The Program Evaluation Standards: How to Assess Evaluations of Educational Programs*. Thousand Oaks, Calif.: Sage, 1994.

Shadish, W. R., Cook, T. D., and Leviton, L. C. *Foundations of Program Evaluation*. Thousand Oaks, Calif.: Sage, 1995.

Shapiro, L. T. *Training Effectiveness Handbook. A High-Results System for Design, Delivery, and Evaluation*. New York: McGraw-Hill, 1995. (ED385725)

Simerly, R. G., and Associates. *Handbook of Marketing for Continuing Education*. San Francisco: Jossey-Bass, 1989.

Sissel, P. A. (ed.). *A Community Based Approach to Literacy Programs: Taking Learners' Lives into Account*. New Directions for Adult and Continuing Education, no. 70. San Francisco: Jossey-Bass, 1996.

Smith, N. L. *New Techniques for Evaluation: New Perspectives in Evaluation (Vol. 2)*. Thousand Oaks, Calif.: Sage, 1981.

Spiegel, M. R. *Evaluating Effective Extension Teaching Utilizing a Comparative Database*. Dallas: Proceedings of American Evaluation Association, 1992.

Spindler, G. (ed.). *Doing the Ethnography of Schooling*. Austin, Tex.: Holt, Rinehart and Winston, 1982.

Strauss, A., and Corbin, J. *Basics of Qualitative Research*. Thousand Oaks, Calif.: Sage, 1990.

Stringer, E. *Action Research: A Handbook for Practitioners*. Thousand Oaks, Calif.: Sage, 1996.

Stufflebeam, D. L. "Metaevaluation." (Occasional paper no. 3.) Kalamazoo: Western Michigan University Evaluation Center, 1974.

Tabachnick, B. R., and Zeichner, K. (eds.). *Issues and Practices in Inquiry-Oriented Teacher Education*. Bristol, Pa.: Falmer Press, 1991.

Thompson, M. S. *Benefit-Cost Analysis for Program Evaluation*. Thousand Oaks, Calif.: Sage, 1980.

Toombs, W., and Croyle, G. E. "A Client Reaction Analysis: Final Report for the Lifelong Learning Center, Reading, Pa." University Park: Center for the Study of Higher Education, Pennsylvania State University, 1977.

Toombs, W. A. "Study of Client Reactions: Lifelong Learning Center, The Free Library of Philadelphia." University Park: Center for the Study of Higher Education, Pennsylvania State University, 1978.

Umble, K., Cervero, R. M., Yang, B., and Atkinson, W. "The Effects of Traditional Classroom and Distance Continuing Education in Vaccine-Preventable Diseases: A Theory-Driven Evaluation." *American Journal of Public Health*, 2000, 90(8), 1218–1224.

Vaille, J. A. *Guidelines for the Evaluation of Instructional Technology Resources*. Stanislaus County Office of Education, California Instructional Technology Clearinghouse, 1998.

Valli, L. (ed.). *Reflective Teacher Education: Cases and Critiques.* Albany: State University of New York Press, 1992.

Verduin, J., and Clark, T. *Distance Education: The Foundations of Effective Practice.* San Francisco: Jossey-Bass, 1991.

Veres, H. C. "From Assessment to Implementation." In F. C. Pennington (ed.), *Assessing Educational Needs of Adults.* New Directions for Continuing Education, no. 7. San Francisco: Jossey-Bass, 1980.

Vicere, A. A. "Executive Education: The Teaching Edge." *Organizational Dynamics,* Autumn 1996, pp. 67–81.

Votruba, J. D. (ed.). *Strengthening Internal Support for Continuing Education.* New Directions for Continuing Education, no. 9. San Francisco: Jossey-Bass, 1981.

Walsh, P. L., and Craft, C. A. *The Train-the-Trainer Program: A Formative Evaluation Report.* St. Louis: Continuing Education Center, Veteran's Administration, 1990.

Weiss, C. H. (ed.). *Using Social Research in Public Policy Making.* Lexington, Mass.: Lexington, 1977.

Wholey, J. S., Hatry, H. P., and Newcomer, K. E. (eds.). *Handbook of Practical Evaluation.* San Francisco: Jossey-Bass, 1994.

Worthen, B. R., and Sanders, J. R. *Educational Evaluation: Alternative Approaches and Practical Guidelines.* White Plains, N.Y.: Longman, 1987.

Worthen, B. R., Sanders, J. R., and Fitzpatrick, J. L. *Program Evaluation: Alternative Approaches and Practical Guidelines.* (2nd ed.) White Plains, N.Y.: Longman, 1997.

Zeichner, K., and Liston, D. *Reflective Teaching: An Introduction.* Hillsdale, N.J.: Erlbaum, 1996.

Zeichner, K. M. *Teacher Research as a Professional Development Activity for 0–12 Educators.* Madison: Department of Curriculum and Instruction, University of Wisconsin-Madison, July 1999.

Ziegler, S., and Sussman, S. B. (eds.). *The Effectiveness of Adult Literacy Education: A Review of Issues and Literature Related to Outcome-Based Evaluation of Literacy Programs.* Toronto: Ontario Literacy Coalition, 1996. (ED399423)

Index

Workplace education programs: evaluation of New York State/AFL-CIO, 141–143; literacy education for union members, 167–168; seven case studies on, 143–144. *See also* Adult education programs

Worthen, B. R., 25, 29, 32, 69, 72, 86, 102, 107, 165, 197, 209, 216, 219, 227, 270, 271, 284

Y

Yang, B., 116
Younkin, W. F., 165

Z

Zaborowski, L. M., 33
Zeichner, K. M., 19, 21, 22
Ziebarth, K., 240
Ziegler, S., 273

Everyone associated with educational programs for adults makes evaluative judgments — consciously or unconsciously—about the worth and effectiveness of the program. But while many in the field continually tout the importance of evaluation, the process is woefully underused in practice. Among the many reasons for this is that there has been a lack of dependable guidelines and useful examples to ensure that program evaluation is worth the effort—until now.

Evaluation for Continuing Education provides the useful and practical tools necessary to ensure a successful program evaluation. The book presents systematic guidelines aimed at enhancing understanding of evaluation concepts and procedures, and offers manageable ways to selectively include evaluation activities as an integral part of program planning, imple- mentation, and justification. Author Alan B. Knox reveals that the key to successful evaluations that improve education programs for adults is a basic rationale for *why* and *how*. He helps readers select and develop their own rationale throughout the course of the book while suggesting fundamental evaluation concepts and procedures. He shows how to distinguish some program aspect upon which a specific evaluation project will focus—including needs assessment, goals and policies, staffing assess- ment, materials development, and more—and summarizes examples of evaluation reports that reflect the various types of providers and scales on which evaluations are conducted. Knox offers a wide variety of these examples, enabling readers to reflect on implications for their own